Sweet Pain

Joy on the Road Less Traveled

Sweet Pain

Joy on the Road Less Traveled

by Nancy and David Norris

Sweet Pain
Joy on the Road Less Traveled

By Nancy and David Norris

Printed in the United States of America.

Published by:

Florissant, MO, USA
Copyright © 2009
By Nancy and David Norris

To order books, see photos, and for other information,
go to nathanielnorris.com

Dedicated to those with pain so profound that it cannot be spoken...

Dedicated to those whose joy is so deep that it cannot be understood...

And dedicated especially to those who live in both of these worlds at the same time.

Acknowledgments

Special thanks are in order to those people who helped turn our rough draft into a book. First of all, thanks to my good friend Mary Loudermilk for setting us in the right direction with her editing. Without her this book would not have been possible. Thanks to Denise Blevins, our first reader, and for the dozens of you who read chapters that I sent you and made suggestions. I am especially thankful for the good work of Janice Rutter. We need a standing ovation for Lisa Stevens Taylor, who along with Mary did the bulk of the editing and for Lee Ann Alexander, our copy editor. Anita Sergeant inspired me with the title, and Laura Jurek did a really nice job designing the cover and laying out the book.

Telling this story had its own set of challenges. Where it was possible, we tried to reproduce conversations the way that they took place, but sometimes we simply had to do the best we could. Some names in the book were changed to protect privacy. Where it was important, we tried to check our facts against the remembrance of those who appear in the story. For Dave, the most significant conversations were those he had with his siblings; their remembrances nuanced the book, and his conversations presented further opportunity for healing.

Like any other child, Nathaniel had many normal days, days that go underreported in the narrative. This story is about highs and lows and is based on our feelings at the time, even when those feelings were not too pretty. That said, I am certain of a couple of things. Life brings us plenty of laughter and tears, and God loves us even when we're ugly.

Nathaniel had a lot of small triumphs along the way, but most of these go untold. Because we wanted the book to be an easy read, Dave insisted we not bog the reader down with too many names and details. I'm telling you, it is a crime how many people do not get mentioned in this book! So, to all of you who are significant in our lives and for all those who helped care for Nathaniel but may not even be acknowledged, you need to know how very special you are to us!

Love and laughter,
Nancy Abshire Norris

Contents

Chapter 1

"We're not sure of all the complications..."

Dave sat alone on one of seven chairs that ran down the length of the wall, all of which smelled of antiseptic. He looked like he had been up all night, which, in fact, he had. He had been told to wait there. He wasn't sure for whom. A metallic clank of some kind made him turn in search of the cause. Peering through the window behind him that spanned the entire top half of the wall, he took a good look into the neonatal intensive care unit, or NICU, as one sign said. Five or six nurses busily walked back and forth checking on this and that, but the source of the noise remained unknown. Meanwhile, machines hummed and buzzed, and displays offered important data on colored screens. Beeps aplenty sounded out the rhythm of the room.

A doctor marched into the NICU wearing that odd colored surgical garb, not quite green and not quite blue; a surgeon's mask still covered his face. He scanned the room, looking this way and that, said something to a nurse, and then came abruptly to the waiting area. "Mr. Norris?" he asked tersely.

"Yes," Dave answered.

"I'm Dr. Raab," said the blue-green mask in a kind of muffled speech. He was much too tall, and when he didn't sit down, Dave stood to his full six-foot height but still had to look up into the surgeon's mask. Dave was twenty-eight-years-old and the doctor a full ten years older. The doctor's bushy-black eyebrows were accented by disheveled black locks that flopped about his surgeon's head. Dave assumed that the doctor would remove his mask, but he did not. It was as if he were about to deliver bad news, which, of course, he was; and as if he wasn't very comfortable giving it; which, of course, he wasn't.

Dave had married Nancy almost eight years earlier. Both had assumed that after they shared their vows that they would one day have a baby—and that having said baby would be something that would just sort of happen naturally. But when it didn't, they began taking steps to get help. First, they went to their family physician, Dr. Bruce Griswold, and then they went to specialists. After visiting clinics to take fertility tests, Nancy went on a selective diet and even used a thermometer that required Dave to be near a phone. More than once Nancy made a phone call, attempting to employ medical science as ally in her quest for a child. "Dave you need to come home right now. I think I'm ovulating."

"It didn't work last month, Nancy... or the month before."

"Just get home and quit arguing."

"Says who?"

"Says the thermometer."

"I'll be there right away."

When the day came that Dr. Griswold finally announced that Nancy's pregnancy test was positive, it was a cause for incredible celebration. Plans were immediately drawn up, calendars consulted, and a strategy unfolded. Nancy worked backward from the projected due date in the beginning of February to plan all of her doctor's appointments. Not only did she not miss a checkup, but Dave dutifully accompanied her to each appointment. Together they saw the first ultrasound, and together they went to Lamaze classes where Dave helped Nancy practice her special breathing techniques. Along with a dozen other compliant husbands, he carried his pillow into class, learning all he ever wanted to know about coaching a spouse to take a clearing breath.

Everything worked according to plan—at least it *had* worked according to plan. It was hard to believe that only the day before Dave stood before this masked man that everything started to unravel. The morning had started innocently enough. Nancy and Dave were at her last scheduled appointment with Dr. Griswold. Not too far into the examination, the doctor got a troubled look on his face. "You're sure, then, about the due date?" he asked, probingly.

Nancy nodded. "Certainly." (Less planning had gone into D-Day.) "Is there a problem?"

"Yes."

"What is it?"

"Well... there is not enough amniotic fluid for a full term baby, and his head is too small."

Dave stepped in. "So what then? What does it mean?

"Well, it could be a number of things."

"Like what?" Dave questioned, not willing to take uncertainty as an answer.

"It could be that... well... it's possible that the baby has no kidneys."

"What? What would that mean?"

Dr. Griswold just shook his head. Dave protested. "But surely it could be something else."

It could be. But none of the other options that the doctor mentioned were a whole lot better than the first one. Nancy and Dave left the office devastated.

It was ten p.m. that night when Nancy went into labor. They were home, getting ready for bed. Somewhere outside was a full moon, but it certainly was not visible in the blizzard that raged. "Get the stuff to the car," Nancy suddenly ordered Dave, pointing to the provisions she had set aside to take to the hospital. "It's time." Dave went out to the car but did not reappear for ten minutes. It took him that long just to shovel a path through the deep snow.

Dr. Griswold met them at their local hospital, less than four miles away. He did some preliminary tests but without much enthusiasm. Presently, he shook his head, resigned. "Nancy, you can have the baby here, but this is a small hospital in a small town. It is almost certain when the baby is delivered he will be taken by ambulance to Milwaukee. I was thinking… well, it might be better if you just had the baby there." This wasn't on Nancy's planner; it was simply not at all what she had envisioned. Reluctantly, she agreed to the suggestion. It was true that she did not want to be far from her baby once he was born.

Under normal circumstances, the ambulance might have made the trip to the city hospital in forty minutes. But these were not normal circumstances. The blizzard still raged, and Highway 41, upon which they were traveling, had been pronounced officially closed due to seventeen inches of blowing snow. Nancy could feel the ambulance fishtailing back and forth on the empty road. Although the eyes of the attendant grew rather large, Nancy made a determined effort not to scream and kept her emotions in check. Dave was supposed to be following behind in their station wagon. He had borrowed ten dollars from the doctor to buy gas.

The siren screamed all the way into the city, and eventually the vehicle faithfully delivered its charge. As soon as the ambulance pulled in, a team of medical personnel immediately dispatched Nancy to the maternity ward. They quickly hooked up all the monitors while Nancy busied herself by concentrating on taking clearing breaths. Months of practice were invested into having this baby naturally, and that is exactly what she intended to do. Soon Dave came in, happy that Nancy had made it and that the baby had not yet made his appearance. He hadn't wanted to miss it.

Dave asked if she wanted water. She did not. Did she need medication? No. Did she need—she needed him to sit down. He did. Contractions were timed and remained constant. A half-hour passed, and then an hour, but Nancy still had a long way to go. And then after two hours, she realized that perhaps the baby wasn't coming, at least not any time soon. All night long she endured the pain of labor, determined to work her way through every contraction. All night long, although the monitor indicated that their baby's heartbeat was strong, Nancy made little progress. Finally, as the sun came up, the nurse became agitated because some of the squiggly lines traveling across the monitor were not now to her liking. "We're going to have to do something. This baby's in distress."

"Can I come in for the Caesarian—" began Dave, but the doctor barked out his refusal before the words were out of his mouth.

Although Dave listened quietly as the masked doctor talked to him about the results of Nancy's surgery, his heart and mind were racing. Pointing through the window, the doctor noted, "This is the neonatal intensive care unit, the place where we bring the difficult cases. They're bringing your baby in right now." Dave stared at a nurse who struggled to handle the purple-faced infant who was howling in rage. The baby was obviously in pain and did not for one minute like being plunked into an incubator.

"Why are his legs all twisted like that?" Dave asked, seeing that the legs and knees of the baby were somehow bent terribly wrong.

Dr. Raab responded, "Well, his hips and knees are out of joint."

"How'd they get that way?"

The doctor shrugged. "It was something that occurred in the womb."

"Oh, dear."

"Don't worry about that. That's something we can fix."

Dave wondered what it was they couldn't fix. "Do his eyes look a little funny to you?" he asked.

"Those are epicanthic skin folds. That is a possible sign of a chromosomal abnormality. It looks like he has Down syndrome. I'm not sure, but we'll test for that."

The purple-faced baby grew angrier and angrier as they poked and prodded him. His howls increased as they began tightening a plastic piece over his nose and mouth.

Dave thought he might be sick. "So what's that plastic mask for?"

"Oxygen," replied the doctor tersely. "We'll put him on a hundred percent oxygen."

Dave shook his head as the baby continued to thrash back and forth. "Look at him fight the nurses. He doesn't like that one bit." They were putting leads on his chest that ran to a monitor that measured his heart rate. The doctor said nothing. Dave continued, "So all that stuff is pretty necessary? Why are they doing that to him?"

The doctor stiffened. "It's absolutely essential. We're working to get things under control."

"Oh, uh… you mean they're not, then… under control, I mean…." Dave said, not sure whether he wanted to hear the answer.

"Well," said Dr. Raab, "we're not sure of all the complications. But we do know that there are some significant difficulties."

"How significant?" asked Dave.

"Well, the first twenty-four hours are critical," said the doctor. "If he lives through that, then he has a good chance."

"A good chance?"

"Yeah, well, we'll see."

It was some time after she had been brought from the recovery room into the regular hospital room before Nancy finally opened her eyes. She looked around without any sort of understanding until she began to recognize a familiar head of dark hair and clear brown eyes staring down on her. Although Dave was more than passable in his appearance, this morning he looked quite haggard and worried. Suddenly Nancy recalled where she was. Although the anesthesia still kept her groggy, she remembered where she was. There was a dull pain where the surgeon had cut into her and presently she asked, "Something's wrong with the baby, isn't there?"

Dave kept his gaze on Nancy. She was twenty-nine, but her face looked younger. With her easy smile and dancing brown eyes, Nancy was animated and inviting. He loved this lady lying here, and now words simply would not come. It was all he could do to offer her the slight nod of his head.

"You saw the baby then?" asked Nancy urgently.

"Yeah. They, uh, brought him into the intensive care unit. I saw him."

"Dave," repeated Nancy, once again attempting to gain information. "Please tell me about our son!"

Dave said something about them monitoring the baby in NICU. But his face clearly demonstrated that he wasn't telling all he knew. He was talking, but he wasn't making a lot of sense. "People are praying, Nancy," Dave pronounced way too weakly.

Dave was glad people were praying. The truth was that he couldn't pray himself. He didn't know for sure how he should pray. He thought maybe it would be better if the baby died. But that thought he simply could not share with Nancy.

In the NICU down the hall, an alarm sounded brashly on an isolette, the incubator that sat across from where the Norris baby lay. Because of this new emergency, the doctor left the little Norris baby and walked over to the other plastic enclosure where a two-pound premature baby lay with tubes protruding from its tiny body. In response to the alarm indicating no respiration, the doctor manually lifted up the board at the bottom of the isolette, flipping the baby up and down a couple of inches. As the infant landed once again on the base of the isolette, the alarm went silent. The doctor smiled and offered to the attending nurse, "The little bugger just keeps forgetting to breathe."

The little Norris baby had his own issues with breathing, but he was helped along by oxygen being forcefully whooshed into his lungs. He continued to thrash against the plastic mask and to scream against the pain, protesting the cold world around him. No human touch soothed him. No comforting voice sang to him. No nourishment filled his mouth. All efforts were concentrated on just one thing: keeping him alive.

Nancy thought about her baby who laid in NICU, that nameless son who was kept from her and whom she intuitively knew was working so hard to live. She suddenly pronounced, "We are going to name the baby Nathaniel."

"Nathaniel?" Dave questioned. "That's a pretty big name for such a little guy."

They'd talked about naming the baby Nate, after a friend. A name book Nancy had found said that Nate meant "gift," but Nathaniel meant "gift of God."

Tears welled up in her eyes. "Nathaniel," she said, "our gift from God. And his middle name will be after my dad, 'Abshire.'"

Dave looked down at his wife who was painfully recovering from surgery and knew he didn't have much room to negotiate. "Yeah," he offered flatly. "Sounds good to me."

A big smile crossed Nancy's face. But just as suddenly as it came, it was gone again. "He's going to be okay… I mean, he is not going to die or anything is he?"

Dave didn't say anything. He just patted her hand.

Chapter 2

"There's a lot we don't know yet, but he's alive"

D
ave had been up for almost thirty-six hours, so when Nancy said she needed to rest, he took this as his cue that it was time to head home. The roads were plowed, and because he was leaving Milwaukee after rush hour, he could easily make it to their condominium in forty-five minutes. But before he could go home, Dave needed to stop at the church office to get his checkbook.

It was dark and the streetlights of West Bend splashed pools of light on the angled parking of the downtown streets. Dave pulled up to the church. It didn't look like a church. It looked like a house because, in fact, that is what it was. They had bought an old house in downtown West Bend and tore out the wall between the living room and dining room. A sign in the front yard indicated the building's new identity.

Something strange was going on. Dave parked next to a half-dozen other cars that shouldn't have been there. He climbed the dozen stairs up the small hill that led to the front door. Passing through the porch area, he came to the commercial wood door that now formed the entrance to the chapel and opened it. Apparently, he was interrupting something. He swung open the door to discover fifteen people kneeling at the metal chairs that served as pews, lost in their petitions to God. Dave noticed Wayne right away. He was a tough customer. A big man in his thirties, Wayne had presence. He didn't talk loud, but he did speak with authority.

Dave recalled a conversation he had had with Wayne when Wayne first started coming to church. "So Pastor, I just want to know what happened."

"What do you mean?" questioned Dave.

"Well, I was addicted when you baptized me. But sixty seconds later, I wasn't. Funny thing...." Then he offered a quiet challenge. "So did you know that would happen?"

Dave smiled. He didn't even know the man was addicted.

Whatever Wayne's opinions, they all came out with the same insistent tone. "Church people shouldn't go to any restaurant that serves alcohol," he pronounced on more than one occasion. Dave didn't argue with him, but he didn't always pass those opinions on to others.

Now, here was something Dave had never seen before. Usually, Wayne sang quietly, prayed quietly, and lived his life quietly. But tonight he was on the front row praying—loudly—he could be heard above the others. There were forty assorted metal chairs facing the front, and Wayne was earnestly pounding the one where he knelt. He was calling out the name of their baby who lay in critical condition in St. Joseph's Hospital. It was a holy moment, and Dave didn't care to interrupt it. He quietly got his checkbook from his desk and quickly left.

Dave was glad others were praying because he still could not. He was numb. Absolutely numb. Then he began to wonder how in the world it came to be that people were there at the church praying. Things didn't usually happen unbidden. "This is likely Dorothy's doing," he chuckled to himself as he pulled away from church.

Dorothy was a lady about sixty-years-old who had shown up to church one day and said that the Lord had spoken to her about moving to West Bend to help. Dave wasn't all that pleased. He and Nancy didn't want to build their church to the detriment of other churches. He tried to discourage her, even calling her pastor sixty-five miles to the south to find out what to do.

"Hello," said Lester.

"This is Dave Norris. I just wanted to let you know that Dorothy was visiting my church this weekend," offered Dave.

"Wonderful," said Lester.

When Dave began to explain how he was trying to discourage Dorothy from leaving this man's church, Lester, a veteran pastor of forty years, suddenly stopped him. He offered evenly, "Let me tell you something. I know Dorothy very well. She has been a faithful member of my church for many years. She has a close walk with God. She has time and doesn't need money. If she says God told her to move there, then He did. Frankly, I don't have much for her to do here. This is just the sort of challenge she needs." So Dorothy came, helping in very practical and significant ways, a lady on a mission. She was like a mother to Dave. Yes, this was likely Dorothy's doing.

Ten minutes after reaching home, Dave was dressed for bed. Fifteen minutes after he was home, he was asleep. It seemed like only a few minutes had passed before the buzzing of an alarm called him from another world and back to consciousness. Dave rolled over to silence the buzzing and go back to sleep, certain it was the middle of the night. But the clock didn't lie. It was 5:45 a.m., time to get up.

Dave didn't bother showering. He would do that later. He didn't pray, read his Bible, or even get a cup of coffee. He groggily got behind the wheel of his car and was at work in less than five minutes. He sat down in the driver's seat of a vehicle that was about half the length of a normal school bus, turned the key and got it running. While the engine purred, Dave did a quick check to make sure that all of the flashing lights, blinkers, and running lights were working. Three minutes later, confident everything functioned properly, he pulled out onto the road.

Twenty minutes elapsed before Dave flipped the toggle switch on the dash that turned on the warning lights, round signals that flashed yellow and then red. He coasted the bus to a stop, threw on the emergency brake, and went outside to the rear of the bus. There he flung open what looked like an oversized emergency door on the side of the bus. Reaching in, he retrieved a metal box connected by a thick cable to the inner workings of the vehicle. He pressed a large black button on the box causing a lift to first unfold from the bus and then lower itself to the ground. As the lift descended, Dave greeted his first client. "Hello, John," he said warmly. The man, twenty-five or so, leaned against his walker, waiting for the lift.

"Hey there, Dave," said John, smiling. He was always pleasant, even at 6:15 in the morning. When the lift settled flat in front of him, John patiently shuffled his walker to stand on it. Both he and Dave rode it up until it was level with the inside of the bus. Then John made his way to his seat while Dave closed the rear bus door.

The bus meandered around several country roads before his next client got onboard. Irving was a heavyset man in his forties, kind of built like a pear with bushy eyebrows. He walked up the stairs and plopped into his usual seat. As soon as Irving was settled in, he doubled over, and held his stomach. "I'm sick, Dave, I'm sick."

Dave responded in mocking derision. "You're not sick, you big faker." At that, Irving suddenly ceased to be sick; he laughed loudly, completely healed and happy. It was their daily routine. He just needed attention. Irving actually reminded Dave of other people he knew. We all need attention; Irving was just a little more obvious about it than most.

As the bus gradually filled up with handicapped adults on their way to the sheltered workshop, Dave thought how ironic it was that his own son would likely ride one of these busses… if he lived… and if he was handicapped, which it seemed quite likely that he was.

"You dummy!" yelled Irving from the middle of the bus.

Dave immediately pulled the bus over to the shoulder of the road and walked back to take care of a situation. "What did you say, Irving?"

Irving looked sheepish. They had only one rule on the bus, and he had broken it. He put his head down, shamed. The single rule for the bus was that everyone must treat others with respect. No one was to be called names, especially names that the clients had heard hurled at them, names like "dummy."

Dave addressed the bus at large. He spoke more sternly than he would have liked, but it was important to press the point. "You all know the rule. We do not call each other "dummy" on this bus! Do you understand me?" They understood. Nodding took place all around, and the bus was summarily in order again. Dave walked back to his seat.

"Sorry, Dave," said the offender, sincerely remorseful.

"It's all right, Irving," Dave said. "Thanks for apologizing." Irving beamed once again. All was right with his world.

Dave got to the hospital by noon. As he looked through the window into the NICU, it occurred to him that Nathaniel had indeed lived a full day, something that had been offered as an important milestone. But the nurses seemed ignorant of his son's accomplishment, or that celebration was in order. They just went about their duties, busy citizens of a small world that hummed along with its own rhythm. Indeed, no one seemed to care that Dave stood at the door waiting to talk to someone. Finally stopping a nurse who walked by, he asked how Nathaniel was doing. She said tersely, "About the same." A doctor could apparently tell him more, but none was there.

Dave wasn't the only one having a difficult time obtaining information. Earlier that morning as Nancy lay on a bed in a different part of the hospital, she attempted to speak to the nurse who was taking her blood pressure. "Excuse me," she said, almost apologetically. "My baby is in critical condition in the neonatal intensive care unit. And I need to go to down to see him."

"That's something that you'll have to take up with the doctor."

"When will he be here? I thought he was supposed to do his rounds in the morning?"

"You just never know with these doctors. Sometimes they have other obligations that keep them away all day."

"But I have to go see my baby. The last thing I knew was that he was in quite a bit of distress. I need to hold him."

"Look, Mrs. Norris, because your son is in critical condition, it is unlikely that they will let you hold him. There's just too much involved. I think they'll probably want you to wait until things, you know, even out a little."

"And you're not sure when the doctor will be in?"

"The doctor will be in to see you when he makes the rounds."

"Well, could you check with the NICU to see how my baby is doing?"

"I'm sure they will notify us if… something happens."

"Please, could you check?"

"Certainly," she said, in a tone that said this wouldn't be her top priority. Nancy didn't really feel too angry with her. The nurse was nice enough. She was just doing her job. The woman was caring for several patients, and her patients had to be her main concern. Still….

Dave came into the room and offered up a welcome kiss. "Hey, Nance, look who has come to visit you. It's Sam." Sam was a minister whom they had met once. He attended one of the Milwaukee churches. Perhaps he had heard a prayer request offered for the Norrises. Perhaps he had even been assigned to visit them. It didn't matter. Nancy had other things on her mind.

"Oh, Sam, thank you for coming. Dave… quick—run down to the NICU to see how Nathaniel is doing. I just can't find out—"

"I stopped down there, but there was no one who could help me."

"Well, get down there right now and find out something!" Nancy urged loudly.

Dave saw that lingering in the room was not a smart option and wisely retreated out the door with Sam in tow. Twenty minutes of pacing in front of the NICU elapsed before any significant contact was made. When Dave finally found somebody who was an authorized person, he didn't waste time with formalities. "Doctor, the nurse said that there was nothing new to report. Is that good news? I really need to tell my wife something tangible."

They were standing outside the NICU looking into the window. Dave didn't know whether this was specifically his doctor, a generic doctor on duty, or just a random person who was walking by, but he did look official. At least this physician was willing to talk. The man was leafing through a chart while leaning back against the glass window. He seemed to be measuring his words. He didn't speak "matter-of-factly," but he wasn't overly compassionate either. "Well, your baby is still on a hundred percent oxygen," he reported, "and he's still in quite a bit of distress. There's a lot we don't know yet, but he's alive, he's a fighter, and he's been alive for twenty-four hours—so that's a good thing."

The doctor looked over at Dave who waited for more. Apparently that was all that constituted news. Turning to enter the NICU, the doctor left Dave and Sam standing there. Silently, Dave watched through the window. It was a funny thing. Dave thought that he was over the numbness that came from bad news. He had accepted it. But the doctor's words seemed like yesterday all over again.

Sam pursed his lips as if to prepare to say something meaningful. "Well, Dave, Romans 8:28 says, 'All things work together for good to them who are called of God, who are called according to His purpose.'" He said it in a lecturing voice, almost paternally, as if he were instructing a Sunday school child.

Suddenly flaring with anger, "Just shut up!" Dave wanted to say but did not. Did this man think that he was being helpful by just simply quoting a Bible verse? Particularly with no feeling or understanding connected with it? And this guy was a minister! The man spoke sacred words tritely, mouthing a truism that was supposed to be taken like aspirin.

Dave remembered another minister who had recently quoted this same verse in a very similar way—himself. Then and there Dave determined that he was through offering pat answers.

"Uh, Sam? Thanks for coming, but I've got to get back to the room to see Nancy. I think I want to talk to her alone."

"Sure, Dave. If there's anything I can ever do for you, you just give me a call."

"You don't mean that," thought Dave to himself as the man left. He was just "checking the box" as a minister. Dave had done it often enough himself. That realization made him feel even worse. He *was*

Sam. And not only was he Sam, but now he had to share his son's meager prognosis with someone who wouldn't like what she heard.

Dave thought of several different ways to present this bad news. His wife had been pretty rattled when he left the room, so he was not too confident that he could talk to her about this in the right way. He was still mulling over the correct approach when his entrance into her hospital room was preempted by someone rushing past him in a blur. "Delivery here for Nancy Norris," announced the aide.

"Oh, that's wonderful!" said Nancy excitedly. It was a rose from three children in their church: Chris, Tim, and Tracy. It joined four assorted arrangements on the shelf by the window. Nancy smiled and shed a tear simultaneously. "Sorry, Mom," she said, speaking loudly into the mouthpiece of the phone. "I just got a single rose— oh Dave, it's my mom—she called!" Nancy reported all of this like she had won the lottery. Animated words flowed into the phone as Nancy told her mom how well everyone was taking care of her. He listened for thirty seconds and then walked out of the room as Nancy was saying, "Yes, and his middle name is after Dad!"

Dave didn't know what to make of Nancy's uncanny ability to live in the present. She had charged him with finding out hard information, which he had reluctantly wrenched from some sort of doctor. Now having consigned him to worry, Nancy was happy again. Dave poked his head back in the room to hear, "Well, if Cathy can't come this Saturday, then just wait. Yes, I would like to see you all at the same time!" Although the phone call was doing wonders for Nancy, it was having the opposite effect on him.

"If that doesn't beat all," he mumbled to himself, fuming. In the last ten minutes he had gotten mad at the doctor, Sam, and God. And now he was mad at Nancy.

Nancy noticed Dave going in and out of the hospital room, but she was just too busy to concern herself with him. People started coming in—streams of people—and Nancy was caught up in the excitement. Dave disappeared. Nancy could not understand him anyway. He had turned into such a humbug that he was getting hard to deal with. During the afternoon, Dale and Betty arrived. They were pastor friends and had been a great blessing to the Norrises. Already they had sent flowers from their church and an arrangement from their family, but now they came bearing additional gifts. For Dave, it was a coffee cup that said "Dad" and for Nancy, there was nice powder and gel for the shower. "Oh, thank you!" said Nancy. "This smells wonderful. I'll use it when I shower. And then when Nathaniel smells me, he will also smell your sweet gift."

Dave didn't seem thrilled with his coffee mug. Nancy decided she was going to have to talk to him. There was no reason for him to have such a sour look on his face, especially after people were kind enough to visit.

At one point twelve people filled the room, taking all the space allotted for two patients. They stood, sat on chairs, and even sat on the other unused hospital bed. Two families from their church drove an hour to the hospital. Minister friends from the area came as well. During all this activity, a nurse brought in two Polaroid pictures of Nathaniel and showed them to Nancy, but there was no time to look at them closely. The nurse taped them on the wall.

As Nancy made her way to the restroom that evening after everyone was gone, she approached the Polaroid pictures of Nathaniel. The pictures, hardly larger than the palm of her hand, were taped on the wall at odd angles. The first photo was hard to decipher. Tubes, monitors, and a plastic piece covered what must have been a baby, one camouflaged by the best efforts of modern science to keep him alive. The baby was easier to make out in the second photo, but his features were indistinct. She couldn't tell what he looked like. Nancy stared for several minutes at the two-dimensional renderings of her boy. She was a visual learner, but these pictures were pretty difficult to embrace, a poor substitute for the real thing.

Someone, somewhere, had apparently made a decision that Nancy was neither needed nor wanted down in the intensive care unit. No one thought that she should be taken down in a wheelchair to have a peek at her newborn son. She didn't want to interfere. Still, it was not as if she even needed to go inside the NICU. It would be enough just to look through the window. Even this had been denied her. Sadly, Nancy's baby had been more real to her during the nine months she had protected him in her womb. Now he might as well have been a million miles away. A tear gently rolled down her cheek as she faced the night. Maybe tomorrow would bring a better day.

Chapter 3

"Why is he taping popsicle sticks to my baby's legs?"

A troop of visitors came through that Saturday morning, two days after Nathaniel was born. The flow of traffic was almost always the same. First, visitors found Nathaniel through the glass of the NICU. They couldn't see much of him, mostly just the tubes and machines and wires going this way and that.

After several minutes of peeking into the window, the visitors would go see the mother, always taking care to mention that they had seen her baby. Nancy was happy for them, even though she had yet to see her baby. They offered information to new visitors who happened in the hospital room because they had important things to share. "Yes, he was five pounds when he was born, but he has lost some of the weight now." "True, he is still on oxygen, but the nurse said that they will try to start lowering the percentages just a little." "No, they don't know for sure what the abnormalities are. They're still doing tests." "Yes, the staff does seem very competent." And so it went.

But no matter how many upbeat comments were recycled in different ways, there was really not a lot to say. Some tried to say too much. One person offered, "God chose you as a special family because He knew you could handle this." Most people were more thoughtful in their remarks, and Nancy generally warmed to the encouragement, despite the busyness of it all.

Dave came in the morning, and while he wasn't as antsy as the day before, he still had his issues. Because he wasn't giving the visitors the attention they deserved, Nancy worked extra hard to make them feel at ease. It seemed rather ironic to her because she was the one in the hospital!

Midmorning, Dave escaped the hospital room to again stare through the glass of the NICU. Inside Nathaniel chafed at the tubes and the mask strapped on him while the insistent thrust of oxygen was forced down his lungs. Half a dozen other infants were situated around the brightly lit room, each receiving one-on-one attention from a nurse.

The doctor from yesterday saw Dave and came out to talk to him. He said he had nothing new to share. The oxygen level had been brought down to ninety-five percent, but that wasn't too significant. Then, instead of leaving right away, this same doctor remained next to Dave looking through the glass at Nathaniel's isolette. Presently another man carrying popsicle sticks and gauze tape appeared on the inside of the glass. Like other medical doctors that swooped into the room, he, too, wore a lab coat, but his beard and scholarly glasses made him appear more like a professor than a doctor. The man walked straight to Nathaniel's isolette and started doing things to Nathaniel's legs, first pulling them one way and then another. Then he began utilizing the gauze tape to attach a configuration of sticks to Nathaniel's legs.

"Who is that guy?" Dave asked the doctor.

"That's Dr. Huizinga."

"There is a reason, I suppose," asked Dave a little pointedly, "why he is taping popsicle sticks to my baby's legs?"

"Dr. Huizinga is an orthopedic specialist. It is easier to take care of issues right away with these newborns."

"So, what is he doing?" asked Dave.

"From what I understand," noted the doctor, "he is working to get Nathaniel's legs situated so that his knees and hips will more readily slide into position—you know, get in the right place so they can go back into joint."

Dave passively stood by watching as the baby's thrashing intensified, his little face darkening in fury. He felt helpless. He knew little about negotiating with doctors or making his own wishes as a parent known. What he did know was that his little baby was suffering and that this doctor was adding to it. He mumbled to himself, "Well, at least he'll have it all together as a corpse."

Slowly and almost imperceptibly during that afternoon, some good things started to happen. The oxygen level Nathaniel required started going down. He thrashed a bit less. It might have been Dave's imagination, but it seemed that the nurses were less tentative around him. Then he thought of the doctor working on Nathaniel's legs and conceded that it was probably a good thing after all. It might even mean that they thought Nathaniel would live.

The afternoon was full of visitors, and Nancy was particularly energized when children came. She laughed, asked questions, and shared stories. She worked to have meaningful conversation with each adult and child that entered the room. Between the phone calls and people dropping in, she had little time to reflect on anything else. It was clear that Dave was spent, so at 7:00 p.m. she sent him home. There was church the next day, and he hadn't arranged for anyone else to speak for him, so he had to prepare.

About 8:30 that evening, a doctor came in unexpectedly—it was hard to keep them all straight since all these doctors were new to her—and he had news. Apparently, this was Nathaniel's primary pediatrician, Dr. Stewart. He began to share their findings so far. "Mrs. Norris, we have ruled out certain genetic anomalies." She smiled, not knowing what he meant, but he continued, undeterred by the blank look on her face. "It appears that your son doesn't have Down syndrome."

"So there's nothing wrong with him genetically?"

"Well, I didn't say that. There could be, but, for certain, we have ruled out Down syndrome. We are continuing to test for other possibilities."

"Alright," replied Nancy nervously. "But how could he have all these problems if it is not Down syndrome?"

"There are a number of possible causes for his condition, including the possibility of some sort of connective tissue disorder." As the doctor explained each possible contingency, Nancy attempted to take it all in. As soon as the doctor left, she picked up the phone to call home. In Nancy's mind, there was no question that Nathaniel would live. She still didn't know what that would mean, but ultimately it didn't matter. This was her boy. It could well be that he would not be handicapped in the way that they feared. Elated, she dialed the phone.

"Dave, guess what? It's me, Nancy.... who else would be calling you...? Oh, I'm sorry. Did I wake you up? Are you in bed already? Sorry... well, Dr. Stewart came in for a kind of *ad hoc* consultation... and it's not Down syndrome.... No! Isn't that good? Well, he's not sure... there is at least a chance Nathaniel doesn't have a genetic problem after all and just has a connective tissue disorder or something.... No, not for sure... no... it needs to be confirmed.... There need to be more tests, but it is really good news! Dave, did you fall back asleep? So don't you think it's good news? Okay... I love you too!"

Nancy began to daydream about raising children. As a teenager, she spent her summers baby-sitting her nieces and nephews. She drove them around, bought them little trinkets, and had a ton of fun with them. Nancy's dad was a church planter in Chicago, and all through her teenage years she taught children in Sunday school. She loved to tell stories and play with children. And now, she was going to have her own child to dress up, play with, and hold.

It could be that her baby would have difficulties. Nancy knew she had to be realistic about this. But her baby was alive and she wouldn't lose him. Nancy remembered going to the funeral of her sister Cathy's baby. The baby was stillborn, and they said it had Down syndrome. What a terrible day that was. So whatever problems Nathaniel had, she and Dave would work through them together. She just wished he would get a bit happier about things.

Sometime in the middle of the night, Dave awoke with a sense of urgency. At first he ignored it, but somewhere between sleep and wakefulness the feeling became more and more intense. Gradually, he recognized the prompting he felt. It was a call to prayer. A dozen families called him pastor, besides the families of the children they picked up for Sunday school. Other times he had felt this summons, a kind of call, and knew that he was expected to respond. Obedience and not knowledge is what was required. So, despite his tiredness, he rolled out of bed and knelt next to it.

At first he didn't speak but listened. Nothing. "Lord God," he prayed, "I am asking You to meet the need.... Who is it, Lord?" Silence. Well, he had asked, so he was doing his part. He waited expectantly. "Lord, I love You. I want to serve You. Help me to hear Your voice, I pray. I ask You to meet this need." Still nothing. He had no idea what he was to pray for or for whom he was supposed to pray.

Finally, he felt the prompting of the Spirit of God. It was insistent, like a command, almost harsh. "Praise me!" came the prompt. That had never happened before. Why would God have to command praise? Praise should be something that happens naturally. It would only make sense if there were something difficult to praise Him for... something that made no sense from a human perspective. Otherwise, there would be no need for a command.

Dave thought about what the doctor had said and the hope he now held that everything was going to be all right. Then it occurred to him. The only good reason God would command Dave to praise Him was if the prognosis wasn't so good... if, in fact, there were severe problems with his son. Then Dave knew... he understood that this would be the case with his boy. He rejected this notion out of hand. He pronounced stubbornly, "No, I won't praise you."

Silence. Nothing. Then gentler this time, the same prompting came once more. "Praise me."

Less pause this time before Dave responded, "No."

And then more insistently, commanding, "Praise me."

After long seconds of silence, tears streamed down Dave's cheeks as he waited in the presence of the Lord. How long he knelt wordlessly he did not know. Finally he relented, gushing out tears of sorrow and submission. "Lord, I don't want to praise You, but

I will. I do praise You. I praise You for what is happening and for whatever will happen. I praise You even though I don't understand You at all. I don't even know You."

As Dave spoke those words, a kind of release immediately washed over him. How long he stayed there, he wasn't sure, but sometime afterward he cried himself to sleep. Yet, when he woke up in the morning, he had a new kind of peace. He wasn't sure exactly how, but he felt he had turned a page.

The next morning, Nancy had no visitors and no phone calls. She knew Dave had obligations Sunday morning and normally so did she. Each month she held planning meetings with new Sunday school teachers to help them become effective in their classes. She typically taught as well as oversaw the program, and she was proud of their dynamic Sunday school classes. But life went on without her this morning.

Dorothy came up first, and she was glad to see her. "Grandma Dorothy!" Nancy blurted out spontaneously, and from that moment on, the name 'Dorothy' could not be spoken without Grandma attached to the front end as a title of honor—a new term of endearment.

Dave came in shortly thereafter. He seemed more settled. Perhaps the church service had helped. Whatever the case, he was there and she was happy to see him. The morning had been more than a little slow.

Hospitals sometimes change their face on weekends. Regular doctor types tend to come up missing, authority figures get sparse, and while there is no direct mutiny by nurses, things just get a bit more relaxed. Nancy could sense it, a feeling that only increased when Sunday's second shift came on duty. It wasn't long before her nurse said in a conspiratorial tone, "That boy of yours is doing a bit better today. Let's see if we can get you down there to see him."

Nancy never knew who it was or what strings were pulled to allow for it, but however it happened, only twenty minutes later, Dave wheeled her down to the NICU with a nurse trailing close behind. Nancy couldn't see in the intensive care window because she was sitting in the wheelchair, so the nurse insisted that Nancy be brought inside. Then, after Nancy and Dave washed their hands and donned the appropriate white hospital gowns, Dave was allowed to wheel Nancy's chair right next to Nathaniel's isolette. They were further surprised as Maggie, the attending nurse, began unhooking things from Nathaniel.

"Won't he need that oxygen?" asked Dave, a furrow on his forehead.

"Nathaniel needs to be held by his mother," Maggie said, rebuking him softly. Soon, Maggie had removed some of the connections, and gingerly and triumphantly picked up Nathaniel. Nancy sat waiting, hardly believing what was happening. Other nurses looked on from their stations with conspiratorial grins, almost as if the whole NICU staff were in on this decision.

Ever so slowly Nancy reached up to receive him from the nurse while a tear of appreciation escaped her eye and rolled slowly down her check. And then she felt him, warm and soft in his blanket. Even though his eyes still hadn't opened, and although Dave doubted it and told her so, she was sure that Nathaniel knew her as soon as she touched him. She immediately felt the tension in him lessen as she cradled him. "You know my voice, don't you? Yes, it's Momma."

At the other end of the NICU, another drama was playing out, but this problem could not be readily fixed. Parents made their way down that aisle to see their son and to say their good-byes. The doctor explained that no brain activity was registering and that this had been the case for some time. Although the ventilator had done its duty, and medical science ensured that the heart still beat, it was all to no avail. The doctor told the family that they must decide, but in reality only one decision could be made—to remove life-support. The nurse disconnected the ventilator and gently handed the tiny infant into the arms of his mother, who sat in a rocking chair. For whatever reason, the nurse had not disconnected the wires that measured respiration and heartbeat. Both husband and wife stared transfixed at the display on the screen. The audible beeps that measured the heartbeat lessened; fewer and fewer sounded. The squiggly lines that had danced regularly across the screen became more and more lethargic. Forty, pronounced the beeping machine, then thirty, then twenty. At some point the nurses mercifully removed the leads from the monitor. The parents sobbed over the baby that had been unable to make it through the day.

Nancy held her son close to her and whispered promises into his ear. Nathaniel was now more than a waiting prognosis. This was not merely "male Norris baby" in bed five. This was her son. "Your name means 'gift of God,'" she pronounced to the little bundle. Eyes still closed, he purred softly at her voice.

"Now, Nathaniel," she continued, "they have to do some more poking and prodding on you, but you're starting to get better." Nathaniel wiggled a bit in her arms. "Remember, Nathaniel," she assured him, "Momma's gonna get you out of here." Suddenly he grimaced and scrunched up his face, wincing. She hurt for his hurt. But he was alive, and he was her sweet boy. Even though her heart ached for the difficult circumstances, it was not a hurt that she would wish away. It was sweet pain.

Chapter 4

"Don't put limits on Nathaniel...
you just never know"

S oft music played invitingly and romance filled the air. Clad in a
tuxedo-like outfit, the waiter bowed slightly, ushering Nancy and
Dave into the candlelit dining room and away from the burden
of a relentless hospital routine. Flickering light from a candle danced
across the starched white tablecloth garnished with real silverware,
the extra forks sitting proudly next to the fine china.

The waiter ceremoniously handled the crystal water pitcher, lifting
it high as he poured water into their glasses. Nancy glanced back at
the sign above the door of their restaurant. She and Dave were dining
at "The Carriage Inn," a "fashionable restaurant" in the heart of St.
Joseph's Hospital that was created expressly for parents of newborns.
It was Monday night, the night that the hospital scheduled this steak
dinner. For a number of parents, this intentionally upscale ambience
would be the last bit of respite before they embarked on the inevitable
stress that came with wakeful nights and a hungry mouth to feed.

Dave gazed across the flickering candle into the eyes of the woman
with whom he had fallen in love ten years earlier. When he and his
Bible college friends held informal summits as to which girls they
should pursue, they had a lot to talk about. With a hundred and sixty
girls to choose from, they needed to work out a short list, so as not
to waste a lot of time. Consequently, because Nancy was attractive,
and because Dave was quite taken with her dancing brown eyes, and
because she seemed to respond to his overtures, it didn't take Dave
long to get pretty serious about her. She wasn't quite so decided about
him. Of course, Nancy was happy for the male attention, something

she never seemed to lack. They dated for some months, but it wasn't until Dave was involved in a van wreck that Nancy realized that she was pretty sure that he was the one. At that point, Dave got cold feet and broke up with her—at least for a while.

They both attended the Bible college where Dave's grandfather was president. Rules were strict, and girls and guys were generally kept apart. Even talking too long in the lunchroom could have its consequences, and Dave had been counseled in more than one private meeting with his grandfather, a man both feared and respected by all.

When Dave and Nancy finally became engaged, it was Dave's intention to marry a year after he graduated from Bible college, the same time that Nancy would complete her teaching degree. But several meetings took place between he and his grandfather during his senior year, and it was decided that Dave needed to get married right away and that he should teach at the Bible school upon his graduation. His grandfather set the date and performed the ceremony. And that is how it happened that Dave graduated on a Sunday evening, turned twenty-one on Monday, and he and Nancy got married on Tuesday.

The wedding was simple but nice. Nancy had many ideas for the ceremony, and her brother even wrote a song. But, apparently, there were limited choices as to how weddings should be done at the church connected to the Bible school. If those ideas were different than hers, well, that's just the way it was. None of this really mattered to Nancy. She was marrying the man she loved. She was happy. The rest were just details.

Nancy had loved everything about being a bride: the flowers, her dress, her dad walking her down the aisle. It was over all too quickly to suit her. Now sitting across from her husband at the candlelit table, it was hard to believe that almost eight years had passed since their wedding day.

Seven other couples dined in the semi-darkness of The Carriage Inn that evening. While the wait staff was formally attired, some of the mothers, like Nancy, were adorned in bathrobes. She ordered her steak medium, and it was cooked to perfection. Other in the room were now in another world and it was just Nancy and Dave. Everything was perfect. Well, almost perfect. Toward the end of the meal, one of the fathers broke the romantic atmosphere with a horrendously loud belch. The music still played and the candlelight still danced off the crystal glasses, but somehow all Nancy could think about was how to keep from laughing. Dave shushed her, giving her a stern look. Nancy knew why. People were often surprised by incredibly loud bursts of laughter that escaped unbidden from her lips. It happened often, usually in just such a situation.

Nancy didn't shush easily. Because both Dave and Nancy knew the risk was real, Dave seemed to be reminding her to keep quiet every fifteen seconds. For Nancy, all of this just added to the humor, with Dave now becoming part of the problem. Even though he shushed her, he couldn't keep a straight face doing it. Indeed, with only the greatest effort did Nancy and Dave succeed in not embarrassing the burpaholic. But not without a price. Just as soon as they escaped the restaurant and headed down the hall, they could hold it in no longer. Both of them doubled over, guffawing and hooting until tears ran down their cheeks.

Manuel and Mary, pastor friends, came around the corner just in time to see Dave sliding down the wall in laughter. "Well now," offered Manuel, "we came to the hospital to cheer you up, but I guess you didn't need us after all."

The next day, Dave's grandmother called. When deciding whether to marry Nancy, it was his grandmother to whom he went for counsel and blessing. He listened closely when his grandmother gave advice. She was giving it now.

"David, it's important for you to hear what I am saying. Not too many years ago, they institutionalized all handicapped babies. I don't know if there will be any pressure to do so, but you need to take this child home and care for him, because he will thrive if you do." Dave didn't know how to make sense of this call. He had been so worried about Nathaniel's survival that he hadn't really thought about what would happen next.

Well enough to be up, Nancy spent most of the day in the NICU. Apparently, the fact that she had already held her son was best left unreported. Nobody on the day shift seemed to think this would be a good idea at all. Although Nathaniel was imprisoned in his isolette, he could hear her voice and feel the touch of her hand on his face if she slid it through the circle opening. As Nathaniel now needed less oxygen, it wouldn't be long before there were fewer restrictions. In the meantime, she would have to content herself with being near him.

Friends came to visit that evening, and after looking in on Nathaniel, they visited for a while in Nancy's hospital room. Abruptly, an official-looking lady popped her head in the door. "Doing okay?" she blurted out. The woman didn't look familiar, and Nancy wasn't sure what she wanted, so, she cheerfully greeted her and told her that yes, she was doing fine. After all the visitors left, the same lady popped in once more. Apparently she was some sort of social worker. "You don't have to be a rock, you know," said the lady. Nancy just looked at her, not knowing what to say. She wasn't a rock. Nor was she holding back any emotions, at least as far as she could tell.

"Well, um, thanks," she replied. The lady left.

"Your son will be completely off oxygen by the end of the day," Nancy's nurse told her.

Because she wasn't sure where the lady had come across this information or why she was sharing it, Nancy asked, "So what does that mean?"

"It means you can hold your baby as much as you want," said the smiling nurse.

Nancy washed her hands with antiseptic and donned the required white gown. After a nurse moved a rocking chair near Nathaniel's isolette, Nancy sat down and waited until the NICU nurse gently straightened the tubes and cables that still fed into the beeping monitors. Finally Nancy felt the warmth of blankets that cocooned the baby who lay in her arms.

Nathaniel's eyes were open, big and brown like his parents'. Nancy assumed that Nathaniel could really see her, that he really could hear her voice. She talked with him, all the while moving the fingers of one hand to see if he would follow her movement with his eyes. At first it seemed that Nathaniel was responding to her, but she couldn't tell, for he quickly lost interest. Nancy gently uncurled the infant's tiny hands. All the fingers were functioning, but there was a scab on one hand that no one could seem to explain, and as she examined him carefully, it looked as if one of his fingernails hadn't quite fully formed. No explanation for that either.

As Nancy started singing a lullaby, Nathaniel turned toward her. It took her by surprise. "So, you can hear me then, and you know my voice, do you, my little man?" She stroked his cheek with her hand. His skin was soft. Suddenly he whimpered. "It's okay," she said. "I know those doctors and nurses have been poking you a lot, but Momma is here."

Nathaniel settled down. Nancy took it as her cue to offer some bad news. "Now listen here," she said softly. "Mom has to go home tomorrow, but I'm coming back for you. And guess what? When you do come home, there is a room that is especially decorated for you. There is a Raggedy Andy on the wall. And we're going to bring you home as soon as we can."

Nathaniel started to cry, and it seemed to Nancy as if he were protesting her going home without him. Once before she had told Dave that Nathaniel understood her, but her husband was an unbeliever and told her to stop projecting on the baby. This time she decided not to tell Dave about the incident, even though she knew Nathaniel was not pleased with her. She would just keep it to herself. "It's just a little extra time," she consoled him. "They're trying to get your legs and knees in place. It won't be so bad." He whimpered some more but finally settled down.

Dave was waiting in the station wagon. Her suitcase and flowers from the room were already packed. As Nancy was signing her discharge papers, another nurse appeared. "Just sit right here," the nurse commanded Nancy, pointing to a wheelchair.

"But I've been walking just fine and—"

"In the chair," insisted the nurse, and Nancy obeyed. They passed an older gentleman with tousled grey hair who slowly shuffled down the hall. He wore a thin hospital gown and rumpled pants and was pushing an IV pole with a fluid bag hooked to the top. He certainly deserved a wheelchair, but the nurse paid him no attention. She continued on her mission, wheeling Nancy out the front door of the hospital and delivering her securely to the safety of their station wagon.

Forty-five minutes later Dave pulled into the parking space and opened Nancy's car door. He took her arm as if she were fragile goods and guided her to the entrance of their condominium. When he opened the door, a floral arrangement welcomed her from atop the kitchen counter. The potpourri that Nancy kept around the apartment was a delightful change from the antiseptic smell that had permeated the hospital. After eight days in the hospital, it was good to be home.

"You just sit right down here in Gramma's lap," insisted Nancy's mom as reached up to take the baby from the nurse. Nathaniel was happy to oblige. Nancy's mom and dad had driven up from the south side of Chicago, along with her two sisters Jan and Cathy. Her mom was in her mid-fifties, but with her slim figure, dark hair, and youthful face, people assumed she was ten years younger. Grandpa Jim Abshire looked on at this grandson who had been named after him. With his silver hair and distinguished dress, on more than one occasion he had been asked, "Did anyone tell you that you look like Senator Moynihan?"

"Yes, I have been told that," he would respond urbanely.

A tear rolled down his cheek. After all the others had cradled the boy, it was finally his turn. He held the baby inches from his face, almost nose to nose. He spoke to him as if he were formally christening a ship. "We've been praying for you, and we are asking for God's richest blessings on your life." Nancy noticed how her dad rolled the "r" when he said "richest" as if he were speaking to a congregation or leading a group in prayer. Nathaniel looked a little surprised by the close-up attention, but then broke into a tentative smile. At that moment, Nancy felt like she, too, was being held.

Nancy and Dave were early for their appointment with their geneticist, Dr Jürgen Hermann. They were nervous as they sat in the waiting room, but once they entered his office, his welcoming manner set them at ease.

"Let me explain what we have found," he began. The doctor spoke slowly, and while for the most part his words were pretty easy to grasp, at odd moments he slipped into language beyond what either parent understood. "Your baby has Cri du Chat syndrome," said the geneticist. "This syndrome was discovered in 1963 by a doctor named Jérôme Lejeune."

"Cri du Chat. What does that mean?" asked Dave, genuinely interested.

"It's French. It means, 'cry of the cat.' Nancy, let me ask you something. Did you ever notice that when Nathaniel cries, he has a kind of high-pitched mew?"

"Yes," said Nancy. "I think it is very special."

"It is. And Lejeune discovered, among other things, that all babies with Cri du Chat have this same high-pitched sound like the mewing of a kitten."

"And that's genetically determined?" asked Dave.

"Exactly. You know that genetic material called DNA determines how we look, how tall we are, the color of our eyes—everything about us. And in every cell of our bodies, this DNA is present in chromosomes. We have twenty-three pairs of chromosomes, forty-six in all. Nathaniel has a little missing piece of one of those chromosomes, chromosome number five.

"So all of the things that are wrong with him physically are caused by that missing piece?" asked Nancy.

"Right. Let me show you this paper that maps out Nathaniel's chromosomes. I have here an image of what we call karyotypes—it's kind of like a little map that shows what Nathaniel's chromosomes look like." Dr. Hermann took a pencil and pointed, continuing to explain. "And this shows what we are looking at." On the paper were what looked to be X-rays of any number of squiggly worms, all of whom had picked a partner that lay more or less next to the other.

"We have enhanced this so you can readily see what we are looking at," continued the doctor, but whatever they did to the image, it still looked like squiggly worms to Dave. The doctor then pointed to the offending chromosome. "You see here. Look at this." Nancy and Dave tried, but no revelation was forthcoming. The object to which the doctor pointed looked similar to the rest of the squiggly worms. Dr. Hermann continued, "Now if you'll look closely here at the short arm of chromosome number five, you'll notice there is a deletion."

Actually, they were looking closely, but they couldn't make anything out. Because Dave's thoughts were starting to wander, he thought he'd better do something to stay focused. He asked a question: "So, you are saying that in each cell of his body, Nathaniel has a missing chunk of genetic material?"

"Exactly," said Dr. Hermann, who seemed to be anticipating the question. At this, the doctor produced a larger blow up of the same chromosome. "You see, Mr. and Mrs. Norris, the problem with Nathaniel is that he is missing material in a critical part of the chromosome. He pointed to the paper with a pencil, sketching out a particular area."

"What does that mean?" asked Nancy.

"I'm afraid that Nathaniel will fall on the lower end of the spectrum in terms of severity."

"Well then, what symptoms should we look for?" asked Nancy.

Dr. Hermann paused thoughtfully. "I'll tell you what. I have a little booklet here that describes the various anomalies that result from Cri du Chat syndrome. I will step out and let you read it together, and then I will come back in a few minutes, and I will answer any questions that you may have. But I warn you. This study was done a decade ago with Cri du Chat children who were institutionalized. What it says about morbidity—that is the incidence of serious health issues—is not nearly so high in children who are cared for in their own homes."

When he left, Nancy and Dave began to peruse the booklet. It detailed a long list of what was likely: significant physical handicaps, severe mental retardation, chronic sickness, and a life span that would be very meager indeed. There was not one shred of good news in the whole booklet. Dave exhaled. "Nance, I don't know how we're going to be able to handle this." Nancy took in the same material, but said nothing. Before long, the doctor reappeared and asked what questions they had.

"What causes this?" asked Nancy.

"Ninety percent of the cases are *de novo.* That is, they just sort of randomly happen. Ten percent of births happen because of genetic material passed down from the mother or father. One of you could be a carrier. If you would allow me, I would like to do some tests to eliminate this as a possibility. Nancy and Dave readily agreed and scheduled a time to give blood. The doctor continued. "Really, if people actually understand all that goes into having a healthy child, they would begin to appreciate what a miracle it is."

Finally, as Dr. Hermann looked empathetically at Dave and Nancy, he offered compassionately, "Mr. and Mrs. Norris, don't put limits on how long Nathaniel can live or what he can learn. You just never know."

Chapter 5

"I dont' care how you have to do this, but we're moving out of here!"

The problem was Nathaniel's hips and knees. They were still out of joint. Dr. Huizenga's earlier efforts to utilize popsicle sticks and adhesive tape as a corrective measure failed, so now the doctor was trying again.

Nancy never knew where he got this new contraption. Perhaps he had a workroom down in the inner recesses of the hospital. However it was that he came up with it, the good doctor now held a device consisting of wooden dowels fastened together to resemble a miniature goalpost. It measured about twelve inches high and twelve inches across. In what way he secured this to the base of Nathaniel's isolette, Nancy wasn't quite sure. Next, the doctor hoisted Nathaniel's feet and legs vertically, attaching them to the top of the goalpost. This maneuver effectively put Nathaniel in traction, something he did not especially appreciate.

Regrettably, it only took a few days to realize that this prescription also failed to yield the hoped for results. That left one alternative: surgery. Consequently, twenty-five days after barely surviving a difficult birth, Nathaniel would be subjected to a surgeon's scalpel.

The night before the surgery, Nancy and Dave stayed in Milwaukee with their friends Dale and Betty. About 6:30 the next morning, the Norrises arrived at the hospital in time to pray for Nathaniel. Already situated on the rolling gurney that would transport him to the operating room, he showed no particular appreciation for the prayer. He only knew that his routine was being altered and showed his distress about it as the nurses wheeled him away.

Nancy sat in the waiting room leafing through two-year-old magazines so stained that some pages were almost illegible. After working her way through a half-dozen or so germ-laden periodicals, she made a mental note to include as a part of her life mission the goal of bringing new magazines to waiting rooms. Dave sat in a kind of fog-like state, not quite catatonic, but certainly not inviting conversation. Perhaps he was recalling the waiting room experience when he first saw Nathaniel. Perhaps a month of crisis had taken a toll on him and he was afraid of more bad news. But for whatever reason, when Nancy talked to Dave, he only harrumphed out a brief yes or no but otherwise stewed in silence. Two competing televisions bombarded the room with racket, while those waiting nervously drank stale coffee. More time elapsed than what they were told it would take, but eventually the surgeon came out to see them, apparently pleased with himself.

"Mr. and Mrs. Norris?" he asked, as if he had forgotten that he had just met them before the surgery.

"Yes."

"It went well. We got his knees in place, but we'll have to wait to see for sure on the hips. We decided that our best shot to make this work was to create a body cast for Nathaniel. It covers him from his armpits down to his toes."

Dave smiled. "Um, I don't mean to appear ignorant, but doesn't Nathaniel have certain bodily functions that need to be taken care of?"

"Well," laughed the doctor, "we made an open area at the bottom. Just put one big diaper around the whole cast."

"You've got to be kidding me," said Dave in amazement. "This I gotta see."

The surgeon then left. The couple would wait another forty-five minutes before Nathaniel came out of "recovery." Eventually, they were informed that their baby had been brought up to NICU for observation. They weren't far behind. "Well now, look at you, Nathaniel," said Nancy laughing. The body cast served like a little chair for him that sat him upright.

Dave tapped the plaster cast with his finger. It was solid. "This thing's a tank!" he said.

After only a couple of days, the doctor transferred Nathaniel to the intermediate care unit. Because the nurses would now allow others to assist in feeding and caring for Nathaniel, Nancy decided that this would be a good time for Dave's sister Pat to come for her promised visit. Dave and Pat had been close growing up, best friends, really.

Pat was eleven months older than him. Like all the rest of Dave's siblings, Pat had brown hair and brown eyes. Pat and Dave were more like best friends growing up, and they spent their teenage years competing together on a Bible quiz team. In their latter teen years, they became leaders of the youth group at church.

Pat was surprisingly trim for having had three daughters in quick succession. She said was going to have six children, and given the pace she was keeping, it was likely to be true. This had always surprised Dave because growing up, Pat was bookish, always at the top of her class at school, and seemed destined to be teaching in a college classroom. But when she and her husband Bill had started pastoring in a small farming town in southern Minnesota, Pat became the consummate pastor's wife and mother. She invested herself into her church and especially into her children.

Pat had somehow arranged for the care of her three small girls and readily made the eight-hour drive across Wisconsin's rolling hills with just a couple of days' notice. When Pat first walked into the hospital room, a nurse was doing a gavage feeding. "I can do that," said Pat, and the nurse proceeded to show her how.

Because Nathaniel had an underdeveloped sucking reflex, Nancy's milk was provided in an unusual way. A very thin feeding tube was lubricated with some sort of water-soluble gel. Then it was inserted down Nathaniel's nose until the end slid down into his stomach. Then mother's milk or formula was allowed to flow by gravity from an oversized syringe through the tube into Nathaniel's stomach. When the nurse told Dave she would teach him how to do the feeding, he got a little green around the gills and left the room.

But Pat latched onto the procedure right away. The nurse only explained it briefly, and she mastered it at once. This was the way she attacked life. When she got an idea and determined that something was important, she poured herself into it. The entire time she was there, she assisted Nancy throughout the days at the hospital. It didn't take Nathaniel any time at all to get used to being held a lot more throughout the day.

Dave and Nancy were about to leave to bring Nathaniel home. Nancy took a last look in the nursery. Not only was it clean and decorated nicely, but like everything else in their condominium, it was new. That was the funny thing about this condominium. Dave never planned to live here. It is surprising how it happened.

Four and a half years earlier they had moved to West Bend to start a church. They first held services in the family room of their rented duplex. A Sunday school class took over Nancy's laundry room and another spilled into the garage. The crowding was remedied only when the church bought an old house in the downtown area of West Bend and began to remodel it one Saturday at a time.

Church services were held on the first floor of the building, but to keep expenses down, the Norrises lived upstairs. Well, not exactly— it wasn't quite as neat and tidy as that. Actually, the kitchen was downstairs too, kind of in the middle of where one would walk to go from any part of the building to the next. As the church grew busier, more and more people marched right through Nancy's dinnertime. It was always for a good cause. They had to paint a Sunday school class in the basement, put up a bulletin board, or participate in some ongoing refurbishing project. At first, all of this was very exciting, but after a couple of years it became a little strained.

People often came to the church seeking money or help. One time a man called for help in the middle of the night. He was threatening to commit suicide. Dave dissuaded him from carrying through on his threat, and then talked the man into leaving his six-pack of beer at the church to keep from further diminishing rational thought.

The preacher and his family didn't drink, so Nancy thought this would be a good time to try a beauty tip she had heard. Supposedly beer nourished hair in important ways. So, while Dave drove his bus route, she improved her shower by dousing her hair with beer, expecting immediate shimmering and lasting results. When Dave returned home from work, she feared the bathroom smelled suspiciously of beer. "You don't smell anything, do you?" she asked guiltily.

Dave sniffed here and there to satisfy her. "No. Is there something I should smell?"

"No. Not really... well... beer." Right then and there true confession was made.

If they had a problem before—how a preacher could throw away a six-pack of beer in the church trash—she had compounded it. How can a preacher throw away the empties? No one might notice, but Nancy still hesitated to put the beer cans in the church trash. So the Norrises drove to another part of town with great stealth. Nancy kept watch while Dave hoisted the offending trash bag into the dumpster behind a business.

Their problem of privacy was further compounded when two young men from the church, Paul and Mark, rented the first floor of the house next to them. The kitchen window from the other house was twenty feet from Nancy's kitchen window. Paul, who needed significant doses of attention, waved across good-naturedly from his window as Nancy finished serving salads and started into the main course. Paul would wave at least once more before dessert, and Mark, the other young man, followed suit. This became something of a ritual. One night, Nancy had enough. "Let's give them something to look at," she insisted and signaled Dave. He understood and the two young men were treated to some passionate kissing in the preacher's house next door.

Dave was never sure what the last straw actually was. All he knew was that when he came home one afternoon, Nancy was waiting for him with arms crossed. "I don't care how you have to do this, but we're moving out of here!" He knew she meant it. Within a week, they had a lease on this condominium.

There were three immediate advantages to the condominium. First, it was only a stone's throw from where Dave drove his school bus. Second, it was only a couple of miles from church. And third, Nancy in particular appreciated the relative distance from all the church activities. "Peace and quiet at last," she noted on more than one occasion, glad for the respite. Given the change of circumstances, it probably shouldn't have surprised the Norrises that not long after moving into the condominium, Nancy became pregnant.

Not long after this discovery, a young couple moved into the empty condo right above the Norrises. It had the same floor plan as theirs. Nancy met them moving in—a young Korean lady named Young and her little baby Deborah. Shortly afterward, she met Young's husband Bill. When this new family discovered that Dave and Nancy were starting a church, they checked it out. Before long, Nancy's nearest neighbors were also members of their church.

One night, after Dave turned the bedroom lights out, he rolled over and whispered, "You know, Nance, the military is moving Bill's things."

"I know that."

"And they haven't arrived."

"They should be here soon," she replied, not knowing why they were both whispering.

"But did you know, Nancy, that while they are waiting for their furniture to arrive, Bill and Young, our upstairs neighbors, are sleeping on the floor with a blanket... and did you know that they are sleeping in the room right above us?" Nancy could only smile.

Nancy had reinforcements waiting when they carried Nathaniel into the condominium. Nancy's mom, Gramma Abshire, took a week off work from her accounting job at the hospital. Dave thought that he and Nancy could handle it fine without her, but Nancy was certainly looking forward to her mom coming. As it turned out, it was good that she came. Things didn't go as smoothly as anticipated. As soon as they laid Nathaniel down in his crib, the crying started. It wasn't a harsh, painful cry. It was more insistent, a complaining high-pitched plea. It went on, and on, and on. They rocked him, fed him, and changed him. Nothing helped. Grandma Abshire took her turn walking the floor with him, trying to settle him down. At 3:30 in the morning, everyone was still up. Finally, Nancy's mom got an idea. "You know, I just wonder... Nathaniel has never slept with the lights out. The NICU was bright as day, and there was always noise. Do you think Nathaniel would be more comfortable if all the lights were on and we played some music?" He was. As a result, so was everyone else.

It was Wednesday night Bible study, and the newest member of the Norris household decided to make his appearance known at church. That night, Bible study didn't go all that well for Dave. He was being upstaged. A six-week-old infant was cooing, laughing, and teasing the audience. Dave decided to speak louder. "And then Jesus told them…" he began but was interrupted with a high-pitched mew talking back at him.

Dave tried to take control. "Nathaniel, I'll handle this one." Nathaniel cooed again, and it was clear that the audience was on the side of the younger Norris speaker.

After church, Nathaniel belonged to everyone. "I thought Grandma Dorothy was watching him," said Nancy, as Dorothy walked out the front door and headed for home. "Don't worry," assured Dave. "That cast is indestructible. Whoever has him, it hardly matters." Only after dispersing the crowd of children that surrounded him were the Norrises able to get Nathaniel out of the building.

Nancy and Dave took Nathaniel in to meet their family doctor. Dr. Griswold had been particularly kind to the Norrises. He charged a pittance for an office call, and sometimes he simply forgot to charge them at all. "So here he is at last," said Dr. Griswold, taking Nathaniel into his arms.

"He's seven pounds and twelve ounces with the cast," reported the nurse, "but I have no clue as to what real weight that translates into."

"You have no idea how many times I have called '334-7770' and got no answer," said the doctor, citing their home phone from memory. He continued, "I'm so glad to see him well."

After a routine checkup, Dr. Griswold turned to other matters. "What kind of insurance do you guys have?"

"Well, Nancy still has insurance through NEA, but it doesn't look like she'll be able to get back to teaching any time soon. In any case, I think we can keep her insurance for a number of months before we have to transfer—"

"They're going to ding you for preexisting conditions and you probably won't pick up any policy nearly so good."

"Well, what do you suggest?"

"I don't have any suggestions about an insurance policy, but I want you to consider something. I need you to think about applying for SSI. Wisconsin has a really good program. They will pick up anything your insurance doesn't pay for and might even give a little monthly check besides."

"And we would qualify because of Nathaniel's condition?"

"Uh… yes." Dr. Griswold offered a tactful pause. "And, uh… because of your income."

Dave and Nancy had never considered themselves to be poor. It was true that they didn't have a lot of money, but all of their needs were met. "Well, I don't know if we really need the check," Dave began.

"So Nathaniel couldn't use a little extra money each month to help with expenses?" asked the doctor. Dave then understood that it was his pride speaking and promised to look into it.

A lot to planning went into their Easter service. The church had rented the auditorium from the University of Wisconsin extension campus and advertised heavily for people to come hear Dr. Ray Kloepper, who was to speak on "The Medical Aspects of the Crucifixion." Nate came from St. Paul to do the music and directed their first-ever choir. They had a record attendance of 110.

Dave invited the mayor to introduce Dr. Kloepper, since the good doctor came as a specially invited guest to the fair city of West Bend. There were, however, a few people that Dave intended to keep away from the mayor. One in particular was Mark. Mark had apparently been on drugs. Although he had a genuine conversion experience, he tended to express his faith in strange ways. Like the time he picketed in front of the police station that Jesus was coming back soon. "Uh, Reverend Norris, there is a man from your church that we're holding right now...."

"I'll be right down."

Another time, Dave received a call while he was traveling. The caller said that Dave needed to return right away because Mark was being "deprogrammed". Sure enough, Mark's parents, who were rather wealthy folks from another city, had Mark captured and had hired deprogrammers to try to help him. Dave only found out about it because Mark had escaped from his deprogrammers and was calling Dave for help. "I'd like to deprogram him myself," mumbled Dave, but then offered to Mark, "How about if we get you and your parents together in the same room and talk this thing through."

"He says we're going to hell," shared Mark's mother, and the father offered additional anathemas that Mark had pronounced upon them. Dave attempted to mediate, but no matter how much he tried to explain that he wasn't the one causing Mark's behavior, and that Mark was actually acting contrary to his wishes, they didn't believe him. It didn't help that Mark sat with his arms folded, pronouncing continued invectives on his parents, proclamations for which he readily credited his new found faith.

Seeing he was getting absolutely nowhere, Dave made Mark leave the room. He then humbly approached the couple who sat across from him. "Look, I don't want you to be offended, but I have to ask you a question so that I can begin to understand. And whatever you say, I accept. Well… uh… did Mark act strangely before he became religious?"

They laughed—a good sign. Apparently his eccentric behavior was nothing new to them. It was just dressed up in religious garb— and his new religion gave Mark a "one-up" on his parents. After all, if God is one your side, who has to listen to other authority figures? It was an important moment, and Dave sensed that perhaps this was a beginning. While it was not exactly trust, at least there was the possibility of dialogue. Dave ended with the invitation, "Call me anytime. Let's work this out together."

Now, here, on Easter Sunday morning, as the service ended and people were shaking hands, Mark began weaving his way over to the mayor. Dave tried to head him off, but Mark only quickened his pace. Before Dave could stop him, Mark slapped the mayor on the back. "He is risen, Mayor!" pronounced Mark enthusiastically. The city official staggered forward.

"Yeah, I know," responded the mayor coolly. "He did that a long time ago."

Chapter 6

"You are the carrier"

"Well, I have good news and bad news," announced the doctor, though his mannerism made it clear that he didn't have good news at all. Nancy and Dave had taken Nathaniel in for a follow-up visit after his surgery, and he was the subject of the doctor's oration. "The good news is that Nathaniel's knees are now in joint. The bad news is that we weren't able to get his hips in place."

There was a pause as Nancy and Dave waited for more information. When none seemed forthcoming, Dave asked, "Are you going to try again?"

The doctor hemmed and hawed around a bit and then motioned for them to follow him to the other end of the room. "Now, if you notice on this x-ray," he offered, pointing with his pencil to the x-ray attached to the lighted glass, "we have a malformation here." He said this, tapping the glass insistently, as if Dave were in the habit of perusing x-rays in his spare time. He continued, "We don't think we're going to be able to readily get his hips back in at all."

Dave protested. "Wouldn't another surgery help?" The doctor said nothing. Dave continued, "You mean, that's it? We went through all of this and now you're just giving up?"

The doctor paused, attempting to sound consoling, which he was not. Rubbing his hands together in a contemplative gesture, he said without compassion, "I wouldn't worry about it. Nathaniel will probably be a 'sitter' anyway." He smiled when he said it and paused once more. Dave felt like the man had slapped him across the face. In one fell swoop, this doctor had passed a life sentence on Nathaniel, pronouncing him wheelchair bound. It was a lot to handle.

The next day, after Dave's bus route, he hung up the keys and talked to his boss. "Say, Ralph," he began. "I know that Threshold is primarily a sheltered workshop for adults, but I am interested in their program that does early interventions with handicapped infants. Does that require a doctor's referral or does someone apply for that here onsite?"

His boss found something very interesting to look at on his desk. The drivers all knew that Dave's wife was going to have a baby, and they also knew that this baby had been born handicapped. "Uh, yeah," said the supervisor tentatively. "I don't know that much about it; it's in a separate part of the building."

Dave walked over to the front of the building and entered an area where therapists appeared to be working with infants, some of whom were decidedly handicapped. His steps felt heavy as he approached the front desk to make an inquiry. The lady readily answered his questions and made Dave feel at ease. "So it is possible, then, that my son could participate?" he finally asked. In response, she nodded, handing him all the paperwork to fill out.

At home, Dave explained the program to Nancy. Yes, it was possible that with a doctor's recommendation Nathaniel could soon be enrolled and attending their early intervention program. No, there was no charge. The program had outside funding. Yes, he could start right away, but they would also do a site visit of their home before Nathaniel could start. Why? He didn't know why... yes... social worker... Mary... Friday... 1:30.

Nancy wasn't happy about the site visit at the condo. Did they want to know whether she was a fit mother? "I'll show them a fit mother," she mumbled with a worried look as she polished the stainless steel sink, determined that it would glisten. The doorbell rang. Nancy sighed. All the dishes were put away. No dirt or lint had escaped her sight. Nathaniel sat patiently on the couch, propped up in his cast. Nancy wiped her hands on a dishtowel and sweetly opened the door, ready with a prepared speech.

The social worker hardly spoke to her. She eyed Nathaniel on the couch and said his name as if she had discovered gold in California. "Oh, Nathaniel!" she cried and slipped past Nancy. She picked him up, cast and all, and embraced him, all the while telling him how special he was. Nancy, still standing with the door open, went unnoticed.

Nancy smiled. This woman was not assessing her housekeeping abilities or even her skills as a mother. Though she may have been a social worker, she evidently truly cared about her son. Nathaniel wasn't just a client, a case number, or merely another infant added to the rolls of the early intervention program. As Nancy stood there, she witnessed Mary holding her son as if her boy were truly precious. As Nancy reflected on her lost hopes and shattered dreams, she acknowledged that a lot had been taken away from her in the last few months. Yet this woman was not taking away; she was giving back. Nancy could not remember having ever received a more precious gift.

Nancy and Dave had other visitors. His sister Linda and her husband Tony came down from St. Paul along with Dave's sister Joanne. Joanne had visited a year earlier when they had a Moped and had cruised around town a bit on it, but that was gone now, and the only interesting thing to see was Nathaniel.

That night Dave took an evening stroll down the road from the condo. The complex was a series of buildings, multiple units that had a pleasing way of jutting this way and that way in identical patterns. When Dave returned from his walk and put the key in the outside door, the tumblers in the lock seemed out of whack. He wondered if perhaps all the bugs in the doors weren't quite worked out. He worked even harder to get the key to turn, but it wouldn't budge. In fact, the key seemed to be getting stuck in the door. Despite Dave's best effort, he could not get inside.

Suddenly the door flew open. It wasn't Nancy—it was some guy in shorts and a sleeveless tee shirt. Something else was amiss as well. Someone had changed all of Dave's furniture around. In fact, it didn't even look like his furniture. Dave looked up at the condo number to make sure it was theirs. It was. And then it hit him. "Sorry," he said, turning to leave. "Right address. Wrong building."

The man at once lost his look of concern and laughed out loud. "Am I happy to hear that," he said. Apparently, he'd been watching a "slasher movie" where someone was just about to get cut up by a chain saw. And while the blood and guts were splattered all over the screen, he heard a key turning in the door as some intruder attempted to get inside his apartment.

Dave and Nancy sat in the waiting room until Dr. Hermann signaled them to come into his office. "Mr. and Mrs. Norris, have a seat," he offered warmly. In his hand he held a manila folder with a half a dozen sheets of paper in it. He also carried a simple, lined pad of paper. Nancy leaned forward to hear his words. "Now, as I explained," Dr. Hermann began, "with Cri du Chat syndrome ninety percent of the cases occur *de novo*. That is to say, it is simply a genetic accident that we cannot explain. I also told you that there is a ten percent chance that one of you is a carrier. Let me explain what I mean by that."

It suddenly struck Nancy that if Nathaniel were the result of a genetic accident they would not be having this conversation—for the doctor would have immediately said so. No, there had to be something more. "Now, when a baby is first conceived, both the father and mother contribute genetic material, twenty-three chromosomes each." Nancy was sure. Either she or Dave was a carrier.

"Although it's rare," continued Dr. Hermann, "individuals sometimes have among their chromosomes what we call a balanced translocation." He then began to draw the squiggly little pieces that he showed them while explaining why Nathaniel was missing part of chromosome number five. He labeled one chromosome number five and another eleven. "That is to say," he continued, "a small portion of one chromosome becomes attached to another." At this, he took part of chromosome five and moved it to chromosome eleven.

"In the case of a balanced translocation, it is possible to go for generations and never discover any chromosomal difficulties, just as long as both chromosomes, in this case chromosome five and eleven, get passed down by the one who has the balanced translocation. However, if only part of the chromosomal material gets passed on, then the child will reflect that deficiency. Mrs. Norris, you are the carrier. That is to say, you have a balanced translocation."

Nancy was too stunned to hear much of what was said next. First, she felt numb. And then, it was like she was someone else watching a couple named Nancy and Dave get genetic counseling. Dr. Hermann was talking, but it was coming from far away… "chromosome five attached itself to chromosome eleven…." The doctor was sketching a chart now. "But Nathaniel got Dave's chromosome eleven… Nancy's chromosome five… missing piece… short arm… that's the cause."

The doctor continued drawing more lines while Dave asked him questions. She could see herself crying, but it was all so far away. Suddenly, she heard Dave ask a question that brought her back to the room.

"What about having more children? I mean, what are our chances of having a normal child?" Nancy saw the doctor draw four lines and heard him talking again, but then his words were just so painful that she could only receive them with great effort. "As a purely statistical starting place, there is a twenty-five percent chance of another balanced translocation… twenty-five percent hydrocephalic—"

"What does that mean?" interrupted Dave.

Nancy began fading again. Dr. Hermann was saying more about chromosome five and eleven, but she didn't care to listen.

"So then, there is only a twenty-five percent chance of having an absolutely normal child?" Dave pressed.

"Well, from a purely statistical starting place. Yes. But there are mitigating factors." The doctor was once again talking from a faraway place. He was saying something about possibly getting other family members tested, and she was nodding as if she were present. First mentally and then finally physically, she left the office to go home.

Now they would never be able to have more children. And she was the cause.

"You are *not* the cause," Dave insisted angrily. "It is something that just happened." But this was meager comfort. Just the words of a man who needed something to say. And she told him so. At this point, Dave struggled to give her assurance. He usually could say the right words. Now, he could offer nothing helpful.

A few days later Nathaniel's cast was cut away. While he was afraid during the procedure, he was certainly happy for the results. He now seemed surprised and even delighted to move parts of his body that for too long had been held in place. He would need therapy to get all the muscles working properly, but he was free at last.

For the first time in his life, Nathaniel had a real bath. Nancy placed him in a little tub that was constructed to support him, a plastic piece holding his back upright during bath time. However, as Nancy took the washcloth and wiped his face, Nathaniel jerked suddenly. He had been accidently splashing, and the sensation caught him off guard. He wasn't sure about this whole experience. Still, for Nathaniel's mother, this was a wonderful mile marker.

It was April. Nathaniel was two-and-a-half-months-old when he started the early intervention program at Threshold. A full-sized

Chevy Suburban picked him up each weekday morning. The driver would gather him up and strap his car seat in, where Nathaniel joined several other car seats already strapped in place. A few hours later he would reappear in the Suburban, generally happy for the excursion. Nathaniel loved people and action, and he especially loved to travel, which was a good thing, too, because Nancy and Dave did a lot of it.

In May, Nathaniel turned three-months-old and had another surgery: a bilateral hernia repair. In June, Nathaniel was formally dedicated at church. It was a special occasion. He had made it to four months.

Because they needed a little more room for the dedication service, they used the community room at the bank. Nancy's mom and dad came as did Dave's sister Pat and her husband Bill. Bill spoke and their three little girls played a trio on small, undersized violins. When asked how three girls under five could play the violin together, Pat explained that the girls had learned to play by the Suzuki method, a technique that apparently had nothing to do with motorcycles.

Grandpa Abshire was asked to pray the dedication prayer. He kept his more-salt-than pepper-colored hair stylishly long, had on his white suit, and a crisp white shirt and tie. "And now, Lord, we ask your special blessing...." Nancy noted how he stretched out the word "special," and how he pronounced other words as well, his rich booming voice articulating every word clearly and slowly. Nancy thought back to her childhood and how her father's voice resonated as he ministered from the pulpit of the church where he pastored. She had to admit that she appreciated his voice less back then. When she was younger, Nancy was primarily concerned with how quickly he would finish speaking so she could go out and play. But today it was particularly important that her dad was here, for it reminded her that God was with her, and that He was with her boy, and whatever difficulties they would have to encounter, they would never encounter them alone.

July came. "Nancy," Dave asked, "should we take Nathaniel with us to these camps?"

"I don't see why not. I mean, if he is healthy enough."

Nancy and Dave worked with a lot of ministry with children. They were in charge of the program for children age six to eleven at family camp in Shawano, Wisconsin. While the parents and teenagers had their own program, Nancy and Dave coordinated a program for the children. The evening service for the adults could be long, and it was the Norris's responsibility both to educate and entertain, making a difference in the lives of the children. Dave's cousin, Ann, was the invited guest who performed each night with large Muppet-style puppets.

Nathaniel came and went, carted around by this or that babysitter. For a five-month-old child, he sure loved the action unless the children became too loud. Then he simply hollered to be excused or have someone install earplugs until the racket settled down.

It was a week later. Two hundred and fifty fourth to sixth-grade children in central Illinois watched the ventriloquist and her dummy.

"I'm just too short," complained the ventriloquist dummy.

"You are not," replied Nancy, encouraging her puppet.

"Yes, I am. Too short. Other kids won't even play with me."

"I saw you playing baseball," Nancy reminded Polly, her vent figure.

"Yeah, but the only thing they let me play is shortstop. And when I grow up," complained the dummy, "the only job I'll be able to get is as a short-order cook... cooking short-stacks." Nancy proceeded to reassure Polly, her vent figure, quickly segueing into the story of Zacchaeus.

Nancy's act was followed by Dave, who was dressed up in a doctor's coat and sporting an oversized fake nose and glasses. "My name is Dr. Albert Schnitzelhouse," he pronounced with a thick German accent. "And I have come to do my greatest experiment ever. I just need a victim—I mean a volunteer—to help." With the help of the children, Dave then used "gospel magic" to conduct some "experiment" that offered a spiritual lesson. Nathaniel didn't pay much attention, but he did enjoy spending the week with Pam, his special babysitter, and he didn't get sick at all.

In August, Nathaniel once again went with his parents to camp in Shawano, Wisconsin. This time they were in charge of the entire camp. As directors, they organized everything from balancing the budget to getting a cook, overseeing the teachers and dorm supervisors, and watching over a large group of nine to eleven year-olds. A very capable team worked together on this project, so most of the time it really was fun.

Dave worked with a team to bring a Bible character to life, and during the course of the week, they would act out the story in dramatic fashion on a stage. Hollywood it was not, as dishwashers, helpers, and anyone who could get a costume on was recruited to act alongside the main characters. Late night practices sometimes became hilarious. Twice a day, 150 children watched in rapt attention as they identified with and internalized the values of the characters that came to life from the pages of Scripture.

One day, a camp worker brought two nine-year-old girls to Dave. They were as cute as buttons. "I can't seem to get these two girls to stop fighting," she reported.

"Well, what's going on here?" Dave offered in his deepest voice, trying to muster a little authority. In truth, he loved these children dearly and had a hard time playing the heavy.

Something about the girls actually meeting the ultimate ruler of camp sobered them, and they hesitated to make their complaint, which now didn't seem so large after all. The first little girl's lip was quivering as she told about offensive words from the other. The other girl defended herself vigorously. Soon they were at it again, fighting right in front of Dave.

"Hold on one minute," said Dave, marshalling conviction in his voice. "You two are at church camp. Do you think Jesus likes what you are doing... how you are fighting?" They stopped abruptly, shaking their heads in contrition. "Well, we need to ask the Lord to forgive us for this. I want you to pray with me." He began to pray for forgiveness, and as he did the presence of the Lord visited that little meeting. The girls began to cry. While Dave never learned if they became best friends after the prayer meeting, they at least made up in front of him.

"I wish pastoring were so easy," he said to Carl, a pastor friend helping at the camp.

"Tell me about it," said Carl. "My wife and I have just resigned our church. We think it is time for a change."

"What are you going to do?" asked Dave.

"Not sure. We'll probably evangelize while we're waiting for the next door to open."

"Hey," Dave offered. "We've got an apartment above our church. It is not much, but you and Barbara can stay there as long as you like."

Dave didn't have much. But then, he didn't really think deeply about possessions either. He freely gave and freely received. When his old car broke down, his brother-in-law Bill sold him a station wagon for a dollar. He gladly took it. The bed of that station wagon was big enough to carry a four-by-eight piece of sheetrock and could also double as transport to pick up kids for Sunday school. For Dave, there wasn't a big line between what was his and what belonged to the church.

He continued with his offer to Carl. "I will have to move a few things around a little, so just let me know when you are coming."

The reason why there were so many things to move around involved another story. Dave had a good friend, Brian Wiseman, who was a missionary. As Brian prepared to go overseas, Dave told him, "If there is anything I can ever do for you, let me know." And he meant it. So it was that Dave handled a few personal affairs for Brian and his wife Joanie. And then, when it came time for Brian to ship off to Brazil, there were a few personal items—well perhaps more than a few—with which Brian could not see himself parting. Bikes, a mimeograph, tables, chairs, and other miscellaneous things all came to the church to be stored. At first Dave placed them in what had been a huge cistern in the basement. But then as the Sunday school grew, they needed that cistern area, and the Wisemans' things were eventually distributed throughout the building, many of them in use. He didn't think Brian would mind.

"We've got plenty of room," Dave told Carl. "Store whatever you want, and bring whatever you need when you come."

"And you're sure it will be all right?"

"Absolutely." Things would just be a little more crowded. Nothing they couldn't handle.

Chapter 7

"Mom... she talked to me.
That lady talked to me!"

Nancy tried to eat the broccoli, but each time she put her fork into it, a little girl tried to grab her water glass to have a drink. Nancy dropped the fork and protected the glass. The girl was seven. She had Cri du Chat syndrome. Dr. Hermann had called Nancy with the name of a couple in the area whose daughter had Cri du Chat. So Nancy had called the mother. "Sure, come on over," she said, inviting the Norrises for dinner. "We'd love to talk to you about our experience."

Their daughter was actually fairly high functioning. She walked and talked and though her vocabulary was limited, she could readily make her wishes known. In fact, from what Nancy understood about Nathaniel's prognosis, this girl was probably functioning at a much higher level than Nathaniel would ever achieve. That's what made it so hard. On a rational level, Nancy knew that her boy was handicapped, but because he was still a baby from whom little was expected, she hadn't emotionally dealt with the prospect of Nathaniel's potential problems. The dinner brought her face-to-face with reality, for this seven-year-old girl was hardly theoretical. "Oh don't mind her," said the mother. "She does that all the time."

Dr. Hermann called again. "I want you to do something for me."

"Sure," Nancy replied before she even knew what he wanted.

"Cri du Chat syndrome is so rare that I think it would be good to try to get some of the parents together—you know, in kind of a support group.

"Ok," she replied. "What do you have in mind?"

"Would you be willing to host some kind of event; a get together for these parents?"

"Absolutely!" she agreed.

Nancy began planning a picnic to be held at a local park and sent out invitations to all the families on Dr. Hermann's list. Two of the families actually lived in Michigan but said they would come anyway. On the last Saturday in August, seven families of infants and small toddlers with Cri du Chat gathered at Regner Park in West Bend.

Cameras captured smiles and laughter while video recorders framed Dr. Jürgen Hermann as he filled balloons from a canister of helium and attached a ribbon to each of them. Balloons of all different colors wafted into the air and were tied down to strollers and car seats.

Each couple had their own story. More than one parent struggled to understand why their child came to have this syndrome. "So you have a balanced translocation?" said one mother to another. "Well, at least you know why your child has Cri du Chat. I mean, I've got a handicapped girl and I don't even know why. Really. I mean, what happened? Was there something in the water? Was it something I ate or did? It's driving me crazy."

At six months, Nathaniel was older than some of the babies there, but age hardly mattered in one respect. When one of the babies cried, all of the parents from every table turned their heads, thinking it was their child making the familiar "mew-like" sound. When one baby cried, it sounded exactly like every other baby present that day.

"You know," said one mother as she left, "I don't feel so alone anymore." Families exchanged information and promised to get together again. Someone even said that they should network and form an organization. Perhaps they would.

Nathaniel didn't have much of a chance to be a homebody. Even when he wasn't traveling to other states, his parents had a lot going on at church. Because there were plenty of babysitters, he had a choice of where to hang his hat—well, to place his rattle. He might stay for a few hours or even overnight with any of six or seven families in the church. He had an open invitation. That's just the way it was. Nathaniel didn't merely belong to the Norrises. He belonged to the church.

As trees in Wisconsin turned to autumn yellow, brilliant oranges, and reds, Nathaniel became more regular in his attendance at the early intervention program at Threshold. School buses crisscrossed the neighborhood, and when the Suburban pulled up with its full load of car seats and babies, he happily joined the mix. If he was healthy, his daily regimen included interacting with a number of different teachers and therapists at school. While the exercises didn't seem to be advancing his developmental skills, they worked to keep him physically strong.

Carl and Barbara held their last service in the church they pastored in northern Wisconsin and made their move down to West Bend. The three small bedrooms upstairs in the church weren't much. The living room was garnished with free carpet samples stapled in colorful patterns to the floor. But it was nonetheless functional and the situation temporary. Carl and Barbara traveled a lot on weekends and sometimes would be gone weeks at a time, but they were often in town during the week. During these times, Dave and Nancy enjoyed getting together with them.

Dave liked missionaries, and for such a small church, they sure had a lot of them stop by for a visit. Having a missionary meant providing a meal, a bed, allowing them to preach at the church, giving them an offering, and if possible, partnering with the missionary in

71

monthly support. Nancy was working on fulfilling their obligation to provide the meal for a missionary that now sat at their kitchen table. She took the Cornish hens out of the oven and placed one of the roasted birds in front of the missionary, Jerry.

"So what do we need to do to reach the world?" Dave asked as the meal was winding down. This sounded like preacher talk, and recently Nancy had heard Dave asking this sort of question to any number of people. She excused herself to check on Nathaniel and came back just as Jerry was saying to Dave, "It looks to me like you're asking way too many questions. Is there a chance you could be called to the mission field?"

"Not me," said Dave. "Not at all."

Nancy observed the way that Jerry was polishing off the Cornish hen. It was disappearing entirely—meat, skin, bones and all. She wondered if this was a skill acquired on the mission field.

"But have you ever volunteered?" Jerry asked Dave.

"Well, no."

"Think about it. God is a gentleman. He won't draft people. He wants volunteers."

"So, what are you saying?" asked Dave.

"Consider this. God may be making you restless. He could be 'stirring the nest' so you will listen to Him. On the other hand perhaps it's nothing," he continued, talking enthusiastically as the last vestige of chicken was consumed. "I'll tell you what. Why don't you set aside thirty days or so? During that time, take a little extra time to focus. Pray and fast, and tell the Lord you'll do whatever He asks you to do."

"Sounds fair to me," Dave said in passing. "I'll sure think about it." Nancy cleared the plates, but little remained to scrape off into the trash.

During the next thirty days, while Dave's focus was on heavenly things, saving the world was hardly uppermost on Nancy's mind. Nathaniel's health required numerous doctors' visits in Milwaukee, specialists interested in this or that aspect of his condition. Nancy noticed something about these doctors' offices. When she was dressed professionally, both nurses and doctors seemed more willing to listen to her opinion. Nancy dressed Nathaniel nicely for similar reasons. Because Nathaniel looked a little different from other babies, people who did not know him sometimes ignored him. But dressing him in attractive outfits tended to break down barriers. The thirty days ended differently for Dave and Nancy. Dave decided that God was not calling him overseas, as a missionary or otherwise. Nancy decided she should go shopping for Nathaniel.

Nancy was wheeling Nathaniel out of the "Osh Kosh b'Gosh" store at the outlet mall, when she spotted a family coming toward her. As she pushed Nathaniel in his stroller, she noted a woman going the other way trailed by a little girl of about six, trying hard to keep up. The mother seemed hurried, unconcerned about the little one lagging behind. Then Nancy really noticed the child. She walked with a wide gate, obviously handicapped in some way. Had Nancy seen that same child before Nathaniel's birth, she may well have turned her head in an automatic response so as not to stare. Now she focused on the child and smiled. "Hello there," she offered warmly, and then walked on. Ten seconds later, Nancy heard the voice of the child as she tried to catch up with her mother to share important news. Calling at the top of her lungs, the little girl tried to get her mom's attention. Her insistent voice echoed throughout the mall. "Mom... wait. Mom... listen. Mom... she talked to me. That lady said 'hi' to me!"

Nancy now lived in a different world, one she had never inhabited before. Everything had changed in the past few months. There was a clear demarcation of life before Nathaniel and life afterward. Before, Nancy had been a teacher at Wayne Elementary. Now, it was certain she would never go back. Before, she had been integral to the running of a number of Sunday school and church programs. Now, others were stepping in to assume some of the jobs she once oversaw. Before, Nancy socialized freely with a whole set of friends. Now, a number of those friends had stopped calling. All of this change was difficult to take. Nancy hadn't signed up for these changes, but it didn't look like her old life would be coming back anytime soon—if ever.

Such a drastic change in Nancy's lifestyle sometimes brought a feeling of deep loss and sadness. Her emotions descended unbidden like a roller coaster plummeting toward the ground. It wasn't exactly loneliness. It was a feeling that washed over her regardless of how many loved ones were around. She didn't like it, but she just could not muster enthusiasm for things that had previously energized her. Nor did she particularly care to have sadness as such a close friend.

Music helped a lot. Nancy frequently played a cassette tape of a Bible school choir from Delaware. The people there wrote much of their own music. Nancy's favorite song on the tape offered the message, "When I am weak, I am strong in the Lord." She sang along with the choir, and it was not unusual to repeat the same tape numerous times in the course of the day.

It was October. Nathaniel was eight-months-old. The Norrises also had other reasons to celebrate. They closed on a new house they had built right outside of town. The home was financed through the Farmer's Home Loan, an agency that offered low-interest loans based on income. Stephanie, one of Nancy's good friends and a real estate agent, discovered a nice big lot. Stephanie's boyfriend built the house. While Nancy picked out their countertop, the carpeting, and even the curtains, most of the nitty-gritty details were taken care of by the builder.

People from the church helped when it came to the actual move. Grandma Dorothy supplied some nice chairs that dressed up their living room. Nancy loved it. The house smelled like new paint and fresh carpet and hope for the future. And it was theirs! Finally, she and Dave were putting down significant roots. After eight years of temporary housing, they had finally come home.

Nathaniel continued to struggle physically. Feedings were problematic. Diaper issues of all sorts were a continual nemesis. First, Nathaniel would have problems because nothing was coming through. Then he would have the opposite problem, requiring so many diapers that Nancy joked about buying stock in Pampers®.

For Nathaniel, even colds could become dangerous, and flu readily led to dehydration. At times, Nathaniel was sick for no determined reason. From what Dr. Griswold and others explained, in one way or another, almost every system of his little body was affected by Cri du Chat. The nurses at the local hospital were now beginning to know him quite well. Emergencies happened fairly regularly, and with Nathaniel's health, almost anything could turn into an emergency. Yet, surprisingly, he had a routine. Although one never gets used to emergencies, the Norris family lived with its own kind of "normal."

One day, something occurred that went beyond any previous experience. The family was out to eat with Dale and Betty. As Nancy fed Nathaniel applesauce, he spit up. But what Nathaniel spit up didn't look like applesauce.

"What is that?" asked Nancy, staring at what looked to be coffee grounds.

"I don't know," said Dave, instantly concerned, "but I think we'd better find out."

Even though Dr. Griswold already knew what it was, he tested the substance Nancy had given him just to make sure. "It's blood," he said.

"Where did it come from?" asked Nancy.

"From his stomach."

"What does it mean?"

"We'll have to do upper gastrointestinal tests to find out," he said.

When the tests came back, Dr. Griswold shared the results. "It looks like Nathaniel has reflux—stomach acids are coming up and burning his esophagus. This causes his esophagus to bleed, and then he swallows the blood. Later, he spits it up. That is why the spit-up looks like coffee grounds."

"What can be done?" said Nancy.

"Well, before we try anything more radical, let's try giving him something that will help neutralize some of those stomach acids."

"Will that work?" asked Nancy.

"We'll just have to keep a close watch on things. We don't want to try anything more radical unless we are forced to."

The drive home from the hospital was pretty quiet. In the back seat Nathaniel was sat pretty still. Nancy and Dave were both discouraged and didn't have much to say. So much for an established routine. "Come on, Buddy," said Dave, releasing the buckle on Nathaniel's car seat. "Let's get you inside." He hoisted the car seat out of the car and carried his boy into the house.

A couple of minutes later, Nancy came in from the mailbox with a fist full of mail. She dropped some bills on the counter and began to open an envelope. "Hey, Dave, look. I got a letter from a missionary."

He didn't look up. He was opening one of the bills. "That's nice. A newsletter?"

"No. I mean ... it is a personal letter."

"Where's it from?"

"Pakistan."

"Who do you know in Pakistan?"

"No one."

"You're sure it was mailed to the right address?"

"Yeah. It was forwarded from the condominium."

Nancy began to read the letter. It was from a missionary named Georgene. The letter began, "I don't know for sure if you will remember me—we met for the first time in Milwaukee in 1981, and again at the General Conference that year. I felt a special kinship with you and have never forgotten the few minutes that we spent together."

Then Nancy remembered. She was with a group of ladies who had briefly met Georgine. They had exchanged a few pleasantries, but that was all.

The card continued, "The last few days you folks have been so much on my heart and mind, and I just wanted to write and let you know that you have been a number one priority on my prayer list. I don't know if you are in need, trying to make a decision, or if you just need a special blessing from the Lord. But He has laid you on my heart and I have done my best to carry your burden with you. So often we feel to pray for others but never let them know. Then they can't share in the blessing. I want to tell you that you're *not* forsaken or forgotten and that God is still very much able to meet all your needs."

It was very humbling to think that someone halfway across the world had been prompted by the Lord to pray for her. It was the best letter Nancy had ever received, and she carried it in her Bible for years.

Chapter 8

"He wants us to move right away"

While lots of things are worth celebrating, some things are worth celebrating in a big way. Nathaniel's first birthday fell into the latter category. Nancy started planning a month early. While shopping one day, she walked into a store that was advertising their first anniversary with a giant paper-maché cake that filled an entire display shelf. "Say," she asked sweetly, "do you know what you are doing with that display item when you are done with it?" Apparently nothing. So Nathaniel's first birthday party featured a two-tier birthday cake that stood five feet in diameter and rose four feet from the floor.

Nathaniel did not seem as impressed with his giant cake as much as he was with the horde of kids from the church who came to celebrate with him. And he really enjoyed the ice cream. For Nancy, there was a lot to celebrate. Nathaniel had probably overcome more challenges in one year than most children encounter in all the years that it takes them to reach adulthood.

Unexpectedly, three days after his birthday, Nathaniel's hands and feet turned purple and he spiked a very high fever. Dr. Griswold admitted him to the hospital and ordered tests. Nancy and Dave sensed his deep concern about the situation. "We have a very high white blood cell count."

"What does that mean?" questioned Nancy.

"We don't know for sure. There is a possibility of leukemia or cancer, but we are continuing to check."

"Happy Birthday!" thought Dave, forlornly feeling sorry for himself and for Nathaniel. Fortunately, it turned out that Nathaniel only suffered from a bladder infection. While that wasn't such good news in and of itself, when compared to what they had worried about, the news was stellar. Nate's week in the hospital seemed like mere "pocket change" when compared to what could have been.

While Dave was out of town, Nancy decided to get the romance back into their marriage. As she picked him up from the Milwaukee airport, she whispered into his ear, "I have a special surprise for you,"

"What's that?" he asked, definitely interested.

"You'll just have to wait to find out," she said. And that was all she would tell him.

In his absence, Nancy had decorated their third bedroom, which was empty, to simulate a picnic at the beach. Everything was prepared— romantic music, a picnic blanket, and sparkling cider. Then, as she was leaving the house to pick up Dave, she realized Grandma Dorothy would be babysitting Nathaniel. Not wanting her to discover the special hideaway, Nancy locked the room. As soon as they got home and could get Grandma Dorothy out the front door, Nancy went to the third bedroom to show Dave the surprise. Unfortunately, the real surprise was that the door was locked and Nancy couldn't find the key.

At the beginning of March, Rick came by to speak at a midweek service. He was traveling to raise funds to go Japan as a missionary. Before he left town the next day, he and Dave went out for lunch. After they finished their meal, Dave stood to leave for his afternoon bus route. Rick continued the conversation on their way out. "Yeah, and that's what I am going to do if I can. It's not enough just to reach American servicemen in Japan. If God opens the right doors, I would love to establish a work among the Japanese people. Some day I would like to have a Bible school to train ministers, because that's the way to reach the world."

As Dave was driving the bus, he mulled over last night's missionary service and his visit with Rick. Rick's last words came to him: "I would like to establish a Bible school to train ministers, because that is the way to reach the world." Dave repeated, "Bible school... that's the way to reach the world... Bible school... reach the world."

Then Dave had a "God moment." It wasn't an audible voice, but it was apparently God's answer to his recent quest of how to participate in reaching the world. He was to teach in Bible school— to train those who would be ministers. The revelation was so sudden and certain that it took his breath away. This was perhaps the most defining moment of Dave's adult life.

Then reality set in. There was one major problem. Dave's only experience in Bible school was working with his grandfather. And then a kind of anxiety washed over Dave. As much as he loved his grandfather, he loved him best from a distance. At that point, Dave decided just to forget the whole thing.

Because the route serviced the whole county, sometimes the landscape was largely random, rising and falling for no particular reason. Dairy farms were interspersed with numerous stands of trees. While trees on either side of the road stretched their branches to form an overhead canopy, he grappled with what it would mean to disregard what seemed to be a clear mandate from heaven. He considered the blessing of God that was upon their small but growing church. He knew that God's blessings were for those who listened to and obeyed His voice. Now Dave was in a quandary. He didn't want the church to suffer because of his own disobedience, but how could the church be blessed if he left it? The bus continued to follow the ups and downs of the road and then banked a hard left as Dave continued to think. The fact was that no one knew these people like he did. It just didn't make sense to leave. Besides, Nancy would never consent to move.

A week passed, and the issue would not go away. Dave mulled it over for hours, but no answers came. One morning after his bus route, Dave sat drinking coffee in the living room. Nancy brought her cup and sat in the chair beside him. She considered how tired Dave looked. "Hey, were you up last night in the middle of the night?"

"Uh, yeah," said Dave, distracted.

"And were you up several times the night before?"

"Yeah."

There was a pause, followed by the inevitable question, "So what's going on?"

Dave was silent for a long time. Then, ever so slowly, he began to explain about his experience on the bus. "And then Rick's words came back to me like a message from God: 'Bible school—that's the way to reach the world.'" He paused, not knowing what she was thinking.

They had spent the first year of their married life working in St. Paul. While they had enjoyed working with the teenagers from the church, they knew it was time to try something on their own. They had traveled as evangelists for two years, working with children and young people. When Dave had felt a definite call to go to West Bend to start a church, Nancy had sensed the same urging and had readily agreed. She had invested as much, if not more than him, these past five and a half years in an effort to see the church grow. Now, for the first time since they had moved to West Bend, they were at the cusp where both of them could spend their full-time efforts in pastoring.

Dave waited for her to offer an objection to what he was feeling. It didn't come. Nancy surprised him. She spoke evenly and without emotion. "Well, you'd better call your grandfather." He did.

Dave went to church and made the call. Later that day, he came home excited. "Nancy, when I explained to my grandfather what had happened, he said, 'You're doing a good work there in West Bend. Just keep it up.'" Now Dave felt elated. He had passed some sort of test—just like when Abraham was told by God to offer Isaac—and because he was willing to leave he wouldn't have to do it. Now they could stay and the church would be blessed and....

Nancy quickly popped his bubble. "He'll call you back," she pronounced. It was the first thing that came into her head. She wasn't sure why she said it, but it seemed right.

"You think?"

"I know it." She didn't say this as if she were sad or resigned or happy. She just said it.

Sure enough, a few days later his grandfather called. He wanted Dave to come to St. Paul so they could discuss this.

Dave headed his car north, back toward the city where he was raised, back to where he had attended Bible school, and to where he had gone to church. As he drove, something else began to take hold—an excitement about the potential of being a catalyst for the faith and dreams of others. He began to feel excited that perhaps he did have something to share. If God had so powerfully called him, then it only made sense that the Lord would be with him every step of the way. The closer he got to St. Paul, the more his faith rose. He dropped off his things at his dad's house and then drove to his grandparents' home for the meeting.

His grandfather had always had a commanding presence. Even though his health was failing, he still controlled every conversation, providing leadership in every situation. They exchanged pleasantries, but soon came down to the important issues.

"So what debts do you have?" his grandfather asked pointedly.

"I think I have about sixteen hundred in hospital bills," said Dave, "but we're making small payments monthly, and the hospital is fine with that."

"And how much do you make a month?"

Dave named the amount. It wasn't much. His grandfather stated he would pay him the same. He also said that Dave and Nancy should find a place to live right away. With that, apparently all was decided. They had not talked about Dave's vision, what he thought could be done at the Bible college, or what potential classes could be taught. They really hadn't discussed anything at all. His grandfather seemed to be thinking of something else. "I'll take you tomorrow," he stated. "We'll get you someplace."

Dave drove back to West Bend the following evening. Arriving home, he began to explain his experience to Nancy. "He wants us to move right away, to be there for graduation."

"Well, we'll have to go up and look at some different places…" she began.

"We already have a place."

"What do you mean?"

"Well, you know my grandfather," Dave offered. "He gets an idea and he acts on it right away."

"What do you mean?"

"He bought a house."

"But you just went up there two days ago."

"Yeah, I know. But he wanted to nail things down."

"I don't even get to look at it?"

"Afraid not."

"So then… what? We'll pay rent or…."

"The school owns the house, and we live in it."

This was a lot to take in. Everything had escalated so quickly. This was March. They were expected to move to St. Paul in a matter of weeks.

"What will we do about the church?" she inquired.

Dave had apparently been considering this. "I was thinking of Jim and Mary," he said.

"They'd be good," replied Nancy vacantly, still reeling from the idea of moving. Jim and Mary would be the logical choice. They were evangelists and had been guest speakers at the church more than anyone else. A number of people had come into their church under Jim's ministry. Dave had known him for years. They were from the same church and shared many of the same life experiences.

"We'll think about it and pray about it," he said finally. Nancy didn't reply. Based on the speed by which things were happening, they wouldn't have long to think about this decision—or any other decision for that matter. Choices would need to be made. Things would have to be done. And Jim and Mary would have to pray about it, too, assuming they were interested.

Nancy wondered what the changes would mean for Nathaniel. He saw a dozen different doctors, all for specific needs, and she knew each one. More importantly, they knew Nathaniel. What about babysitters? Here she could call anyone at anytime, and they would gladly step in to help. She even had people who would help with laundry and house cleaning. Some months back, Grandma Dorothy said, "Just leave your husband's shirts in a basket and I will wash and iron them." Like magic, they reappeared on hangers, sometimes accompanied by Dave's favorite sugar cookies.

It seemed to be a usual Sunday night as Dave stood to preach. He began his message by telling a story about something that had happened on his bus route, or so the listeners thought. Gradually, it became apparent that he was explaining to them why he was going to resign as their pastor. "I know that God has blessed this church," Dave continued. "But God's blessing goes beyond a person or a family leading a congregation. God has continued blessings for the church in the future. He will provide and meet every need, and He will continue the work that He began in us." Good words. Tough service. Lots of crying.

Afterward, a father of three small boys came up and asked whether Dave had given any thought as to who would be their new pastor. It was all too awkward. Dave had not wanted the church to hear about his leaving from another source, but not everything was quite together yet. He didn't know how much to share. "Well, I would really like Jim and Mary Booker to come. But the church would have to vote them in, and they haven't given me an answer yet as to whether they would consider coming."

"Well, if that's what God is doing, then that is what it will be," replied the man. Jim and Mary did decide to come. The vote at the business meeting was a mere formality. Bookers would move from the Twin Cities to West Bend at the same time the Norrises would be moving in that direction.

Nancy opened a letter from Social Security. "Oh no." she said. "What?" asked Dave.

"It says here that we have to repay the three hundred dollars that they sent for Nathaniel last month. Why is that?"

Dave looked at the demand for money. "Well, I have to report any extra income, and when I was in St. Paul, my grandfather gave me a check for five hundred dollars."

"Great!" she said, clearly upset. She threw the demand for money onto the table, sat down, and got very teary. "So, will this SSI stuff be the same in St. Paul?"

"No. Every state has a different program. We'll have to apply again and see what benefits they offer, but it could be that they won't offer anything."

"Great," Nancy said again, more weakly still.

The last church event for Nancy and Dave was set for a Sunday evening in May. The service was held at a local bank's community room that had a kitchen attached to it. The main event was to be a dinner along with a program. Others planned everything. There would be singing, laughter, and times of sharing.

Jim, a charter member of the church, got up to speak. "I remember when I heard from my sister that the Norrises were coming to town. She had told us how God had changed her life. Then she told us about the Norrises. That's all it took. We didn't go to church, but we decided that we would start going very soon. About the same time a Lutheran Church was starting in our area. The pastor knocked on our door, asking if we wanted to be a part. 'No, my pastor is coming to town,' my wife told them.

"When I saw Dave get out of the van, I thought, 'This guy is really young. Is this the pastor, or is the pastor his father?' Well, we began Bible studies in our home. Dave taught my wife and me at the kitchen table while Nancy taught the kids downstairs. After a few weeks of Bible studies, right there at the kitchen table my wife was baptized with the Holy Ghost."

Alan got up to share. "My father-in-law is Italian. He doesn't impose his will much, but when he does, people listen. He is from Milwaukee, so we don't see him too often. But when he told Carol and me to take a Bible study from the Norrises, we didn't argue. If that's what he thought, then that's what we would do. My father-in-law came out to our house to introduce us to the Norrises. When they came in, we realized that Nancy was one of the teachers from the kids' school. The next week we started Bible studies. Dave would teach Carol and me while Nancy taught the kids. We loved it. But when their car broke down, I suggested we come to their apartment for the Bible study. When we saw the chairs set up for church in their family room, I knew they were holding out on us. 'Hey,' I said, 'do we have to wait till all the Bible studies are done before we can come to church?'"

Several people shared that while they didn't mind if Nancy and Dave left West Bend, they could only go so long as Nathaniel stayed. They shared this for good reason. He was their baby. They had invested a lot of prayers in him, and now it just seemed wrong that he would be moving six hours away. Although they smiled and laughed, they didn't care one bit for Nathaniel's inevitable move to St. Paul.

Chapter 9

"This boy is dehydrated. We have to admit him to the hospital"

The first time Nancy saw her house in St. Paul was the day that she moved in. It was an older home and needed a little sprucing up, which wouldn't be a problem because paint was easy to come by. Yet, as she directed boxes here and there, a profound sense of loss descended on her. It wasn't just the fact that their house in West Bend still smelled new and this house smelled old. Rather, it was more fundamental than that. In her West Bend house, she had picked out the drapes, the countertop, the carpeting, and the kitchen floor; at this house she had not picked out a thing.

Men from the church in West Bend had moved the Norrises' belongings to St. Paul, while some of the locals gave an additional hand at distributing items into this or that room. Because Jim and Mary's things were stored at the house where Jim grew up in Richfield (a suburb of St. Paul-Minneapolis), the plan was that these same men would then help move Jim and Mary's things back to West Bend in the rental truck. Then the Bookers would follow the truck back to Wisconsin so they could oversee the unpacking of their household goods. The plan should have worked without a hitch, but it didn't. Instead, something totally unthinkable happened.

Jim was an only child. During his childhood and teenage years, his mother, who had been stricken with polio, developed first one and then another complication with her health. Jim knew what it was like to make plans not knowing whether or not they would be affected by his mother's serious health concerns. In the past few years, her condition had declined considerably, and had become almost bedridden. Her health was very fragile indeed.

Jim had lived in the family home all his life. Even when he and Mary graduated from Bible college and began to evangelize across the United States, he never really had another home. His things were stored there, he visited often, and in a very pragmatic way, the home in Richfield was still his home base. Now Jim and Mary were leaving town to assume the pastorate of a church six hours away. In the past, Jim had always come home; now his leaving would be permanent. Unfortunately, the very day he was to leave town, Jim's mother died.

Dave's grandfather preached the funeral. He painted the picture of a runner who faithfully finished a race. He rightly explained that Victoria was a godly woman, and now her suffering was done. While all of this was true, the funeral service was bittersweet.

Nancy immediately set about finding a primary physician for Nathaniel. Protocol dictated that one doctor transfer files to another, but she was able to procure all of Nathaniel's files from their several different sources. She thought it would be helpful not to waste time in getting things together. She handed the thick stack of folders to the man who would be her son's pediatrician. He muttered something about this being "highly irregular" and she knew that they had gotten off to a bad start. "Cri du what?" he said. "I'm not familiar with that. I think you're going to need to establish an on-going relationship with a geneticist."

"Okay. And the reason would be...."

"Nathaniel should have his diagnosis confirmed and a treatment plan mapped out and...."

Nancy thought this should be the job of her pediatrician and almost said so but then thought better of it. The doctor continued, "This infant is only twelve pounds, and he is eighteen months old. I think we have some issues here."

Of course they had issues. That was just the point. That is why she was coming to see him. "Where would be the best place to take Nathaniel to the emergency room?"

"Does he need to go?" the doctor asked nervously.

"No, but he will," Nancy responded. "His health is very tentative, and almost certainly I will have to take him a time or two this summer for pneumonia."

After "tsssking" a couple of times, Dr. Smith explained that he had privileges to practice at a couple of different hospitals, but Ramsey Hospital would be best for emergencies. So it went. To every question Nancy asked, the doctor provided meager answers, answers that she could only pry out of him with a great deal of effort. Did he know of schools? No. Nancy would have to ask someone else. Did he know about SSI? He had no idea. How about early intervention programs? They were not his specialty. "Thanks," she said and left.

The phone rang. Dave picked it up. It was Jim. "Hey, Jim, how are things going? You're getting settled in all right?"

"Well, to tell you the truth, things are a little crazy."

"Oh, what do you mean?"

"Well, half of furniture in the church has the name 'Wiseman' on it. And I am not sure what to do about that."

"Well, like I said, there are a few loose ends. The church is storing things for them, but it is okay to use those things while the Wisemans are on the mission field."

"So you've been using things that don't belong to you."

"Yeah. Pretty much. Hey, the Wisemans are great!" offered Dave. "I love Brian's faith. He is bold as a lion. One time he was visiting this farmer who said God wasn't alive. The farmer told him that if

God was real, then just like Jesus promised that they could move mountains—Brian should be able to pray and move his barn. Do you know what Brian said?"

Exasperated, Jim said, "What?"

He said, "'Where do you want it?' And the farmer said, 'Oh, just forget it.'"

"And one time we were in the park, and Brian and I walked up to this kid—"

"Uh, Dave?" said Jim, clearly not in the mood for Brian Wiseman stories.

"Yes?"

"You know Carl, the minister who you said could stay in the upstairs of the church temporarily…."

"Yes, he's a great guy."

"Well, I was sitting in the office today, and he says, 'I am not sure why Dave didn't have me take this church.'"

"Jim, I called him and explained that to him. He was traveling at the time. I told him that I thought that you were the one for the church, and that we had voted you in."

"Well, I get the impression he was disappointed that you didn't give the church a chance to vote on him."

"Jim, you are the pastor. No one is voting for anyone else."

"And Carl says to me, 'Well, that is my desk chair you're sitting on.'"

"Well, Jim, actually, I think it is."

"Dave, don't you own *anything* in this church?"

"Hey, Jim, I am so sorry this happened."

"That's not the worst of it. I receive a call that Bonnie has attempted suicide. And all of this is facing me the minute I walk in the door."

"Jim, I am so sorry that happened."

"Well, when you said there were a few loose ends, I had no idea there was so many!"

"Hey, Jim, I am so sorry."

Dave thought about their conversation the next day as he went to work on the kitchen at the Bible college. Dave wasn't exactly handy, and the best thing to do when working on a project was to keep him away from any tools that might be dangerous. Consequently, he was doing grunt work, ripping up the old tiles from a cement floor.

He wasn't too worried about the Wiseman stuff or Carl. That would blow over soon enough, but he wept openly for Bonnie. Nancy and Dave had taught Bonnie and her husband Bible studies for a couple of years, and at one point, had dealt with a bundle of their personal issues, even supervising their checkbook to help them get out of debt. Nancy and Dave had been there when a couple of their kids had been born. Dave knew there were issues—issues that would not readily go away—but that was what the church was for, to minister to people with issues.

And now, Jim, reeling from the loss of his mother, would be asked to own all of these challenges at once. No doubt Jim would have a different style of pastoring than Dave. Actually, Dave was pretty sure that not too many people operated according to his personal pastoral style. Dave's pastoral philosophy was what someone might kindly call "laid back"—what others less gracious might call "negligent."

As Dave ripped up the tiles on the floor, he wondered if there was anything he could do to help Jim. But no answers came to him. As Dave continued to slide the giant metal crowbar underneath the tiles, the task of grieving the loss of his church began in earnest.

With regard to the question of who was in charge of telling Dave what to do at the Bible school, the answer was, well, pretty much everybody. Dave mostly worked for the school, but he also worked for the church. He received one paycheck from the school, but that salary assumed he would do specific work for the church as well.

Dave's grandfather had become pastor of the church fifty years earlier and a few years later had founded the Bible college. In the beginning, both church and college were one entity. During those days of the early Depression, one building functioned not only as home to Dave's grandfather and his family, but also as home to all the students: The building provided a sanctuary for church worship services and classrooms for the Bible college students. Over the course of time, two very impressive parallel institutions rose from those small beginnings.

A dozen years earlier, Dave's grandfather had divided the responsibilities of the church and school between two men, Robert and Wendell. Robert became the pastor of the church, and Wendell became the president of the school as Dave's grandfather pulled back… well, for a week or two.

Because he simply had been unable to release the reigns of responsibility, Dave's grandfather took back the leadership of the school and once again became its president. Robert remained the pastor of the church, but Dave's grandfather continued on in his position as the chairman of the church board.

How much had changed in the last decade Dave had no way of knowing, and in a way, it didn't matter to him. Dave had grown up in the church and had gone to the Bible school. He really was happy to be involved with both school and church. While he respected his grandfather greatly, Robert, the pastor of the church, was a father figure to him as well.

Dave would oversee the youth program and would also serve as a minister at the church. While this might include an occasional hospital visit, it mainly involved speaking for one of the many services. Dave's uncle now largely superintended the day-to-day affairs of the school, but Dave's grandfather clearly had the final say.

Dave and Nancy easily transitioned back into the church. Because Dave had grown up there, people already knew him. They knew Nancy as well since he and Nancy had been one- time youth leaders in the church. Now many of those former teenagers were married and raising their own families. Further, Nancy was by nature a people person and made friends easily. Since Dave was a project kind of guy, he immediately started to work on a couple of different things at the church.

Dave's time that summer mainly involved ministering at the church. That was good, but it was when school started that Dave became energized. The first month of school, Dave approached one of the class officers in the student body. "Say, Jennifer, I want you to speak in chapel."

"But girls don't speak in chapel."

"They do now."

"I refuse."

"I refuse to let you refuse. You'll be great!" And she was.

"John, when are you going to start your Bible study?" Dave asked. His class on outreach required that each student be actively involved in teaching someone who was unchurched. Dave had explained that it was easy because all they had to do was just be friends with people. But John was not convinced.

"I don't know anyone that will let me give them one," he objected.

"You don't know anyone who doesn't go to church?"

"Sure, but I asked a couple of people, and they told me no."

"Well, I'll tell you what, then. Just make people feel sorry for you. Tell them I will flunk you if you don't teach a Bible study." Dave said this with a smile, but he was sure John got the point.

"Well, I think I can do that," John replied. As a matter of fact, he did.

And so it went. Saturdays were full of activities as Dave took students out doing ministry kinds of things. He felt that he was living his call and in some small way contributing to a ministry beyond himself—that of reaching the world.

Old Testament Survey challenged Dave. Because it required a sweeping understanding of the entire Old Testament, he never felt like he knew enough. He worked hard to make the class interesting and to provide real life applications. For him it wasn't enough to teach about things. He wanted the Bible to be spiritually transforming for his students, and in the process of study, he felt like the Bible was transforming him.

Dave also taught a survey of the Book of Hebrews, a book he had memorized as a teenage Bible quizzer. This time, however, the book spoke to him as it had not earlier in his life. He felt like he was on a treasure hunt and that he was discovering incredible things about Jesus Christ. He regularly discussed what he was learning with Robert, the pastor of the church who also taught in the school. He too was on his own quest to go deeper in this kind of study. Dave came home energized and full of excitement for each day, completely engrossed in what he was doing.

Even when he was at home, he sometimes continued to work on projects. "Hey Paula, can you call the restaurant at the hotel? We want to do a Christian fellowship breakfast there in October as an outreach. Get seating for eighty."

Roles were being reshuffled at the Norris household. At various times in their marriage, Nancy and Dave had each handled the bills. When they first came to West Bend, he worked full-time so she paid them. Then when she began full-time work as a school teacher, he paid them. Now, things shifted back to Nancy because she was home all the time while Dave was out. Dave didn't have regular hours at the school and church. He was sometimes gone ten to twelve hours a day.

Other things seemed to fall back on Nancy as well. So far, there were no programs, no babysitters, and no support system for Nathaniel. When Nancy called for information about school programs, the lady was indifferent to her concerns and said they must wait until fall to begin Nathaniel's paperwork. Even when the school year began, it took awhile for things to work out.

Nancy sat in the kitchen feeding Nathaniel carrots. These were, of course, strained, tasteless, and quite orange. Nathaniel seemed to do okay with their bland taste and was working his way through the jar. Then, just as Nancy was about to spoon the last little bit from the jar into his mouth, Nathaniel hurled out the entire contents of his stomach in what could only be called projectile vomiting. Strained, tasteless, and very orange carrots splattered onto the wall several feet away. Nancy wasn't sure what to do. She checked Nathaniel for a fever, but when there was none, she decided to keep an eye on things. No sense creating emergencies when real ones readily appeared on their own all too often.

Nancy's pediatrician seemed competent enough, but she had to be proactive about getting Nathaniel additional care. After obtaining a recommendation, she made an appointment with Dr. Susan Berry, a geneticist who had an office across from the University of Minnesota Hospital. Nancy kept Nathaniel occupied in the waiting room until they were called in to the examination room for Nathaniel's initial consult. When the doctor came in, and one of the first orders of business was to draw blood. Soon after the doctor began drawing Nathaniel's blood, she urgently announced, "This boy is dehydrated. We have to admit him to the hospital right away."

Nancy was shocked, but if Nathaniel was dehydrated, she was glad that something was being done. Dr. Berry called over to the university hospital to admit Nathaniel. By some fluke, the hospital's power was out. They had only emergency lighting and backup power. Office personnel told the doctor in no uncertain terms that Nathaniel could not be admitted. She insisted. The person on the other end also insisted that it could not be done.

Fortunately, Dr. Berry was not a person easily deterred. She ignored the functionary on the phone and went into action. Immediately, she inserted an IV into Nathaniel's arm and marshaled an orderly and a nurse to follow her. The group walked Nathaniel across the street as a team. The orderly carried Nathaniel while she held the bag of fluids over his head. "Quickly, now," she ordered, "to the fourth floor." Nancy followed doctor, nurse, and orderly up four flights of stairs. Ignoring anything like normal protocol, they somehow managed to get Nathaniel settled into a bed. Then Dr. Berry marched back to the nurse's desk to check him in. As she talked to the nurse, the electrical power came back on, and lights shone brightly around the building.

This was a good sign. Nancy was sure that things would now even out.

They didn't.

Chapter 10

"We'll just close the top of his stomach"

"How many months has Nathaniel been thirteen pounds?" asked Dr. Berry.

"I'm not really sure," said Nancy. "He's twenty months now. I would guess that he hasn't gained more than a pound or two for the last ten months."

"This projectile vomiting that you described—does he do that often?"

"Well, not like where it goes all over the wall or anything, but, yes, he does spit up a lot."

"And you say that Nathaniel has been admitted to the hospital for pneumonia since you have been here in St. Paul."

"Well, a couple of times this summer, but it hasn't been so bad this fall."

The doctor wrote a couple of things down, and then leaned back in the chair, getting ready for some sort of oration. "Mrs. Norris, let me explain to you what is going on. Because of Nathaniel's disability, there is a malfunction of the lower esophagal sphincter muscles. That is why stomach acids go up into his esophagus, causing him to bleed and to ultimately spit up dried blood. That is why he can't keep food down. Furthermore, that is why he is not gaining weight. Just as importantly, because of this dysfunction, Nathaniel is getting junk into his lungs, which is contributing to his episodes of pneumonia."

Nancy wasn't sure what to say. After a couple of seconds of silence, she finally asked, "Well, is there anything that can be done about it?"

Dr. Berry seemed to be expecting the question. "As a matter of fact there is," she began. "I would like you to consider letting us do a Nissan fundoplication on Nathaniel."

"What's that?"

"We would do an operation that would work to correct the problem. Essentially, we'll just close the top of his stomach."

"How would he eat?"

"We would put a tube directly into his stomach, and he would be fed through the tube."

"And this would be permanent?"

"In some cases, this sort of operation is temporary. But in Nathaniel's case, I can't foresee that there would ever come a time when he wouldn't need it."

Nancy stared at the floor. She knew that Nathaniel was not normal. Until now, it hadn't been so bad. He couldn't do very much, but neither could any infant. He had to be pushed in a stroller but that, too, was pretty normal for babies. However, by doing what this doctor was suggesting, she would definitely be crossing a major line. Other babies did not need to receive nourishment through a tube. Simply put, this was too much to take.

"Talk to your husband about it, certainly. You may want to consult other doctors. But in my opinion, this is the only wise thing to do." Nancy and Dave did talk about it. And they did talk to other doctors, but in the end, they realized that what Dr. Berry had said was correct.

Since Nathaniel's surgery was the next day, Nancy would soon be required to have new skills to care for him, so she went to the hospital to receive instruction. A nurse brought Nancy into an examining room. Before her on a table was a "demonstration doll." The doll was unclad except for a diaper and a miniature rubber hose poking directly into its stomach area. Though it was hard for her to tell because it was coiled, the full length of the tube appeared to be about sixteen inches. It was a quarter inch in diameter, except at the furthest end from the doll where it flanged out a little. Nancy couldn't help staring at the place where the tube quite unnaturally intruded into the doll's stomach.

"Now it is important," said the nurse, opening a can that appeared to be formula, "that you do not feed the baby too rapidly." The nurse picked up a sterilized package and removed what looked like a giant plastic syringe, nine inches long and an inch in diameter. The syringe had a plastic plunger with a rubber tip inserted into it. The nurse pulled the plunger all the way out with a pop and at once inserted the lower end of the syringe into the tube attached to the doll. The nurse then held the giant syringe vertically and began to pour formula into the top of this device. The syringe held a couple ounces of formula, and gravity allowed the formula to flow down the tube and into the doll.

"Now... not too fast," said the nurse, watching the formula's gradual flow out of the syringe and into the tube. "You can actually control the speed of flow by how high up you hold the syringe. The higher you hold it, the faster it flows." She lowered the plastic syringe almost level with the baby doll, and the flow slowed and then almost stopped. Nancy listened. She watched. And then she wanted to run.

The nurse droned on. "Now, if the formula is moving too slowly, you can help it along with the plunger here." She put the plunger into the syringe, forcing the formula more quickly into the doll's stomach. "Now you try it."

Nancy held the tube in her hand and began to pour the formula into it. The nurse encouraged her. "Now take the plunger and...."

"I have to sit down," said Nancy. "I'm feeling a little faint."

"Certainly."

Nathaniel was slated for an early morning surgery. The staff had invited her to stay overnight, and Nancy slept on a cot in another room. At least she tried to sleep. The cot was very hard and uncomfortable. Dave arrived early the next morning and they watched as the orderlies wheeled Nathaniel down the hall toward surgery. The surgery took longer than what the hospital staff said it would, but eventually the surgeon came into the waiting area.

He informed them that the surgery went fine and Nathaniel was resting. "Now what I've done," he said in review, "is cut a hole in his stomach and inserted the tube. The tube is held in place by a metal flange that should not come out. If for any reason it does, get Nathaniel to an emergency room right away."

Visitors came from the St. Paul church and others drove six hours from West Bend to see him. Alan and Carol arrived with their children, as did Grandma Dorothy. She held Nathaniel lovingly. Nancy thought of all that Grandma Dorothy had done for their family when they lived in West Bend and reflected longingly on what were now the good old days. Dorothy rocked Nathaniel tenderly, but then her forehead creased as if she had a lot on her mind. Abruptly she asked, "Do you think I should move here to St. Paul to be with you?"

Dave was quick to speak. "No. Stay there. That's where you're needed." Nancy said nothing.

Working with the tube was not as neat and tidy as the nurse had indicated it would be in her demonstration. Several ongoing issues presented themselves. First of all, the tube was held shut by a nondescript metal clamp that didn't seem to be made specifically for the task. The clasp tended to leak if it were not tightly screwed shut or if it was not clamped in exactly the right place. Messes were the norm. Further, the site where the tube entered Nathaniel's stomach had to be cleaned often; it seemed as if stomach acids could somehow leak up to the site. It became sore and got infected easily.

Nathaniel needed to "eat" every four hours. The cans of formula were self-contained, holding all the liquids, solids, and nutrients that he needed. They were merely poured in. Nathaniel supposedly should not be able spit up—but for some reason, he still could. Not a lot and not often, but it was enough. At times Nancy couldn't tell if Nathaniel was doing okay with the tube. Because Nathaniel was not typically a whiner, when he did fuss, Nancy knew that he was in pain. The problem was that she could not always tell where the pain came from, whether from the tube or from some other complication.

Dave preached on Sunday morning. He had thirty-five minutes to make his point, for the main service was slated to be finished at the same time as the Sunday school released children to go home on the buses. The auditorium seated about a thousand on the main floor, and with the high arched beams, things tended to echo. Dave had read a text, told a story or two, and was just getting to his main point when the computerized air conditioning kicked off. As Dave paused for a breath, a loud snoring sounded out from the front row and echoed throughout the building. One of the good brothers from the church, a single father who worked hard all week long, was truly making the Sunday Sabbath a day of rest. His snoring resounded for all to hear. Though Dave was certain that his next point was a good one, he doubted if anyone really heard it for all of the snickering among the young people in the front rows.

Nancy was finally able to get Nathaniel into a school program. He had graduated from a Chevy Suburban to a small school bus. At 8:30 each morning, she or Dave carried him out to the bus in his car seat, where he would happily get buckled in for the ride. The school was actually a half-hour away, but there was no program that was any closer. Nathaniel returned about 2:30 in the afternoon, happy that he was finally getting some action in life.

With Nathaniel now settled into a routine, Nancy was ready to do more at the church. Dave asked, "Do you think you could come with me next Friday for my Bible study?"

"I'd be happy to if I could get a babysitter."

Dave went to his uncle and explained how much more effective he and Nancy could be together if they could get a little help with someone to watch Nathaniel. His uncle said that the school would pay two dollars an hour on the bill of any student who would babysit. Dave wasn't sure how many takers they would get at that wage, but a surprising number of students made themselves available.

It wasn't as if a babysitter could just give Nathaniel a bottle. Things were quite a bit more involved than that. Anyone who watched Nathaniel for more than a brief span of time had to learn how to give him a tube feeding and how to administer his medications, both of which could be scary. Still, there were now willing helpers. All Dave had to do was ask.

"Joyce, can you come this Wednesday night while we give Tom and Darcy a Bible study?"

"Lynn, can you come Tuesday night? Nathaniel is sick, and Nancy has to direct the children's choir."

"Lisa, can you watch Nathaniel while Nancy does her Bible study with Sylvia?"

It was a Friday evening, and Nancy heard some commotion out in the driveway. When she opened the side door, she saw a pair of legs sticking out from under their white Pontiac Sunbird in the driveway. It was up on some kind of metal deals, and since Dave didn't have any metal deals and she wasn't sure he could identify a spark plug, she assumed the metal deals belonged to the legs underneath the car. Dave was standing there, looking at the car as if he was supervising, but obviously, he wasn't doing anything. She called him into the house for an inquisition. "What's going on?"

"Tony's working on the car."

"Who's Tony?"

"A student."

"You're going to let a student work on our car?"

"He's done it before. He usually works at school. And he's a good mechanic. Besides, I didn't really have the money to take it to the service station. It was running a bit rough. Don't worry. It will be fine."

She did worry, but it turned out fine. Nancy decided that Tony had better get supper out of the deal in any case, because it didn't sound like Dave would be paying him too much. In the meantime Dave was on the phone talking to Greg, the student he was mentoring as the youth leader.

"Okay, so the youth choir idea is good," said Dave, "but if you were to dream big, what would you do with it?"

"Okay. Yeah, we could do a weekend tour, but what would it look like? The kids would have to come up with some kind of program."

"Uh huh. No. I think that November might be too soon. What about a December tour? Okay, yeah. Maybe do a Christmas theme? There was a pause on the other end of the line. Then Dave was talking again. "I think two vans wouldn't cut it, not with forty kids. How about the school bus?"

"Well, no… that's true. I know it wouldn't be all that comfortable, but come on—it would be an adventure, after all. I bet I could get us some churches in Wisconsin that we could go to perform. But the kids might have to rough it a bit for sleeping accommodations. Maybe they could bring sleeping bags."

To Nancy it seemed that for Dave, the crazier the idea, the more appeal it had, and the more projects he could get himself involved in, the happier he was. She stirred the tomato soup and flipped a grilled cheese sandwich. "Go get Tony and tell him to wash the grease off his hands. It won't improve the flavor of the grilled cheese."

Nancy sat in the gastrointestinologist's office at the University of Minnesota Hospital explaining the issue to the doctor. "I thought that you said Nathaniel wasn't supposed to be able to spit up."

"Is he having the projectile vomiting again?" the doctor said, looking worried.

"No. But when I go to his crib in the morning, I see spit up on the sheets, usually quite a bit. He just doesn't seem to be tolerating his night feeding.

"That is not so unusual for those who have slow motility," he said.

"Sorry," said Nancy, challenging the doctor to slow down. She was learning that it was important to insist that doctors speak in

English. Dave was coming to believe that the more unsure or insecure the doctor was, the more complicated their vocabulary became.

"In this case, motility relates to how fast a person can digest food," said the doctor. "This little guy has problems with his whole system, and he digests food very slowly. It hangs around in his stomach longer than it should. That's an important factor in his spitting up."

Nancy was glad for the switch back to English but was more than a little concerned. "So what can be done about it?" she asked.

"I'd like you to try a drip feeding throughout the night. That will go in a lot slower and should really help."

"How do we do that?"

"It is just like they do at the hospital with an IV. There is a kind of pump that allows it to drip in slowly."

"Do you mean that Nathaniel would have to have an IV?"

"No. You would pour the feeding into a plastic bag, and there would be a plastic tube that connects directly with the tube that Nathaniel already uses for his feedings." Nancy began to envision Nathaniel's bedroom looking more and more like a hospital room, but she agreed to try it.

Nathaniel's spitting up at night ceased, but this kind of feeding had its own sets of problems. A week after they began using the pump, Nancy came in one morning to see that the feeding bag had somehow become disconnected from his tube, and formula was caked all over Nathaniel's bed, crusted in his hair and was all over his face. Nathaniel was laughing as Nancy ran the bath water.

Nancy saw Sylvia come in for Sunday night service and head toward a pew at the back of the auditorium. Nancy walked back to greet her. "Mind if I sit with you?" she asked Sylvia.

"I'd love it."

Sylvia's parents had taken her to church as a child, and recently she had started coming again. Nancy had taught her a couple of Bible studies at the house, and last Sunday night Sylvia was baptized. She invited her husband to see the baptism, but he declined. Then when she got home that night, he told Sylvia that he had slipped in the back of the church to watch. He said he was happy for her. Nancy pulled up the stroller next to the end of the pew and held Nathaniel in her lap as one of the ministers began to lead the song service.

Nancy noticed something unusual taking place on the platform where Dave and a few other ministers were sitting. An usher came up to him and whispered something into his ear, and Dave exited off to the side of the platform and did not reappear. Before long, Gary, the usher who had gotten Dave from the platform, tapped Nancy on the shoulder. "Do you need me?" she asked.

"Yes, and your friend as well," he said. He didn't explain further.

Nancy could see by his face that something important was happening, so she walked across the aisle and handed Nathaniel over to Joyce, a student who was a regular babysitter for him. "I'll be right back," she said. Joyce didn't mind at all.

Dave stood in the usher's office with a sober look on his face. He motioned Nancy and Sylvia to come inside, and as he shut the door he said, "I have just received some bad news that I need to share. Please sit down."

Nancy and Sylvia sat quietly. Dave began. "We just received a phone call. It's about your husband."

Sylvia was alarmed. "What? Was he in an accident? Is he all right?"

"There's been a shooting."

"He's shot?"

"Yes. I'm sorry."

"Is he going to be all right?"

"No. I'm afraid not. I'm sorry."

Nancy embraced Sylvia as she sobbed freely. What Dave had not said, but which he would share with her now in bits and pieces, was that her husband had committed suicide. He had used a shotgun and had killed himself in their home. The carnage was terrible.

Nancy ran back into church. "Joyce, take Nathaniel home after service and watch him until I call. Okay?"

Nancy drove Sylvia in her car while Dave followed in theirs. Sylvia's husband was a Vietnam War veteran. He had never gotten over the war and the aftermath of coming home to a nation that did not value his service. Now this man's name would be added to the long list of those whose lives had ended because of such a tragedy.

Dave was in conversation with the law enforcement officials. They told him they would clean things up a bit more before they would let Sylvia come inside. There was no wind, but it was bone-chilling cold. Squad cars filled the driveway, so Nancy and Sylvia stood on the snow-covered grass. Soon, the next-door neighbor invited them into her house for coffee. Friends and family began arriving, filling up the neighbor's home.

The funeral was held at the church. Full honors were bestowed upon a man who had not only given himself in service to his country, but who, because of life's circumstances had also paid the ultimate cost in the end.

Several people watched Nathaniel that day. Once again he was making himself everybody's baby.

Chapter 11

"Did daddy leave you here?"

Dave was out to eat with Robert, his pastor. As he waited for his food, Dave lifted Nathaniel from his stroller and cradled him on his knee. Then he popped the top off a can of formula that he had procured from Nathaniel's diaper bag. He continued talking as he poured the liquid down the giant syringe and watched it trickle into Nathaniel's g-tube. After a few minutes, he then clamped the tube shut and tucked it into his son's shirt. As always, Nathaniel was glad to be with people.

"Dave, I think you should think about having another child," said his pastor.

"Can't," said Dave. "The geneticist says there is only a twenty-five percent chance of having a normal child."

"Is that really true?"

"What do you mean?"

"Well, if you do have a child who is a balanced translocation, then that's still a normal child. So right there, you are up to fifty percent. And didn't you tell me that most children with these genetic defects don't make it to full term?"

"True. Nathaniel is a bit of a miracle to get as far as he did. He's a fighter."

"Okay. Would I be wrong in saying that if a baby lived to be full term, the chance of him being normal might be as high as eighty percent, or maybe even higher?"

"Well, if you look at it that way, then, yes, I suppose so."

"I'd like you to think about having another child. You certainly have a supportive church environment. And the way you and Nancy care for Nathaniel is a testimony of God's love." Nancy didn't like people spiritualizing about Nathaniel, but Dave didn't mind that kind of talk. Still, he wasn't sure about the logic of the pastor's proposal. He had come to notice when people get to be of "grandparent age" they are much more in favor of the doctrine of "be fruitful, and multiply, and replenish the earth." Yet, as the pastor said, the church was supportive. Dave promised to think about it.

Dave somehow resurrected his ability on the trombone and took a number of students out on a brass tour over spring break. When Dave returned, he carried his suitcase into the house only to discover a new babysitter. Sally hadn't been coming to church too long, but she had volunteered to help. She now sat in a chair holding Nathaniel but said nothing. Apparently, she wasn't big on social skills. Nancy was no doubt attempting to help her even as Sally was helping Nancy to care for Nathaniel. Dave was friendly and talked to her, but somehow Sally made him feel as if he were an intruder in his own house.

Dave couldn't quite figure it out. He wondered if Sally was reflecting Nancy's mood because he had been gone for a week. He had worked pretty hard to make this tour happen, but in retrospect he wished he had just dropped it altogether. Just then, Nancy walked into the living room and greeted Dave sweetly. At least one person was nice to him in his home. He wanted to hold Nathaniel, too, but decided to wait until Sally was gone.

The church was planning its 70th anniversary celebration. Even though it wouldn't take place until October, there was a lot to arrange. The event would be advertised as a "homecoming." Although there were a number of church board members on the planning committee, Dave and Nancy were the only ones on the ministerial staff who were participating. And after only one planning session, Nancy dropped out. She didn't care much for committee meetings.

On more than one occasion, Dave noticed some sort of tension in the room. "Why can't we spend money on that?" one of the board members said in an angry outburst. Another of the board members cautioned against any lavish expenditure, an expense that would be frowned upon by others. Apparently understanding the implication, the first board member retorted, "This is our church, and the Bible school shouldn't be in charge of what we do!" Others agreed.

Dave could tell that these feelings didn't originate in this particular meeting but rather represented some sort of ongoing undercurrent of discontent. Such pronouncements flashed up infrequently during the planning, but Dave had an uneasy feeling about where things were heading. He was sympathetic to what the church members were saying and thought that they were making some legitimate points. Still, Dave was conflicted for his very ability to be on staff at both the school and church resulted from the church paying a significant portion of his salary.

Dave had been listening to a speaker who was saying, "So we send out lots of promotional material in July, no matter what anybody says, then…." when he faded out of the discussion. Embracing a daydream as a welcome escape, Dave was once again a little boy at his family's cabin. He and his dad had just come in from a night of bass fishing. The boat drifted toward the dock as his dad cut the outboard motor. Dave, in the bow, prepared to step out of the boat. Instead of settling in toward the dock, the boat started to drift back out into the lake. With one foot in the boat and another foot on the dock, Dave was in a precarious position. If he did not quickly make a decision as whether to get up on the dock or go back into the boat, he would end up plunging into the water. As the discussion in the room swirled around him, Dave felt himself that little boy all over again.

The end of the Bible college year brought its own sets of challenges, and Dave was right in the middle of them. Nancy had already put Nathaniel on the bus and was sitting at the table with her Bible and a cup of black coffee, when Dave resurrected. Nancy observed the dark circles under his eyes as he poured cream into his own mug. Nancy was not sympathetic. "A phone call would be nice," she noted. "You were out until 2:00 a.m."

"I know. And I'm sorry. It won't happen again. But you should see the great scene I've got worked out!" Dave chimed. "I use this one Amy Grant song as background, and then I have three little vignettes going on simultaneously!"

Nancy was far from impressed. When Dave got into these creative jags, he lost all track of time, social skills, or any knowledge of the greater world around him. He was producing a play for end-of-year graduation weekend, and he hadn't been normal for at least a couple of weeks. "Nathaniel hasn't seen you in days!" she protested.

"Well, I'm sorry about that. I'll tell you what. I'll take him with me to drama practice tonight."

"Oh, no. Not a good idea. Who will watch him? Change him? Feed him?"

"There are several girls in class who babysit for Nathaniel already, and if I can't find anyone else, I will feed him myself."

Nancy was a little suspicious as to how much attention Dave would actually give Nathaniel, but she let him go. As soon as Dave got to the room where the practice was being held, he parked Nathaniel near the front of the room. There were fifty people present, and Dave needed to work out some sort of market place scene.

Soon, one of Nathaniel's babysitters came over to his stroller. "Did Daddy leave you here?" she asked, picking him up. Nathaniel responded with a happy cry and a big smile. And then, Nathaniel disappeared down another row where a second young lady picked him up and carted him off. Then someone else held him. With all the attention, Nathaniel was in heaven.

At home, Nancy opened the drawer and pulled out a stack of medical bills. Since Dave was so busy changing the world, the mundane things in life fell upon her. Normal bills were easy enough to handle, but hospital bills were more difficult. Some statements of different amounts seemed to reflect the same bill. In any case, in whatever form the bill came, it was submitted again and again to their insurance company. Unfortunately, insurance companies are not always personable, nor can they always adequately explain why some procedures were denied payment. Phone calls didn't seem to help, and now the tone in the letters from the hospital was getting angrier.

Dave phoned from the drama practice at 9:00 p.m. to say he would be home soon. At 11:30 he carried a sleeping Nathaniel to his bedroom. "I thought you said you'd be home soon," Nancy said.

"Well, tomorrow's Saturday, so he can sleep in," said Dave guiltily, as he laid him in his crib.

The following week, on a Tuesday morning, the doorbell rang. Dave was teaching, so Nancy looked out the window to see who it was. Parked in front of the house she saw what looked like a police car. Nancy opened the door. It was a sheriff. "Is this the home of David Norris?"

"Yes," she replied.

"Is he home?"

"No, he's not."

"And who would you be, ma'am?

"I am Nancy Norris, his wife."

"Well, then, these are for you," the man said calmly, serving her papers. He turned and left while she stared at the court summons she now held in her hand. The Ramsey Hospital was taking them to court. She didn't think a hospital would be this aggressive, but apparently she was wrong.

"What are we going to do?" she asked Dave when he came home.

"Maybe I can get a loan," he offered.

"We are not going to do that," said Nancy stubbornly. "We are going to pray one more time and resubmit these to the insurance company."

"That's not how those things work," Dave said, knowingly. "If they've refused us twice, then I don't think—" but now he could see that was Nancy was in no mood to be contradicted, so he relented in midsentence. "Fine. Just go ahead and resubmit them."

After over a year of completing and filing paperwork, Nancy finally did get one benefit from the SSI in Minnesota. They offered what they called a "respite program" where Nancy could drop Nathaniel off overnight at someone's house and the family would watch him. However, dropping Nathaniel off required giving two sheets of instructions on feeding and caring for their boy to complete strangers. They tried it twice, but they worried the whole night while Nathaniel was away. In the end, they decided that it was hardly worth it.

A few weeks later, Nancy came in with the mail and waving it in Dave's face said, "I told you. Didn't I tell you?"

Dave looked up from whatever he was working on, only half-interested. "You told me that...."

"That they would take it. And they did!"

"Who took what?"

"Blue Cross/Blue Shield," she continued. "They're gonna pay the hospital."

"Let me see that," said Dave, grabbing the bill suddenly. After a minute of looking through the papers, he shouted, "Thank you Jesus! Eighth wonder of the world. An insurance company relenting."

"I have other news, too."

"And what would that be?"

"The blood test came back positive. We're going to have a baby."

It was the end of August, and they scheduled the ultrasound for the middle of September, a couple of weeks after the school year started. Nancy lay face up on the table as Dave stood by her side. The technician put the gel on her and lifted up the transducer, a metal implement attached to a machine of some sort with a big screen. It was cold to the touch. She pressed it firmly against her skin, sweeping it back and forth.

Both Nancy and Dave watched the screen next to the bed. It was so blurry that Dave couldn't make anything out. "It looks like radar measuring a bad storm coming in," he joked.

"There it is," said the tech. "See his heartbeat?"

"Yes!" pronounced Nancy immediately, and after a bit, Dave echoed the pronouncement.

Because the pregnancy was certain and was confirmed by the ultrasound, Nancy called Dr. Berry, her geneticist, sharing the news. Dr. Berry seemed genuinely happy for her. "Nancy," she offered. "I understand that you won't abort the baby under any circumstances, but sometimes it is good to know about him. There is a test that can be given very early to determine whether or not there are genetic issues."

"Really? What is it?"

"It is called Chorionic Villus Sampling—CVS for short."

"Okay. Would I come up to your office and take the test?"

"No. It is relatively new. In fact, there are only two places that give the test. One is in Chicago, and one is in Philadelphia."

At the end of September, Nancy flew down to Chicago on a Friday evening and stayed with her parents. Her test was scheduled for the following morning, and her dad would drive her to the downtown office where the test was to be performed.

Reaching the office, Nancy was shown into a room where she changed into a hospital gown. She stepped to the examination table. A number of screens and computers on various shelves and carts were collectively marshaled to record important data. A nurse was present, but the doctor was clearly in charge. "All right, Nancy," he said. "I want you to lie on this table face up. Before we do the CVS, I need to do another ultrasound, just to make sure of locale."

Nancy situated herself onto the table and the nurse applied the gel. She then placed the transducer on Nancy's stomach. She moved it around a bit, and then she adjusted some things on the computer. Then once again she moved it this way and that, but it remained mute. The doctor stared impatiently. After thirty more seconds, the nurse went over and spoke with the doctor in muffled tones. Nancy couldn't make out what they were saying. The nurse tried one more time with the transducer, and then looked over to the doctor, shaking her head.

"Uh, Nancy, are you sure you are pregnant."

"Yes," she said weakly.

"And this has been confirmed?"

"Yes, I saw the baby's heartbeat two and a half weeks ago."

"I see; well, you see, that's just the problem. We see no heartbeat."

Nancy bit her lip. It was hard to think. "And that means…"

"A fetal death in utero occurs in ten to fifteen percent of all pregnancies. It can actually occur in up to ninety percent of cases where there is a genetic anomaly."

"My baby is dead inside of me?"

He shook his head, affirming this.

"What will happen?"

"Nothing. You will have a miscarriage. You just have to wait for it to occur."

"When will that happen?"

"I wouldn't be surprised if it didn't happen fairly quickly. Maybe within a week or two."

There was no emotion, no consoling, not even a gentle voice. Five minutes ago she was the happiest woman alive. Now, everything was gone—and her loss was being described with medical gobbledygook. Nancy quickly dressed and found her father in the waiting room. She didn't need words. She just sobbed as he held her.

She would have stayed longer with her parents, but Nancy was to direct a children's musical at church on Tuesday night. There were fifty or sixty kids singing, and Nancy felt good about herself as she directed it. Mary, a doctor's wife at church, had taken Nancy on as a project and found her a matching scarf for her new dress. After the performance, the performers celebrated downstairs with a cast party.

Someone went to find Dave. "You'd better come and get your wife, now. You need to take her to the hospital. She's having a miscarriage."

At the hospital, Dave sat glumly in the waiting area where they told him to sit. Soon, Sally came in and plopped herself down. Dave didn't really want to see Sally right now. "Who's watching Nathaniel?" he asked tersely.

"One of the students," came her equally terse reply. Both sat silently for a few minutes of waiting.

"Are you a relative?" asked the nurse to Sally.

"No," she snapped.

"Well, you really don't have to wait," said the nurse. Sally said nothing but continued to stay parked in the chair. She looked at Dave like he was the cause of all of this. In a way, he was, at least in part. He said nothing. She said nothing. Nancy came out. Dave took Nancy home. Sally went home. It was a sad night.

Dave gently opened the door to their home and let Nancy go in first. A young lady from the Bible college sat reading a book. He thanked her for staying so late with Nathaniel but made little further conversation. She left to go to the dorm.

Although in the strongest way all that Nancy wanted to do was just go to sleep, there was something she needed to do first. She entered the second bedroom of their home and walked over to the crib. A cabbage patch doll sat on the dresser, while a little stuffed bear shared the crib with Nathaniel. She stroked Nathaniel's cheek softly. Presently he smiled in his sleep.

Now Nancy was ready to get some rest.

Chapter 12

"Don't 'hi' me, 'Mr. Stay-away-from-home-man' "

A month had passed since the miscarriage. Very little communication was going on in the Norris household. Dave managed his emotions by getting busier. Nancy was having a hard time coping at all. It all came to a head on a Wednesday night when Dave came home late. She was waiting for him. She had already laid Nathaniel down, but now he was in pain, whimpering in his crib.

Nancy wasn't exactly sure where Dave was, and she began to think about all the times he was away from home. He had a meeting about something or another, no doubt with some important person. Apparently it didn't matter that he had left her fourteen hours ago… and had been gone all day without telephoning. Or in the other room lay a whining boy who may have to go to the emergency room if his fever got any higher.

Dave opened the door. "Hi, Nance—"

"Don't 'hi' me, 'Mr. Stay-away-from-home-man.' You think I'm happy sitting in this old house by myself with a sick boy while you run around like a hot shot? You move me away from people who care about me and then you are gone half of the night—"

As she grew louder and louder, Dave was caught off totally off-balance by the tornado that was whipping itself up in the living room. Some of the points Nancy raised were absolutely true, while others deserved a good argument. He wisely opted out of such a strategy. He wished he could leave, but it was 10:30 at night and he had no place to go.

Nancy continued, "I didn't choose this house, didn't choose this city, and I don't have a say in anything. You're out there saving the world but are so inconsiderate of your own wife and handicapped child that you don't even call to say...." Dave wasn't sure why Nancy had chosen tonight to uncork her hurts, but all he could do now was listen.

Home wasn't the only place there was tension. At work, there was back-and-forth talk between the church and the school about what the future would hold. Nothing was said publicly, but there seemed to be plenty of rumbling behind the scenes. Rumors and innuendos flowed this way and that and seemed to be quite intense. It reminded Dave of a family squabble—no, of a coming divorce.

Nancy was surprisingly better the next morning. Nathaniel's fever had come down, which helped her mood. She was drinking coffee and reading the monthly newsletter from Nathaniel's school. "Dave, they are advertising a special marriage weekend for parents of handicapped children."

"How much is it?"

"It says they are sponsoring it. So, apparently it doesn't cost anything."

"When is it?"

"In three weeks."

"How long is it?"

"Starts Friday night and ends Sunday night."

Nancy could tell that her husband was trying to think of an excuse to get out of this but couldn't quite come up with anything. So they went. Sally babysat Nathaniel.

The Marriage Encounter® weekend serviced ten couples as participants with another four couples functioning as leaders. Friday evening began with a mixer, but although the couples were allowed to share trivia, no one was allowed to tell their profession. The leaders wanted the emphasis for each couple to be their spouse.

The couples taking the lead at the weekend meeting took turns teaching biblical principles and sharing their own personal stories, which they read aloud from scripts. The sharing was so authentic and self-deprecating that it tore down walls and defenses. After the couples in charge shared with the larger group, the participating couples were instructed to write down their feelings; they were sent off by themselves for a set period of time to reflect and write. When the bell rang couples would then come together privately and read what each other had written and dialogue related to their issues and concerns. Dave was not at all looking forward to such reflections. But as he wrote, feelings came out unbidden that he didn't know he even had. Nancy had a similar experience.

Dave wrote about how Sally sneered at him when she saw him and how he felt like a stranger in his own house. Nancy wrote about how hard it had been to leave West Bend. He wrote about how much he loved his wife. She wrote about how much she missed working together with her husband in ministry. When they read what each other wrote, healing began. They talked. They cried. They laughed.

Dave had to miss part of the Sunday morning session because he was slated to speak in the morning service. Apparently one of the couples noticed that he was gone because during one of the afternoon writing sessions, a husband came up to him as he was writing and said, "You've got to settle something for me, okay?"

"If I can."

"My wife and I have a bet. She thinks you must be a minister because you had to leave this morning. I said to her, 'No. Remember Eddie? He was a pizza man and had to get up early to get all that dough ready, so anyways—'"

"Shhhh… go back to writing. No talking please." Dave was saved by one of the "hall monitors" and was thankful for their strict policy.

"All right then," Dave told Nancy when the time came for private couple dialogue. "Let's look for ways that we can be in ministry together, and I promise never to make life decisions until I am sure that we have worked through everything to each other's satisfaction."

At the end of the session, the leaders asked for volunteers who wanted to be involved in writing for future Marriage Encounter® sessions. Nancy and Dave looked at each other only briefly and then together they simultaneously lifted their hands to volunteer. After what they had committed to each other, this chance to work together on a project seemed like an answer to prayer. They were especially drawn to helping in Marriage Encounter® because it seemed like a safe place to work, and it had already been a lifesaver for the two of them.

The Norrises went through training to become part of a leadership team for Marriage Encounter®. Dick and Jan were instrumental in mentoring them. They helped the Norrises get started by directing them how they should write, and on several occasions they critiqued their work. Norrises not only drew principles for their talks from a teaching manual; they also sprinkled their presentations with personal stories. Dave found it easy enough to write about marriage principles, but personal sharing turned out to be a lot harder than what he thought it would be.

"That sounds like too much pride in those statements," challenged Dick, upon reading Dave's talk, pointing to the second and third paragraphs. Dick focused in on the offending statements, and Dave went back to the drawing board. Eventually, after painful reflection, the paragraphs were replaced by a more humble approach.

Nancy's talk was more acceptable. She wrote about getting rid of masks and not utilizing "games" as defense mechanisms. Nancy finished her presentation on authenticity by utilizing the story of *The Velveteen Rabbit*, the story of a stuffed rabbit who wants to become "real." In a conversation with another toy as to how it is that one becomes real, the other toy, a skin horse, defines how it is that one becomes real. He offers that being real has nothing to do with how you are made. He even allows that sometimes becoming real hurts. The rabbit asked if it happened all at once, but the Skin Horse advised him that this wasn't the case at all, noting that it only happened gradually so that by the time one became real, "most of your hair has been loved off, and your eyes drop out and you get loose in the joints and very shabby. But these things don't matter at all, because once you are Real you can't be ugly, except to people who don't understand."

Norrises met the other couples with whom they would be working. Assignments were given and decisions were made about the prescribed order of the talks. Nancy and Dave were incredibly gratified to be acting as the clergy couple for their weekend session and could hardly believe the difference in demeanor between couples on Friday and the same couples on Sunday afternoon. Lives were being changed right in front of their eyes. All they had to do was be vulnerable.

Sundays held a specific routine for the Norris household. There was the hubbub of getting ready for Sunday school, then morning service, and then Nancy and Dave would go out to eat with someone. It was hardly ever the same group. It might be family, friends, a colleague from the school, someone from the church, a big group, or a small group. It didn't matter. It was always a good time.

Nancy and Dave's life had not always followed this pattern. In fact, when they were first married, Dave brought Nancy into his life-long childhood Sunday routine. His mom, Dorothy, made the same meal each Sunday that she had made all of their growing up years. Salads marked the beginning of the meal that then featured potatoes and carrots, which had simmered in a broth all morning, to complement the roast beef dinner. Dessert followed.

Dorothy was half-Swedish and half-Norwegian, and her warm smile and even temperament had no doubt contributed to attracting Dave's dad. When the kids were little, she worked part-time and was home when they arrived home from grade school for lunch. But as they got older, she added a full-time job to the task of raising six kids. Somehow the laundry was miraculously churned out, though it was incumbent on each child to locate and fold his or her own clean clothes that were scattered across the ping pong table in the basement. Her daily routine was the same. Arriving home from work at 5:20 in the afternoon, she would without fail have a cooked meal on the table by 6:00 p.m. so that the family could sit down and eat together. Children were required to do dishes, though she refereed who was supposed to wash or dry. Dorothy wasn't one to mention her own needs.

The first year of their marriage, Dave took a singing group from the Bible school on summer tour. Because Nancy had one more class left to finish her elementary school teaching degree, she couldn't go. Norrises lived in a walk-in basement apartment and had a nosey neighbor for a landlord. When she berated Nancy for throwing food away after having gone through her trash, Nancy came over to her mother-in-law's house and shared this with Dorothy. This was the only time she ever saw Dorothy angry. She insisted that Nancy come live with her and drove her over to get some things. She wouldn't let her go back to the apartment until Dave got back into town.

There was only one time that Dave ever remembered his mom ask him for anything. She had cancer, and she asked him to move back to St. Paul to be closer during that time, but they did not. She was gone now. She had died four years earlier. Coming back to St. Paul after living in West Bend didn't quite seem like coming home, because now his mom was gone. Dave missed her. She had been a rock whenever things were difficult. And in her quiet way, she had showed affection to both her children and her husband. One of Dave's earliest memories was that of his mom kissing his dad good-bye when he left for work.

His dad would say, "See you later, alligator."

His mom responded, "After while, crocodile."

Dave opened the car door and put Nathaniel in his car seat. It was Sunday afternoon and it was time to go eat. "Too bad your mom isn't still around," said Nancy. "We'd know where we were eating for lunch."

"Let's go to Baker's Square," said Dave.

"You're not meeting anyone there?"

"No. Everyone left before I could ask anyone. Where were you, anyway?"

"Oh, we had a planning session for our Tuesday night children's program."

"So what are you going to do now?" asked Dave.

"Guess what!" said Nancy, gushing with enthusiasm. "I talked them into doing a short unit on the Book of Matthew!"

"And that's good because...." prompted Dave.

"It's the same chapters they are using for Junior Bible Quizzing!" said Nancy. She was working up to something, Dave was quite sure. So Nancy explained. She would have a six-week program for the larger group, and then if some of the children wanted to continue, they could.

"And that would be good because...." continued Dave.

"Because you could coach the children, just like you did the children in West Bend." Bible quizzing is similar to a college bowl, only instead of someone asking a series of questions about academic subjects, a series of questions is asked about specific Bible verses. Questions may include asking about specific information contained in verses or they might even require participants to quote verses verbatim. Although the teenagers in the church had been involved in Bible quizzing for years, the idea of grade school children being involved was relatively new, and the church had never before had a Bible quizzing program for children. For Nancy, it would be an exciting six weeks of competition, prizes, and fun.

Nancy enjoyed working with children. For an hour and a half each Tuesday night, students reviewed verses and then answered questions on what they learned.

Dave would have liked to help, but his focus was on Bible college students. He busied himself with teaching classes, overseeing chapels, and investing in the college students' ministerial development. All the while, though, an ever-present undertone of a deep distrust grew more tangible more tangible in the building where he worked.

For Nancy, Tuesday nights started with a bang. After a short prayer, children blended a lot of learning with a load of fun.

For Dave, faculty prayer meetings were anything but a bang. And they certainly were not fun. As unspoken suspicions hovered in the air, loyalties were tested to their limits.

Nancy orchestrated a group of Bible school student helpers who created team spirit as they coached children to answer questions from the Book of Matthew. The six-week program for Bible quizzing ended with several children wanting to continue with quizzing. It also ended with a big party to celebrate the accomplishment of all the children who had worked so hard.

That same six weeks ended for Dave in a very different way, a way that was not good.

It was decided by Nancy that Dave was needed to be a junior Bible quiz coach.

It was mutually decided by Dave and his grandfather that his skills were no longer required at the Bible college.

For the Bible quiz team, Dave would be needed right away.

At the school, it wasn't just that Dave would not be returning to teach in the fall. He wouldn't be needed for the remainder of the school year.

Dave drove the church van two hours to St. Cloud for a Bible quiz tournament. On the way there, he turned from the wheel, yelling out to the eleven-year-olds in the back, "Who wants to stop at McDonalds?" The junior Bible quiz team happily reported that they all did. The team entered McDonalds dressed alike—in pink, unfortunately. The team was made up of mostly girls, so it sort of made sense. At first, Dave's masculinity felt threatened by the pink tie, but Dave's youngest sister Joanne, who was his assistant coach, convinced him that it was actually mauve.

The team had a good day. They beat a couple of teams but ultimately got crushed by a Bible quiz team from Grand Rapids, Minnesota. The kids from Grand Rapids were simply unbeatable. On the way home, the van stopped at McDonalds again. The kids pulled out the team mascot, Gumby, and had him dancing across the table. They were laughing and joking, all the while twisting Gumby every which way so he would be eating French fries. Dave laughed until tears streamed down his face. Then it occurred to him: This was the most normal thing in his life right now.

Dave went into the pastor's office for advice about what to do next and was greeted with a surprising offer. Robert said, "A man from a church has contacted me recently; they are in need of a pastor. They have about a hundred and forty people who attend regularly. You would have to interview with them and speak at the church, but there is every chance you would be voted in as their pastor. It is a pretty decent income."

Dave nodded, glad for the generosity, but he was not really interested. He wasn't sure exactly how to put it without sounding ungrateful. He paused and then said, likely sounding ungrateful, "If I took the church, would I just be a hireling?"

"I have no idea what you are talking about," replied the pastor. "You have already been a pastor. You certainly have the gifts to do it."

Dave squirmed uncomfortably in his seat. "God called me away from pastoring a church that I loved. I would never have left that church just to go pastor another church."

"Look Dave, sometimes we do what we feel impressed to do. And other times there are times of waiting, while we prepare to once again do what is in our heart to do."

"God called me to teach. It was very specific."

Although the pastor frowned, clearly not impressed with his idealism, Dave continued, "Surely there is someplace I could go to teach?"

"Well, there are other schools you could go to, but I wouldn't recommend it."

"I'm pretty much done here; wouldn't you say?"

"This is a family squabble. People get over things. But if you teach at a competing school, you will have burned your bridges."

"Do you think another school would have me?"

"There is a school or two that would, certainly."

"Could you inquire for me?"

"I don't recommend it. It's not a good idea. But if you want me to, I can make a preliminary phone call. You would have to do the actual inquiring yourself. Just don't bring my name into this." In the last several weeks Dave had been getting this caveat more and more from anywhere he sought advice.

Chapter 13

"Our lives are surreal"

Nancy and Dave disembarked from the plane in Baltimore, picked up their rental car, and drove the two hours that it took to get to Dover. After calling for directions, they headed out of town on a county road. There was little to see. While rural Delaware features an occasional Amish buggy, the landscape more typically sports little three-bedroom ranches and random house trailers. When after four miles or so they found the turn, they proceeded another quarter of a mile as instructed.

Sure enough, across from a Amish school house were several upscale homes. They knew they were in the right place. They turned into the driveway and followed the long curving drive to the front of the home. It was not quite a southern mansion and not quite a plantation house. Janet greeted them warmly and escorted them up the stairs to the guest room. Dave parked his suitcase in a room that could have been featured in *Country Home and Garden*.

"How was your flight?" asked Janet. It had been uneventful, good really.

"Any trouble finding the house?" A little, but it wasn't too bad.

"Let me show you around." A lot of brick and wallpaper met their eyes as they toured the home's many rooms. While the formal living and dining room could be described as elegant, it was clear that a whole lot of living took place in the family room and kitchen.

Janet didn't linger but offered, "I'll take you for a tour of the church and school. Right now it's all housed in one large building."

The Norrises both rode to the school with Janet. As soon as they turned onto Highway 13, the large sign announced the complex. The church and school sat on a good chunk of acreage at Dover's northernmost point. On a paved parking lot sat an oversized two-story building. Majestic brick archways extending thirty feet into the air repeated across the front entrance of the building. The entrance led into an oversized lobby. A second set of glass doors opened to a large multipurpose room, which apparently served as both school cafeteria and church sanctuary.

As with their home, Janet's husband Wayne had been the builder and Janet the decorator. Janet took them beyond the sanctuary to spacious executive offices where she dropped off her things. Oversized desks were situated in the middle of plush, well-coordinated offices—wallpaper with the cornices and furniture. Dave couldn't help but think that the combined square footage of Janet and her husband's offices was probably larger than the house in which he lived.

Down the hallway from the offices was a full-sized gymnasium featuring some kind of special cushiony floor. Upstairs, the second story unfolded into a seemingly unending set of classrooms punctuated by a few plush offices. Lastly, Janet took them back down to an open area on the first floor, which had one time apparently been used for daycare. She pronounced, "I'm going to subdivide this to make you a nice office." She didn't use the language "if you come" or "if we can work something out," even though the whole trip was still in the exploratory stage. "You will have a full-time secretary in the office in front of you. You will never have to type another letter again."

Dave actually was not much into typing letters, but he thought that now would not be a good time to mention it. Janet gave him a leather pad with his name engraved on it as well as the name of the school. He smiled and thanked her, promising that they would really consider coming.

On the way back to the airport Nancy reported, "Well, I'm ready to move."

Dave was about to launch into a warning about how that it was normal for people to put their best forward when recruiting others to come. He was going to talk about how there was a whole staff who already worked there and question how they would fit. He had a lot to say, but he wanted to approach it logically. He began, "Nancy, this isn't real."

"Well, it looks real to me." There was silence the rest of the way to the airport as the driver of the car went into one of his melancholy moods. He had promised Nancy that whatever it was they were going to do, it would be someplace where they could work together in ministry. Further, they would make their decision jointly. But now her vote was being swayed by outright bribery. Janet said that if they decided to come, she would pay their way to the staff retreat at their villa in Jamaica.

Dave knew he needed input from others in his life right now, but he felt isolated. Some godly advice had to be available from somewhere, someone who could keep confidences and might serve as a sounding board. One night after a church service, he approached an elder in the church: "Do you have some time when I could talk to you?" The man replied that right now was a good time, so they looked for a place where they could have a private conversation. They stepped into a conference room and Dave began to explain his situation.

Before he was sixty seconds into it, the elder stopped him. "Look, I don't want to hear complaints about any of the ministers from the church or the school." Dave convinced him that this was not his intent and the elder allowed him to explain. When he finished speaking, the man stood cautiously, perhaps not altogether certain why he had to be the victim of this needy man asking for advice. None was forthcoming.

"Well, at least pray about it with me," requested Dave, and although the man nodded, Dave supposed this to be merely an obligatory gesture.

Dave also called Jim in West Bend. Jim had been a good confidant, knew more about the issues than anyone else and had promised to pray about the situation. Dave called him back, and he said, "Dave, given everything, you don't really have a lot of choices do you? I think you should go."

About a week later, after a church service, the elder that Dave had spoken to unexpectedly came up and stood next to him. He was not quite looking at him, and it took Dave a second or two to realize that the man was actually speaking to him. He offered simply, "I think you should go." Then without another word, he turned and walked away. Like others from whom he asked advice, the message seemed to be clear. It would be better if his name were not mentioned.

Dave's pastor Robert worked things out so that the church would pay Dave's housing and salary for as long as he wanted to stay in St. Paul. District playoffs for Bible quizzing were to be held at Grand Rapids in the middle of June. That was still over a month away, but he would like to coach the kids there. Robert said he could stay as long as he wanted, but it was clear that Dave's time in St. Paul was drawing to a close.

After getting off the plane in Montego Bay, Norrises were driven on what appeared to be the wrong side of the road, first on a fairly good road, then on a mediocre road, and then on not much of a road at all. Finally, after they had settled into their room at the villa, they sat on a portico next to the pool eating lobster bought from a local diver and nicely prepared by the resident cook, Thelma. "No problem," people kept saying to them, and this seemed to be the mantra of the entire island nation of Jamaica. Nancy was having a great time at this staff retreat, lost in the moment. All the while, Dave kept thinking of possible disasters that might still befall them. He took another bite of food and said to Nancy, "Pass the lobster. Our lives are surreal." She wasn't listening.

"If you can, I need you to come right away," said Janet. Those were the very words uttered by his grandfather two years earlier.

Dave suddenly chafed. He said, "I have some obligations with the church, so it is possible I could come at the end of June, but more than likely I'll need to stay until the middle of August." In truth, he had no real obligations at all with the church, though he was still coaching the junior Bible quiz team, and would like to stay until their district play-offs in June. On the odd chance that they beat the team from Grand Rapids and went to national competition, the team wouldn't compete until August. Yet, it hardly mattered that this was incredibly tentative. Right now, he needed some space. He was very much afraid of the unknown, no matter how celebrated things seemed to be at the moment.

Dave's quiz team drove to Grand Rapids on a Friday for district play-offs. The first round of the finals came down to the St. Paul team against the Grand Rapids team. And something very surprising happened. Dave's team won. Unfortunately, it was double elimination, and the next day, at the end of a very long morning, they played Grand Rapids again. This time, Grand Rapids won, and it all came down to a play-off quiz between the two teams for the state championship. Before the quiz, Dave brought their trusty mascot, Gumby, to the table. Gumby had a few tricks to show them to lighten the mood, and at least he got them laughing a little.

Soon it was time for the final quiz to begin. Three quizzers sat at the table in front of him, just as three competing quizzers sat at an adjacent table. In front of each quizzer was a wooden block upon which sat a button looking very much like a doorbell. When a quizzer knew the answer, he or she hit the doorbell. Immediately a buzzer sounded and a display light illuminated indicating which particular quizzer was the first to respond. A quiz official would then call on the quizzer's color and number and the quizmaster would wait for him or her to answer.

This was the first year for Dave's church to participate with this younger age group. For the children, the competition was all great fun. Not for Dave. His future hung in the balance of this quiz. If they won, it meant eight weeks of reprieve until national playoffs before he would have to move. And now that it came down to it, he was more reticent than ever to leave the familiar. Joanne, his sister and the assistant coach, sat beside him keeping score. It was back and forth through the six ten-point questions with Dave's team pulling ahead during the twenty-pointers.

Dave called a time out and talked to his team. "If you get this next question, just relax and don't hit anymore," he said. He had good reason for such a strategy. Points are taken away if the individual answering the question gives an incorrect response. Furthermore, if a quizzer interrupts the question and gets an answer wrong, then the other team is eligible to answer the same question and gain further points. It is actually possible to lose a quiz that was already a guaranteed win. Dave emphasized once more that if they answered the next question, they would have a guaranteed win, provided they didn't do anything stupid.

Their team got the right answer, and Dave knew that the match was iced. That is, they did have the quiz won until the next question was read, and Joylynn, his team captain, interrupted the question and attempted to answer. Dave held his breath. The officials deliberated and finally the question was ruled correct. Joylynn went on to answer the last question too. "So much for listening to your coach," said Dave after the quiz, but he couldn't keep from smiling.

July was a blank slate when it came to Dave's schedule. In truth, for the first time in a decade, he had little to do. He would speak in church for this or that service, but there were no daily responsibilities. For the first time in his life, Dave had a very unique routine. His days consisted of showing up at the homes of quizzers, repeatedly asking the same Bible questions, doing speed drills, and listening to eleven-year-olds quote the same Bible verses over and over again. While he couldn't really explain this adequately to anyone, these weeks in his life were an incredible gift. The feeling of "joy" is not something that most people associate with drilling children over and over on the same Bible verses, but then most people were not in Dave's shoes either. For him, the team had already won.

Four children were on the team. Joylynn always smiled broadly when she answered questions. Her cousin Krissy was also on the team. There was a friendly rivalry between the two of them, which he actually thought helped them study more. Tracy regularly argued with him about whatever came to her mind, and Dave loved her spiffiness. Steve was their fourth quizzer, and it was his dad who had actually created and manufactured the buzzer system that was now used nationally. Steve was more reflective and analytical about quizzing than the girls, and he lacked that intuitive killer instinct possessed by his female counterparts. He was glad to sit peacefully on the bench as a substitute, even though he knew the answers.

Joylynn's mother Cindy found the quiz team amazingly cheap plane fares to St. Louis for national play-offs. A van was too expensive to rent, but Cindy was able to get them an upgrade to rent an upscale car cheaply. Dave and his sister Joanne, along with Nancy and four quizzers, managed to stuff themselves into an oversized Lincoln Continental to drive around in during finals.

Their quiz team won the first couple of quizzes and then there was a long enough break to go mini-golfing. They were right in the middle of the mini-golf course when they met some other quizzers who told them that on the matrix their team was scheduled to play right then. Dave dropped his clubs, gathered up his flock, and swooped them into the Lincoln. It was a good thing, too, because they would have forfeited the next match had they been any later. For some reason, the team kept on winning. Gumby the mascot regularly appeared, making them laugh, and before they knew what hit them, they were second place in the nation.

The quizzing took place in an auditorium at the denominational headquarters building, and as a special treat, the general superintendent read the names of the quizzers on the winning teams. When he announced Krissy's last name, for whatever reason, he mispronounced it. Although the spelling doesn't look like it on paper, her last name is actually pronounced, "Win-ar'-chek." When the superintendent pronounced it, he said something like "Winterchuckle". Nancy spontaneously laughed very loudly. The superintendent gave a stare that let everyone know that he did not really appreciate such an outburst. Then when Dave and the quiz team lined up to have the official photograph taken, the general superintendent shook his hand and said, "I want to see you in my office after the ceremony."

Dave had never met the general superintendent before, much less been in his office. It was quite large. Dave was directed to the chair right in front of the very large desk behind which the general superintendent sat. The superintendent began, "First, congratulations on being second in the nation." Dave thanked him. Then he abruptly added, "Second, I need to talk to you about this whole St. Paul situation. Now I've known your grandfather a long time. I remember the time...."

Dave had voted for this man in the very first conference where he was eligible to vote. The man was a strong leader with charismatic gifts, and Dave was glad he was in office. In fact, this man was on Dave's short list of heroes. One time, Dave randomly wrote him a letter and sent him a check to take his wife out for breakfast. Somehow, this gesture now seemed provincial. "Remember that your grandfather is a pioneer, and he thinks differently than most," the general superintendent was saying.

The year after this man was elected to office, he had decided to serve communion to the whole General Conference, some twenty thousand people. Dave was a little nervous about this because he knew that there was some disagreement as to how communion should be done. There was the wine faction, and there was the grape juice faction, and each faction thought the other to be in error biblically. He was curious as to how this would be worked out for the conference.

Dave sat with his arm around his wife in the coliseum where communion was soon to be served. An announcement kept flashing on the screen. More ministers were needed to volunteer to serve communion. Those willing to volunteer were to meet in a room in back someplace. The announcement kept flashing, but Dave readily ignored it. Nancy kept poking him until she finally shamed him into going. He walked back to join a mass of several hundred ministers, who were just then receiving last-minute instruction as to where they were to go. Maps had been distributed, assignments given, tasks laid out. It only remained for the volunteers to pick up the elements of communion and go to their assigned areas. "So, are there any questions?" asked the man who appeared to be overseeing the sacrament.

"Yeah, I've got a question," yelled a man, who did not at all seem as if he were sincerely asking a question. "Is it wine, or is it grape juice?"

Dave waited to see how the fellow would answer him, but the man overseeing this distribution seemed genuinely surprised by the question and couldn't seem to come up with an answer. He simply stood there. Suddenly Dave found himself yelling out. He wasn't sure why, but he heard himself saying, "It doesn't matter." Everyone turned to look at him. "It doesn't matter," he repeated. "Our general superintendent is trying to do something to bring unity; he wants revival. *That's* what matters. I think we ought to pray!" Dave said this more authoritatively than he felt, but for some reason they listened and they prayed.

And now the general superintendent was speaking to Dave. "And so, you need to remember that even when your grandfather is wrong, he is right." Dave thought about the first years of the general superintendent's tenure. He had started a program... well, more than a program, really. It was more of a quest—a quest as to how to have revival. He had called for fasting, all-night prayer meetings, and specifically for each minister to ask God for direction. Then each minister was to send him what he believed God was saying to him. Dave had participated. He really felt that God had showed him some important things, and he sincerely wrote them down. Some were things that had already changed him personally. While some might have called him idealistic, he was sure this program would make a difference in the progress of their denomination. Now, sitting here, it struck him that the superintendent had probably not even read what he wrote. How could he have read that many?

"And so that's what I want you to do," finished the speaker behind the desk. Dave had missed that last bit.

"I'm sorry, what was it you want me to do?"

"To write a letter of apology to your grandfather."

"Sure. I'd be glad to do it," said Dave getting up. He'd be glad to do anything that would get him out of that office, out of that building, and out of that city.

Chapter 14

"We're going to live in a barn?"

"**W**e're going to live in a barn?" Nancy asked her husband incredulously.

"It's not like that," said Dave. "They're remodeling a place for us to live. Apparently, they used to raise Arabian horses and peacocks but now it seems that they are turning the barn into a guest house."

"It's not done?" asked Nancy.

"Well, they're working on it. And believe me, when it is done, it will be really nice."

Nancy accepted this readily and suddenly made a quick mental jump. "Dave, Sally wants to move with us."

"What are you talking about?"

"She wants to go to help with Nathaniel."

"Nancy, she is a strange person."

"Dave, do you remember what happened when we first moved to St. Paul? It was months before I had any support. Do you suppose that Dover will be any different? I know there are some issues with Sally, but are you willing to turn down good help?"

"Nancy, it is my understanding that we are going to stay at the big house until things are finished at the barn, so I just can't ask them to put someone else up."

"And that's because…?"

He paused. His wife was unrelenting. Moments passed where nothing was said. No ready excuse came to him, and finally cornered, he relented. "Okay, I'll see if there is room. Maybe she can come out a bit later, once we get settled."

Nancy was making lists of what to do to get ready for the move. "I don't want to move this furniture across the country," she said to Dave.

"What are you talking about?"

"We've had some of this furniture since we got married over ten years ago, and some of it was used then," she pointed out.

"Not all of it."

"Dave, let's give it to Joanie." Nancy knew that Dave couldn't say no to this idea. There had been a tragedy. Brian Wiseman had been diagnosed with advanced stages of cancer on the mission field. Now he and his wife Joanie and their two kids were coming back to the United States so Brian could be treated at Mayo Clinic. Joanie was getting an apartment in Eau Claire, Wisconsin, and she would commute to Mayo with Brian. They were starting this season of life with very little. Dave agreed as she knew he would.

It was Dave's last time to speak in St. Paul. Dave's father was in church that Sunday morning. Dave's dad hadn't attended church all of Dave's growing up years. He came for the annual Christmas program, but that was about it. Something had happened when his dad was only a teenager. There had been some kind of argument between Dave's father and Dave's grandfather. Stories were all third-hand. He may have been kicked out of the house. He may or may not have come back, and that is when Dave's grandfather may or may not have gotten him a job as printer, something that his dad had now done for over forty years at the same company.

Dave Sr. was fairly introverted and hardly eloquent with words, but he had a common sense approach and knew what was what in life. Dave never knew his father to tell a lie—ever. He was a hard worker and didn't have vices. But he didn't possess what you might call warm fuzzies either. He said no to anything he deemed questionable. As far as church was concerned, he was in favor of the kids going to church and listening to what the minister said, he himself stayed away.

All of this worked to turn the family dynamics on its head. Because the kids went to church and he did not, it had been an unspoken truism that it was Dave Sr. who was in need of prayer—the lost sheep of the family.

Dave's mom had died almost six years ago. It was after she died that Dave Sr. had started coming to church. He generally sat in the back, mostly with family. Dave had never seen him respond in church, at least not until that day. Dave would never know why he came forward that day when the invitation was given, but it happened that on that particular Sunday morning that his dad came down the aisle to the altar. Seeing his father pursuing God in his life was for Dave a happy moment, a truly great gift.

Nancy looked around the house one last time at the boxes that were ready to be packed into the U-haul truck. Nathaniel was waving his rattle around excitedly. He knew the routine was different, and he enjoyed the action. After Dave had squeezed the last suitcase into their car, they headed to the airport. Nathaniel made happy noises in the back seat. Checking her luggage at the curb, Nancy wheeled Nathaniel down to the plane, checked the stroller at the entrance to the jet and held Nathaniel on her lap. As the plane touched down, they became new residents of the East Coast.

Later that day, the truck came and some fellows loaded up the furniture that Nancy would be giving to the Wisemans. Then Dave picked up his U-haul truck, and with the help of friends, loaded up what little remained to take to the East Coast. Dave vacuumed the house and put the vacuum cleaner into the truck. The truck had plenty of room left inside. The truck held boxes and boxes of books, but no couch or chairs. Nathaniel's crib was safely stowed inside, but they hadn't moved so much as a mattress.

After Dave put the last item on the truck, he walked back into the empty house. A feeling of melancholy began to settle over him. Materially, he didn't have much to show for thirty-two years of living. Not much at all. And prospects didn't look promising for an immediate change.

A severance check was coming from the school; and he had expected a significant gift from the church. There had even been some talk that they would get him a car. Given that the car he was driving might not make it cross country, Dave had promised to give that car to Tony, the student mechanic who had kept it running. Tony had done more work on keeping it running than it was actually worth. But things didn't really work out for Dave when it came to going away gifts. Instead of a car, he got a punchbowl. And the check from the school certainly would not allow him to buy new furniture. Dave climbed into the truck, turned the key, and pointed the truck east.

As he headed across Wisconsin on Interstate 94, he tried to see the bigger picture. There were different ways to invest, and it wasn't up to him to figure out what value to place on the specific time and effort he had given to one thing or another. In particular, he wouldn't try to assign a value to the last couple of years. He would have to give it some time before he could think clearly about it. But there was one thing he could evaluate. The value he would assign to the last couple of months he had spent with the children: priceless.

Driving across the Midwest, Dave began to leave events in Minnesota behind and began looking forward. He started to think about all the unknowns in Dover. He was a Midwesterner to the core. He was going to a culture that wasn't quite Eastern and not quite Southern, but some unusual mixture of both. On the previous visit, he had noticed a lot of "yes, ma'ams" and "no, sirs." He made a mental note to try to work that language into his vocabulary a bit more.

For Janet it was no problem that Dave and Nancy came without a car. She was energized by a crisis, and although he brought more than a few with him, she didn't break a sweat addressing them. She said she would make arrangements for them to borrow a car, and if there were other needs, she would take care of them as well. It was soon decreed that the Norrises could borrow her daughter Jeanette's car when they needed it. Jeanette was one of two married children that lived on the property.

Who all actually lived on the property was something of a mystery. Tom, who seemed to be a yardman of some sort, worked around the house, but his position wasn't altogether clear. Apparently, he was just getting out of the Air Force and was used to being told what to do rather loudly. Carolyn was a kind of cleaning lady/family friend who didn't live there but appeared regularly to clean and rearrange things for this or that visitor.

The house was constantly alive with comings and goings, and various rooms were always getting changed out. One man named John, who seemed to be an inventor and was apparently a millionaire of some sort, largely came and went at will. Raphael, a beekeeper from one of the Dakotas, also made appearances. A number of ministers were regulars at the house, mostly women. There was the taller Dawn, a short-term missionary, the shorter Dawn, an evangelist, and Nannette, also a minister of some sort. From what Dave could figure out, they were all involved in self-directed ministries and used Dover as their base of operations. And then there was Lisa, a very competent young minister. She seemed to be more permanent, a sort of worker bee. While she readily worked in the academy, there didn't seem to be a single job description that fit all the things that she accomplished.

As best Dave could figure it, the house was less a bed and breakfast than a headquarters building for those who came in and out of the dreams of Janet and Wayne. The population of the house ebbed and flowed as easily as the tide.

Even the living arrangements of Wayne and Janet's children seemed rather fluid as well. There was Jeanette, a daughter in her twenties. She was married to a minister and had a little girl named Stephanie. While a house was in the process of being finished on a couple of acres sitting to the right of the main building, the couple lived in the guesthouse adjacent to and yet connected to the main house.

Anthony, son of Wayne and Janet, was also a minister. He, his wife Tammy, and their infant son Ryan lived to the left of the main house in a home built a few years earlier when he was planning to getting married. These three nice homes stood looking down on the one-room Amish school house that squatted across the road from them.

It was September again, time for Amish boys wearing suspenders and straw hats to roller blade past these homes on their way to school. Oddly enough they carried Superman lunch buckets. The eldest among them didn't look to be older than junior high age, so it was not too surprising that the boys largely ignored the girls who were forced to amble along behind them. Amish horses and buggies regularly passed by the homes, often leaving remembrances of their journey in the middle of the road.

The third night the Norrises were there, everyone who was around gathered in for a large family dinner. Apparently they were eating the cow that used to walk the grounds. It had made its home in the barn in which the Norrises were going to live, but it had to be sacrificed during remodeling because it kept trying to get back into what it thought was its stall, and this was largely hindering the work.

The following Monday Nancy heard a loud beeping noise outside. She looked out the window of the guest room to see Nathaniel's school bus not quite able to make it up to the house. Neither the bus nor its driver was happy. To the driver's reckoning, there were three cars that prevented her from making complete passage through the curved driveway and back out onto the street. Car keys were sought and found and the offending cars moved. Finally, Nathaniel was dutifully loaded onto the bus for his first day of school.

The office that Dave would occupy was now being decorated. Janet's son Anthony had framed it out with sheetrock that was currently being covered by wallpaper. The office was given the feel of an outside wall with a faux window; the "non-window" was hidden by a drapery and valence that matched the wallpaper. A large executive desk sat directly in front of the faux window. Matching bookcases partially offset by beveled glass doors occupied the wall to the right of the desk. An expensive love seat, complemented by a chair, completed the ensemble. A very nice picture that hung on the wall brought together all the room colors. Apparently, this was just the beginning of the coordinating effort. Janet insisted that Dave immediately bring in his books so she could arrange them by color on the shelves. Book jackets were violently torn from the covers and the library was sorted out and arranged by color and size. A particular set of commentaries was featured under the lights in the middle glass shelf in the credenza.

Services at church were compelling. Worship was sincere and expressive. Music was wonderful and quite loud. It was a mixture of genres, but mostly had a black-gospel feel. The choir was incredible. Sermons were almost always evangelistic, and a steady flow of visitors along with compelling altar calls loaded the services with a sense of expectation.

Announcements in the church services were less giving of information than pep rallies, where new, world-changing programs seemed to be introduced constantly. It shouldn't have surprised Dave, then, as to how he was introduced to the congregation. Janet began offering his qualifications, inflated by more than a little. Then, when it came to a job description, while not exactly the messiah, she explained that Dave would make considerable changes and cause growth and prosperity in almost every facet of the church. All of this was revealed to Dave at the same time as it was to everyone in the congregation. Dave wondered if perhaps Janet were thinking of additional things even as she was speaking. The litany of productivity that was yet to come would result from Nancy and him overseeing youth, young marrieds, and outreach. From there, Dave lost count. The Apostle Paul would have been hard pressed to fulfill the role. Afterward, he asked Janet about her impromptu announcement, and she responded sincerely, "Well, haven't you done all of those things?"

"Not all at one time."

Some weeks after their arrival, Nancy sat in the audience during the mid-week service with Nathaniel beside her in his red wheelchair. While it could be folded down into a car seat for travel, it could also be extended to its full size to support him for other functions. Dave was the speaker, but when the service was over, someone told Dave and Nancy that Wayne wanted to see both of them in his office. Nancy felt more than a little apprehensive. Offices had a particular connotation to her. They meant rebuke and correction. They meant threats. Sadly, they had only been here a couple of months, and already there was trouble. She gathered Nathaniel and put him in his chair, obediently wheeling him behind Dave. They entered Wayne's office, and he invited them to sit down. "So, how are things going?" he asked.

"Fine," said Dave warily.

"And the classes are good?"

"Yeah, uh, yes sir. They're just fine. Good student body. We're enjoying ourselves." Nancy was sure this was leading up to some significant drubbing, but the conversation stalled as her husband sat defensively in the chair, waiting for the worst. After a couple of minutes, Jeanette, Wayne's daughter came in hurriedly and said that Dave and Nancy were wanted down in the gym for something. Suddenly, Wayne was no longer interested in conversation as Nancy wheeled Nathaniel into the gymnasium with Dave following.

Nancy was instantly taken aback by the streamers and decorations that hung from the ceiling. Then she noted that the entire front of the gym was decorated with a seaside theme—an anchor and waves and such. A sign read: "Welcome Aboard, Norrises." And there were presents. Not just little presents either. There was a beautiful oak dining room table and chairs, and there were all kinds of assorted wrapped gifts that held matching dishes, towels, and household utensils. It took twenty-five minutes to open everything. People watched them like it was a wedding shower. Dave felt glad but embarrassed. Nancy felt warmly welcomed. Nathaniel liked the attention and, just as importantly, the taste of the ice cream.

Chapter 15

"Dave, I think I'm pregnant"

No matter what car he was in, Nathaniel always rode in the front seat. There was a very good reason for this. Nathaniel had outgrown both his stroller and a smaller wheelchair in Minnesota and had been fitted with a fire-engine-red wheelchair that had a very special feature. The back wheels folded up so that it doubled as a car seat, a really, really heavy car seat. Reinforced steal bars crisscrossed the undercarriage to make the wheelchair impregnable to anything but a nuclear attack. In order for Dave to get Nathaniel into the car, he collapsed the wheelchair with Nathaniel still in it, then grunted and groaned the wheels all the way to the front of the floorboard while subsequently wrestling the back of the chair across the front seat. Finally, a seatbelt looped over the whole contraption. Dave was buckling in the Eiffel Tower.

The only person in the world really happy about this gargantuan effort was Nathaniel. To him, the red wheelchair meant no more rides in the back seat. Nathaniel loved the view from the front seat. While being strapped in, Nathaniel made happy sounds, laughed, and waved his arms. He would shake his favorite oversized rattle, spinning the little red balls around the transparent plastic bubble that topped the rattle, a little scepter indicating that he was now in command of the road.

While Dave was busy teaching college classes, right down the hall Nancy was busy teaching in the academy. She worked as a reading teacher for second to sixth graders. "All right then," said Nancy to the sixth graders in front of her. "The exercise in this book calls for you to write a civic official."

"What's a civic official?" asked Kelly.

"Well, a civic official is like a mayor or city council member. Hmmm…that sounds kind of boring to me. Why don't we expand this? What if you could write anyone in the whole world? Who would you write?"

"Do you know who I think would be cool to write?" asked Susan.

"Who?" replied Nancy.

"John Wooden."

"Who is John Wooden?"

"You don't know who John Wooden is? UCLA Bruins coach? Unbeatable? John Wooden? Hello?"

"Great," said Nancy. "Write him. And who else should we write?" Other students chimed in with this or that name as the class became noisy and enthusiastic. Nancy didn't mind noise. She had taught reading before, both for "gifted and talented programs" and "remedial reading." Along the way, she discovered that learning takes place best when children have fun. Ever since, Nancy worked hard to make sure her students were having a good time.

When Nancy came down to the cafeteria, Dave was already there eating lunch. She brought her tray over, sat down, and asked, "So how's it going?"

"Good," said Dave. Nancy nodded, waiting for more. He was not a detail man when reporting his daily activities. He could have five appointments, work on a half a dozen projects, and stomp out a crisis or two; but when she would ask him how his day had gone, he would always just say "good."

Chitchat was minimal for about ten or fifteen minutes. "So did you do a live class or did you proctor?" she finally asked, probing. In the past, the Bible college was set up to allow for the maximum amount of flexibility. A student tended to work at his or her own pace. While there were video classes that were proctored and "paces" that students worked their way through at prescribed times, if a student was out doing ministry or had a job conflict, it was easy enough for them to get the video or audio tape and work through the material independently.

Dave zoned in enough to talk. "Well, I'm sitting in the Old Testament class, and after a half-hour, I ask if anyone has any questions. Some do. So, I answer the questions and we turn the video back on. Five minutes into it, someone wants to ask a question. I stop the tape and answer it. Then ten minutes later, the teacher himself has a question about a particular verse in the Old Testament to which he doesn't know the answer. I stop the tape and explain what I believe the verse to mean. One of the students then asks, 'Why don't you just leave the tape off and teach us yourself?' Now I am asking myself the same question. I think we have to change this program for it to go to the next level."

"That's nice," said Nancy, grabbing her tray and heading out. It was her turn to be brief. In five minutes she would have a group of fourth graders waiting for her in the reading lab.

At the same time as the Norrises were handling their own particular challenges, Nathaniel was busy at Kent County Orthopedic School. The aide from the bus would push his chair onto the wheelchair lift, lower the lift, and then wheel his red chair into the classroom. As soon as Diana, his teacher, had time, she or her aide would lift Nathaniel down from his chair.

The class was roomy, with plenty of objects and tools for learning to give each child a full complement of sensory experiences. Nathaniel was not merely joined by the teacher, but a half-dozen preschool classmates and a teacher's aide spent their days there as well. Further, throughout the week, the classroom was visited by an occupational therapist, a physical therapist, and a speech therapist, among others. Nathaniel might be placed in a walker, on a giant wedge, or put in a container full of plastic balls. On occasion, he would spend time on a mat.

The children in Nathaniel's class were all handicapped to some degree; yet they were all higher functioning than he. Nathaniel was categorized as SMR; that is, he was severely mentally retarded. He was on a level of about a three to six-month-old infant. Most of Nathaniel's classmates could crawl or walk. A few of the children could verbalize pretty well, and most could make their needs known.

However, Nathaniel required total care. Perhaps Nathaniel's teacher Diana was drawn to him because of his neediness and the challenges of teaching someone like him. Although teachers don't have favorites, it did seem that Nathaniel was getting extra special care from her.

"If you sign up for this program and pay up front," Janet was saying to the church, "you can be a part of the first graduating class in Jerusalem." It was a Sunday night and enthusiasm was high. The audience cheered, but it would remain to see whether there were any takers. It was Janet's new idea. She was going to start an external studies program—ESP for short.

Janet explained how the program would operate. She would bring in people who were most competent in their field, film them teaching a course, and then make the video tapes available for class. As an added bonus, students of the very first class would graduate in the Upper Room in the city of Jerusalem. As she explained it, the program sounded like an opportunity that no one should miss. "It only costs five thousand dollars and you can be a charter member of this program."

Together Janet and her husband pastored the church in Dover, Delaware, and another church an hour away in North East, Maryland. Janet had already pitched this same promotion to the North East church that morning and had a dozen takers. She had also made a few phone calls to likely participants. Apparently, there was interest from the Dover church as well, because the next day she had a meeting with Dave. She reported that based upon the level of interest, they were going to build a recording studio in one of the classrooms and get professional cameras for taping. For Janet, visions had only to be shared before they were quickly on the road to becoming reality.

"He wrote back!" said Susan. "Can you believe it? He wrote back!" Nancy's reading class gathered around as Susan waved her letter from John Wooden, the famed coach of the UCLA Bruins and dynasty builder of legendary status. Nancy had them all sit down. The class listened attentively as Susan read the sincere reply from a man who no doubt had a whole lot on his plate, but who had taken the time to speak into the life of a sixth grader. A hushed silence passed over the class as Susan finished. After a few minutes of awe over Susan's success, Nancy glanced at her watch and quickly shuffled the sixth graders out the door. She had to be downstairs to get Nathaniel when they dropped him off from his school bus.

The bus pulled up and an aide was loading Nathaniel onto the lift that would lower him to the pavement. Nancy ignored the aide and went straight to driver. "Excuse me, Ma'am, but I just needed to have a little talk with you about yesterday."

"Yeah?" said the bus driver. "So talk."

"Well, I got involved in a conversation, and by the time I got downstairs you were gone and Nathaniel was missing. I looked all over for him, but he wasn't in the office where I usually pick him up if I can't meet the bus."

"Well, I dropped him off," said the driver.

"I know. But my regular person couldn't be there, and as I said, I got delayed. Who did you give him to?"

"I don't know. There was a group of children standing there. I asked a student to take him in."

"Yes, but who was it?"

"I don't know. Just one of the children."

"This is an elementary, junior high, and senior high school. Not every one here knows Nathaniel, and I don't know all the children. You can't just assume that a child will be responsible and bring him to me."

"You said you would have someone to meet him."

"Can't you bring him into the office?"

"No."

Janet and a group of four others, including Dave, went to New York City to a ministers' meeting. They took the train. When they got off the train, there was a limo waiting for them. Apparently Janet had a friend from Jamaica, and she traded off the rental of his limousine for the use of her villa. The limo took them to a church someplace in New York where Janet was allowed to promote the new ESP program. Janet had a gift of being able to help people visualize what could be possible.

As Janet began talking, what started as a promotion for ESP suddenly morphed into something else entirely. What she was proposing began to sound more like an extension campus. If someone did not know Janet, they would have thought that what she was relating had gone through committees, had been the product of surveys, and had ultimately been produced after months of rigorous thought. However, Dave could see Janet creating it in front of his eyes! Then she was mentioning his name and how he would be involved. Janet was the most incredible dreamer he had ever met! And although he could buy into the vision of others and did some dreaming of his own, he was having difficulty keeping up with all of this. Dave decided that they needed to have a talk when they returned to Dover.

"Well, this may be a new record for shortness of stay at any institution," said Dave to himself, going into Janet's office. He began to offer some plans that he had for the school and to suggest parameters that needed to be created to allow things to happen. Then Janet did a thing that he found very unusual in administrators—she listened. Apparently, she was not only capable of dreaming her own dreams, but she was also capable of believing in the dreams and visions of others. Amazingly, she thought everything he suggested was a good idea. He decided to push the envelope a bit more and stated, "So, if we are going to have live classes, we need to protect the integrity of the class period."

"Alright," she said, "but I'm not sure what you mean."

"Well," said Dave, "I am teaching the other day, and your husband comes in and pulls out ten students to go pick peaches."

"Well, he needed them," said Janet. "There is a man who owns an orchard who will let us pick for free when the peaches are ripe. As many peaches as we want. We'll make dozens and dozens of pies and bring in hundreds of dollars."

"That's good," he said. "But here's the problem. Before, all the students who missed a class had to do was to watch the video lecture later. Because each class period was recorded and available for viewing, that sort of thing worked very well. But if we are going to have live classes, there is no way for students who are picking peaches to make up that particular class."

"Alright," she said supportively, "he won't do that anymore."

Dave was more than a little pleased that he still had a job and that he found someone with whom he could create things. "Okay," he said. "Let me give you five names of people who could teach live classes, people that I believe would be effective." At that moment, he not only gave names of instructors, but also cast a vision of what the school could look like in five years.

A week before their denomination's General Conference, Dave was a little surprised when he went into his office and found the academy's art teacher sketching his bookshelves. Beside this, someone else was taking a picture of his bookshelves. he didn't want to be rude, so he simply said, "Hey, how's it going?"

It apparently was going fine, and they left. At lunch a couple of days later he found out more. Janet told him, "I'm taking your office to set up at General Conference. But don't worry. I know where every book is on every shelf. It will be reassembled exactly as we found it."

For Dave, it was very strange to see his books on display along with his entire office at conference, but there was more! A week before conference he saw the color brochure that was to be used as promotional material. "You can't use this," said Dave to Janet.

"What do you mean?" asked Janet.

"If you use this, it will really hurt me," he said.

Janet had designed the full-page color brochure advertising their new ESP program. It also advertised something else. Bigger than life was a picture of Dave and under it the words, "The Young Legend." The previous year the conference had honored his grandfather in a special service, and he had been described verbally and on a banner as a legend. This was playing off that celebration. He explained that people might not understand what she was doing and would certainly question his motives. However, Janet had already spent a lot of money producing thousands of these brochures and it was too late to do anything different. She was sorry but they really had to go with it.

Dave was standing at a booth at conference and a man who obviously was making assumptions came up to him. "You know, I never really liked your grandfather either," he began. "Do you know that one time he—"

"Excuse me, but I have to run," said Dave, and took off walking down the corridor of the arena. The last thing he wanted anyone to do was criticize his grandfather, but his actions had seemed to indicate to this man that this was exactly what he was doing. Then, Dave saw some friends that he had known for years and waved. They nodded slightly and then quickly passed him by as if he were a leper. It would be a long conference.

Nathaniel's parents both went to school for an annual review of his Individual Education Plan (IEP). This meeting featured a round-table discussion with all the teachers, the physical therapist, the occupational therapist, and others. Several pages detailed Nathaniel's progress and their goals for him. He was functioning at a three to six-month level even though he was a few months short of his third birthday. The goals for him were actually the same goals that they had for him a year before. While Nathaniel could verbalize happy sounds, there was little else that he could do. He couldn't roll over, had no fine motor control, and randomly threw his hands in the air when he got excited. His one accomplishment in life so far was to be able to move big rattle from one hand to another. "Hand transfer is a good step," offered one lady, smiling.

Dave found it difficult to come to this school and have these meetings. Nancy did better. To him, all the other handicapped kids in the program were somehow in a different category than Nathaniel. Nathaniel could show his feelings. He loved to be snuggled. He demonstrated his opinions when being carried off to bedtime. He happily made himself a part of any size group. So, from Dave's perspective, the label "handicapped" just didn't apply to Nathaniel.

One night, Dave was almost asleep. The lights were already out when Nancy spoke to him. He heard what she said quite clearly, but he was hoping he had heard wrong. He turned on the lamp on his nightstand and sat straight up in the bed. "What did you say?"

"I said, 'Dave, I think I'm pregnant.'"

"Nancy, we haven't really talked through what we want to do about that."

"I know, and I'm not sure how it happened, but I think it did," replied Nancy.

As the possible implications of having another baby raced through this head, Dave had more questions than answers. "But Nance, we don't even have a doctor yet." He wasn't asking for a response, but after fifteen seconds, she spoke from the other side of the bed.

"We'll get one."

Chapter 16

"Mrs. Norris, we cannot find the heartbeat"

"**H**old this for me, Sally," said Janet, unrolling the wallpaper trim. Janet was putting the finishing touches on decorating the barn where the Norrises were going to live. Sally had driven out from St. Paul preparing to move to Delaware to help with Nathaniel. Janet had set up a bed for her in the formal dining room that was not used too much.

The barn that had now turned into a house sat a half-acre behind Steve and Jeanette's house. In between the two houses was a pond where a blue heron sometimes landed to scoop up a fish or two. Although on the outside the house still vaguely resembled a barn, inside it had the feel of a nice country home.

The house that had been born out of the barn actually rambled in two different directions. While the main body of the house went in one direction, jutting out from it at a right angle was the large living area with a fireplace and above it on the second floor was the master bedroom. This section of the house had a little porch on either side of the front portion of the home.

Janet was hanging wallpaper and trim in the living room. It matched the draperies and the cornices, which Janet had on order. These custom made items also complemented the wallpaper in the kitchen, and together they featured a country theme. Nancy's kitchen dishes that she had received at their "Welcome Aboard" shower matched the wallpaper.

"And your brother died, too, then?" inquired Janet, as Sally continued recounting her family history.

159

"That was after the fire, and before my sister died of leukemia," said Sally.

"I see. Yes, I see," said Janet, pasting the last bit of trim up in the corner.

The next day, Janet caught Nancy privately in the house. "Nancy, I need to ask you something. Do you believe all those things that Sally is telling you about her life and her family?"

"Yeah, sure," said Nancy. "It's tragic."

Janet then recounted the list of tragedies that was longer than a two-year plot in a soap opera. As Nancy listened, her face flashed with understanding. "Now that you lay these stories out end to end, it does sound incredible. I heard them piecemeal, one story at a time."

"Nancy, you are a sympathetic listener, and I am sure that you gave Sally a lot of attention when she told these things to you. Perhaps when you were so responsive, she thought of the next story, or perhaps she went back to embellish the first story. It looks to me that Sally thrives on your attention, but something is not quite right here."

The next day Dave called Sally into his office. Intent on getting to the truth, he started by telling her a story. "Sally, when I lived in St. Paul, I got a call at my house from a man who was an anesthesiologist about to start at the University of Minnesota Hospital. He named people I knew, and talked about a number of ministers with whom I was acquainted. He told me that he had just gotten into town and had lost his wallet and wondered if I could help him out. I told him that I would happily put him up for the night and work with him to get everything straightened out. 'Where are you?' I asked, assuming he was at the airport."

"'I'm right in downtown Minneapolis across from the bus depot.'"

"I started out the door and got in my car when it occurred to me that there was something a little bit fishy about an anesthesiologist calling me from a bus depot. But I drove over to downtown Minneapolis and found him. And things started getting a little harder to believe when he handed me an old suitcase. I flipped up the back of my Sunbird and stuck his suitcase inside.

"He opened the passenger door and got inside. His clothes did not appear to be the clothes of an anesthesiologist. Nonetheless, I began driving him toward a motel. He turned to talk to me, and I smelled liquor on his breath. As he explained the story of how he was on the bus and his wallet was lost, the narrative became harder and harder to believe. I asked, 'Is that liquor I smell on your breath?'"

"'No, someone gave me candy that had liquor in it.'"

"It was night. He was not a tall man. He didn't look dangerous, but a person never knows. I said to him, 'Look. I need you to tell me the truth. If you tell me the truth, I promise I will get you a motel room and help you out. I don't care who you are or where you came from. But we can't go any further unless you tell me the truth.'"

"He looked at me and said, 'I am telling the truth.'"

"I repeated, 'I promise, if you simply tell me the truth, I will get you a motel and help you out. But you can't lie to me.'"

"'I'm an anesthesiologist, I tell you.'"

"I stopped the car right there, in front of a fire station. There were several firemen lingering around at the bay where the fire engine was. It seemed like a safe place. I opened the back hatch and repeated once again, 'All you have to do is tell the truth.'"

"'I'm an anesthesiologist, I tell you,' he said, but without much conviction."

"I slammed the hatchback shut and started back toward the car. 'Aren't you going to even drive me back downtown?' he asked. I said nothing but drove away."

Then Dave turned to Sally and spoke with assurance. "Sally, you can stay here and help with Nathaniel on one condition. I have to know the truth."

There was silence. Finally Sally admitted, "All those things I told Nancy weren't true."

"Thanks," said Dave, waiting for the real story. But he would never know the real story, because that was the only information that was forthcoming. Sally left the next morning.

A young man in the church at Dover named Greg operated a waterbed store in the mall. He invited Norrises to visit the store to find a bed. When they walked in they saw Greg but not much else. There wasn't much in the store.

"Most of what people get comes out of these catalogs," said Greg, pulling out a stack of them.

Nancy and Dave began leafing through the catalogs but were more than a little lost. "This is what I would recommend," said Greg, pointing to a blue sofa and chair. "And this burgundy piece is quite nice as well."

"I'm not sure how much living room furniture we can afford right now," said Dave. "What we really need is a bed and maybe a couple of pieces of furniture in the bedroom."

"Well, let's just pick some stuff out and go from there," said Greg, leading them to a waterbed with a brass headboard, some nice bedroom pieces, as well as some living room furniture.

As Greg tallied numbers on a list, Dave began to feel nervous. Nothing in the catalogs had actual prices on it – only codes. Greg explained that there were any number of tiers to pricing, and then he said that he would see what he could do for them. When he finished calculating, Nancy and Dave had ordered all of the furniture for what they might have otherwise spent on a really good sofa. Greg told them not to tell anyone.

Several men in the church bought and sold cars at auctions. One man explained that he could get them a car for a very reasonable price, but there was a risk attached to it. Indeed, the car that Dave bought from this man was deemed by a mechanic to be what he called "a lemon." While the lemon seller didn't offer any immediate solution, there were other men in the church who were able to help. A man named Richard really helped Dave, not only getting rid of the lemon but getting him something that ran decently. And then Dave got to meet Fred, a likeable man from the church in North East, Maryland. Fred was incredibly gifted but not too optimistic about fixing his car. Twice he told Dave he probably couldn't fix something on Dave's car and then proceeded to fix it while he talked to him. Dave decided that this was a man he could trust.

November 15 was moving day from the main house to the barn. The move was rather uneventful as the Norrises were only moving from the guestroom at the Trout home to a home about a hundred yards away. Dave brought over Nathaniel's crib. That same day Greg delivered a bed for the Norrises. The bed had a nice brass headboard, and while it wasn't a waterbed in the traditional sense, the mattress was filled with water. All other furniture was still on order. Even though the house still seemed pretty empty, this hardly mattered to Nancy, for to her it seemed complete. "It's so pretty I don't want to put one nail hole in the wall for a picture," said Nancy appreciatively.

After church on Sunday morning, Nancy approached one of the students from the college. "Say, Joy, how would you like to babysit for me?" Joy was a pretty brunette with a built-in smile. And she was incredibly resourceful.

"When would it be?" asked Joy.

"Well, two weeks from now we have been invited to Connecticut to do a children's program. Because it will be such a quick trip, I was hoping to be able to leave Nathaniel home."

Joy noticed Nathaniel looking at her out of the corner of his eye. When she turned to look at him, he turned his head the other way, suddenly shy. "Well, is there a lot to learn?" she asked Nancy.

"Yes, quite a bit," Nancy said as Joy noticed Nathaniel sneaking his head around to take another look at her. "But you can come over once or twice before then, and I'll teach you."

Joy then knelt down beside the wheelchair and spoke to the boy in the fire-engine-red chair. "Well, Nathaniel, looks like I'm going to be coming over to your house."

Nathaniel waved his hands excitedly and let out some happy cooing, finally convinced that this attention was truly for him. Knowing that he deserved it, he then offered eye contact, fully expecting that there had better be some sort of response. "We're going to have some fun," Joy said, and Nathaniel laughed out loud, agreeing.

"Dave, I can only get into Philadelphia for the genetic test on the fifteenth of December."

"How come?"

"Well, the CVS has to be performed from nine to eleven weeks, and that is the only day that they can fit me in their schedule."

"So, let's do it then," said Dave. "I will go with you." They had already seen the ultrasound and watched the baby's heartbeat. Now, they were going to go up to Philadelphia for the same procedure that Nancy had flown to Chicago for a year earlier before her miscarriage in St. Paul.

Nancy was looking at the calendar again and said, "Nathaniel will be admitted into A. I. duPont for a battery of tests for half of that whole week. I will need to be with him most of the time, but maybe we can find a way to slip away for that appointment."

The DuPont family had built a state-of-the-art children's hospital in Wilmington, Delaware, forty-five minutes away. It was one of the best children's hospitals in the world, a fact that Janet had explained to Nancy to convince her that coming to Dover was a good idea.

Greg delivered the living room furniture. The colors of the blue couch and burgundy chair were beautifully accented against the country wallpaper. That same day Greg brought some more bedroom furniture as well, a credenza and matching nightstands. Nancy thought she was in heaven. Afterwards, he went into Nathaniel's bedroom as Nancy was reaching down to get Nathaniel out the crib.

"You shouldn't have to do that," said Greg.

"Do what?" returned Nancy.

"You don't want to keep stooping down into that crib. What if I make Nathaniel a bed? It would be almost chest high. We could put drawers in it and have room for storage in the back. I will attach a rail that can be raised when he's sleeping so he doesn't fall out or lowered when you want to pick him up. That way you won't have to bend over. We can also get him a mattress like yours, one with water in it."

"I can hardly wait," said Nancy.

Nancy wheeled Nathaniel into the outpatient entrance of A. I. duPont. The ceiling was high, the colors inviting, and the atmosphere warm. Life-sized stuffed animals were perched in the lobby, along with oversized wooden and plastic structures that children could use for play. Nancy went to the front desk to fill out Nathaniel's paperwork. Even the lady who checked her in was pleasant, something that is usually not the case with such a high-stress job.

First they met Dr. Miller. Nathaniel kept staring at the doctor's beard like he wanted to pull it. Dr. Miller was the doctor overseeing the team that was running the battery of tests over the next several days. Nancy answered familiar questions, but unlike some other doctors, this one did not seem surprised by her answers. Usually, whenever Nancy was required to take Nathaniel to an emergency room and was required to explain details about Nathaniel's Cri du

Chat syndrome, doctors would excuse themselves, returning later after having looked up a paragraph or two on the implications of the syndrome. Unfortunately, their reference books sometimes utilized outdated information.

Over time, Dave's opinions of doctors had begun to slip. One too many had pronounced this or that as the likely cause of a problem when later it turned out to be something else altogether. "They're just glorified auto mechanics," he lamented, "just trying to figure out what is going on under the hood." Dave was more likely to make these kinds of comments when a doctor was aloof or haughty, and Nancy would shush him, embarrassed. On the other hand, A. I. duPont impressed Dave with their well-run hospital and knowledgeable doctors. He was not merely impressed because of their expertise, but also because of their genuine care.

"Nathaniel will first go to the gastrointestinologist," said Dr. Miller. "Then, he will have his first appointment with orthopedics. After that, we'll get him settled into a room. That will be enough for the first day."

"Alright," replied Nancy, glad that Nathaniel would finally be getting some broad oversight of his medical needs. She helped Nathaniel through his first day of appointments, got him settled in his room and then drove home. She would return the next day for a nine o'clock appointment with a neurologist.

The third day Nathaniel was at A. I. duPont, Dave went with Nancy up to Philadelphia for her test. They got a little lost but finally walked into what looked like a doctor's office. Nancy was expecting something like the skyscraper that she went to in Chicago, particularly for such an advanced test as the CVS, but the place where the test was conducted looked from the outside at least like a rather ordinary doctor's office.

An attendant led Nancy back to a room where she laid down on an examining table. The room was stuffed with equipment and appeared a lot more complex than the usual examination room. She looked around at an array of electronic gizmos, monitors, and computer screens attached to this or that implement. Like the last time she had this test, they explained that they were going to do an ultrasound to locate the baby before they would perform the actual test. Like the last time, they had the same sort of implements that they used on her when she had undergone an ultrasound a year and a half earlier in Chicago. She was on the table, and Nancy recognized the sequence of the procedure. Nancy recognized something else as well—the rather blank expression on the technician's face before she suddenly left to get the doctor. For that reason Nancy had already discerned what the doctor was about to say.

A scream was locked up inside of her. She was never sure whether it came out or not. "Mrs. Norris, we cannot find the heartbeat."

The doctor told her to go home and wait for the baby to miscarry.

Dave held her, but there was no comfort in his arms. Once again, the baby was dead. They wanted to perform the CVS anyway to determine whether it was a genetic anomaly, the sex of the baby, and so forth. She declined. She simply couldn't bear it.

Dave got a motel that night. It was a luxury they could ill afford given that they were only an hour from home, but tonight the house was just too empty. Nancy was numb. Only a handful of people even knew about her pregnancy. And even those people who did know about it would be hard pressed to mourn her loss. They would console her with statements like: "This is the will of God." Or "It is a good thing that the baby died." Or, "Now you will be spared from caring for another handicapped baby." On one level Nancy understood all of this, but on another level she was suffering a very real loss of a very real baby. It was especially sad because this was a baby for whom no one would mourn.

The next day while Dave was teaching, Nancy was back up at A. I. duPont with Nathaniel. A nurse walked by and saw Nancy crying. "Hey, what's wrong?" she asked.

When Nancy poured out her story, the nurse suddenly became very nervous. "This is a children's hospital. If something goes wrong, we can't care for you here. You need to get this taken care of right away."

"But Nathaniel needs—"

"Nathaniel needs his mother taken care of. We can certainly take care of Nathaniel. Please, attend to this right away."

DuPont Hospital kept Nathaniel a couple of extra days. Nancy went into another hospital as an outpatient for a DNC. After the procedure, Nancy spoke to the doctor. "I lost a baby in St. Paul, and they analyzed the genetic material and found that it was a Cri du Chat boy. I was wondering if a test could be done to—"

"What difference does it make?" said the doctor crassly. The pregnancy is over. There is no baby. There was probably a genetic issue, but it hardly matters, does it?"

It did matter. But something about the abruptness of the doctor and Nancy's feeling of vulnerability stopped her and she dropped the issue then and there. Dave drove her home but had to go back in to the college to teach. He had made arrangements with Jackie, who along with her husband Robert oversaw the dorm, to come and stay with her.

Nancy and Dave went in to see Nathaniel at A. I. duPont later that night. He was fine. Like other times when they had left him in the hospital, he took a few minutes to warm up to them. "Hey, Nathaniel," said Dave excitedly, but he turned his head away as if to ignore their presence.

Nancy stroked his cheek and talked soothingly to him. "Oh, were Mom and Dad being mean to you? Did they leave you here by yourself? Oh, poor, poor little Nathaniel." After a couple of minutes a smile insinuated itself on Nathaniel's face, then a full grin. All was forgiven.

Dave picked up his boy and held him in his arms while Nancy continued talked to him, stroking his cheek. "When your momma was a little baby, she had a hole in her esophagus, and she couldn't breathe right. But then some people prayed, and your momma was healed. It was a miracle."

Nathaniel was more impressed with being held than his mom's story. But she continued. "Nathaniel, it's a miracle that you were born, and that you stayed alive, and that you're still alive today. Don't let anyone tell you that you are weak."

Nathaniel cooed with happiness for the attention.

Chapter 17

"There is something coming out of his chair"

N ancy pushed Nathaniel out to the car after the Sunday morning service. On the trunk of the car was a large package of diapers. She looked around but couldn't see who had left it. The week before, there had been a package of diapers in Dave's office, and the week before that there had been one in the back seat of their car.

Because Nathaniel was getting bigger, diapers were becoming more and more expensive. Yet, when Nancy inquired with their health insurance providers whether diapers could be considered a medical expense because of Nathaniel's condition, they finally decided that diapers could be covered, but not until Nathaniel's fourth birthday still some months away. While they were never sure how, somebody must have found out about this and organized a kind of diaper brigade at church. Each week diapers appeared from nowhere. A package might be found in Dave's office, on the hood of the car, or even in the back seat. This continued until Nathaniel's fourth birthday.

In church, Nancy would either hold Nathaniel or sometimes he would sit in his chair. One Sunday morning, a lady sitting behind Nancy poked her. "I don't mean to bother you, but there is something coming out of his chair." To Nancy's dismay, Nathaniel's clamp had come loose and he was indeed leaking all over the floor. Not only that, but Nathaniel was sopped with formula. Nancy hunted through her rather large accessory bag for help and quickly wiped up the spilt formula. Then she wheeled Nathaniel out to change him. Utilizing her reserve clothing stashed in the supply bag, Nathaniel was first cleaned up and then received a head-to-toe change of his wardrobe.

As Nancy wheeled her boy back in to the auditorium, Wayne was delivering his sermon. As usual, this was an evangelistic service. His message was entitled "Death Throes" and featured a rather stern charge for people to get right with God. Stories of deathbeds and lost opportunities punctuated the sermon. As he was winding down, Wayne called for musicians to play softly in the background as he told the story about a horse who was dying, and he described in detail its death throes. Both Wayne and Janet could tell a good story, and Wayne could readily get people to come to the front to pray.

A woman came sobbing to the altar and Nancy immediately went to pray with her. The woman stayed for a long time, just crying. Nancy was glad to see the woman getting things right with the Lord, and simply remained nearby being supportive. The woman stayed until the service was dismissed and continued praying. Nancy was ready to offer spiritual counseling about conversion. "Are you doing all right?" she finally asked, handing the woman some Kleenex.

"No," the woman said.

Nancy compassionately touched her shoulder, offering, "Tell me about it."

"My horse died," the woman said, and then broke down sobbing again. Although not exactly what Nancy was expecting to hear, the sermon had indeed been effective for the story about the horse dying had allowed the woman to grieve.

One Friday, Nancy packed up her puppets, put together Dave's children's ministry stuff and had the suitcases waiting by the front door. Connie, one of Nathaniel's favorite babysitters, was sitting on the couch with Nathaniel, waiting for the Norrises to leave. They were doing a weekend children's program in Lexington Park, Maryland, and had to get on the road. Dave said good-bye and gave a couple of last minute instructions. He saw that Nathaniel had grabbed Connie's long blond hair and was happily chewing on it. Connie, who was reading a magazine, was oblivious. Dave started to say something but thought better of it. He took the last suitcase out to the car, and he and Nancy were on their way.

Second semester Dave recruited a staff of people to teach live classes. Nancy taught Child Evangelism along with Child Psychology.

"Nancy, what do you think about going back to the University of Delaware to get your Master's Degree?"

"We have money for that?"

"We can work it out."

"When would I go?"

"Well, you can start this summer."

"Well, what about you? You've wanted to go to seminary for years."

"I've been looking into it. I'm contacting a number of seminaries in the area. I'm trying to see if they will accept my Bible college work."

Karen, a young lady from the church, told Nancy she wanted to babysit Nathaniel. Nancy welcomed the help. Karen was a spunky redhead with freckles, and while she wasn't exactly a tomboy, she seemed to be willing to trying just about anything. She quickly learned how to tube-feed Nathaniel and soon began caring for him whenever her schedule allowed. Karen was comfortable bringing Nathaniel with her wherever she went, so before long, Nathaniel seemed to operate independently from his mom and dad. Sometimes she watched him at the house, and sometimes she would just take off with him for parts unknown. Nathaniel's adventures would only later be discovered through the pictures that Karen took.

"So, Nathaniel, it looks like you had a good time down at the ocean!" Nancy commented. Nathaniel waved his arms in delight.

Nancy didn't think she would enjoy teaching college students, but she had a blast. "So, what drama would be effective for a four-year-old class?" she asked. Answers came back like popcorn. Ed had an idea, as did Pam.

"Alright," she continued, "how could the same story be adapted for teenagers?" First one student, then another would respond.

"I know what we should do," said Pam. "Why don't we write a play in this class?"

"Well," said Nancy, "I don't think it would be enough to write a play. We'd have to perform it for somebody. Otherwise, it wouldn't be a good exercise."

"We could put it on in church," said Ed.

"Let me see if we can get permission," replied Nancy.

After that, the play took on a life of its own, and students were energized beyond what she dared to dream. She was thankful as well for their creativity. They called their play, "Hell Requires No Reservation." She obtained the proper permission, and the class planned to perform it for church on a Wednesday night.

The first time Nancy saw the play was when they performed it. She had seen them practice some of the funny parts, but as it turned out, the play as a whole was pretty scary. Some of the teenagers in the church were affected in a positively way, but a few parents complained about performance scaring the younger children. Nancy decided not to share any of the criticism with the students. They had put too much work into it for her to be critical.

Nathaniel's babysitters were multiplying. As students and friends from church got to know him, any number of people participated in watching him. Sometimes they would sit with him for just a short time, but a few others were willing to learn all the intricacies of caring for him so that they could spend longer periods of time with him.

One day, she was home from school less than an hour when the telephone rang. "Is this Mrs. Nancy Norris?"

"Yes."

"Well, this is Mrs. Plankton from the County Nursing Program. I am calling because at the recommendation of your doctor and the school where your son attends, you are now eligible for four hours of nursing a day during the week."

"What? How does that work?" asked Nancy.

"Well, typically, a nurse's aide comes out to the house and gives you some respite. We have an LPN or RN that will care for Nathaniel on a regular basis."

"How soon can we start?" was all that Nancy could think to say.

Nathaniel turned three-years-old. Ryan and Stephanie, Janet's grandchildren, came over for cake. Rhonda, a friend and staff member from the school, brought her little two-year-old Eric and her baby Elizabeth. A couple of kids from the church came along with their parents. There were cake, candles, and helium balloons. Although Nathaniel loved any kind of helium balloon, Nancy found that the Mylar balloons were tougher and could take more abuse, especially since Nathaniel had learned to chomp down on things with his teeth.

It was morning and Nancy had to get to school. Dave had called for Nancy to get into the car a couple different times. Finally he came up to the bedroom and found her staring at the closet. "I can't think of what to wear."

"Nancy, when I left to go put wood in the fireplace and get my stuff together from downstairs, you were trying to decide what to wear. Are you still deciding?"

"Yeah."

"And when I made those telephone calls you were still deciding."

"Yeah."

"That was twenty minutes ago."

"Yeah, I know."

Two days later, Dave was calling up to Nancy. "Okay, we're ready to go," he said.

"Okay," she returned.

"How're you coming?" he asked.

"Good," she said.

"How much longer?" he asked.

"Pretty quick," she replied.

"Nathaniel and I have been in the car for fifteen minutes, and it's almost time for church to start."

"Be right down."

They were forty-five minutes late for church. Dave was beginning to realize that this behavior was not going away.

Dave found Janet in her office and asked for a couple of minutes of time. "I think Nancy is clinically depressed," he offered, describing what was going on.

"It's hard to find a good counselor," replied Janet. "I know a good one, and one that can keep a confidence, but he is a bit of a drive from here."

"That's not an issue," said Dave, taking the number.

Nancy and Dave left Nathaniel with a babysitter and drove to Lancaster, Pennsylvania. It was a little less than two hours away.

They found the motel where they would be staying, dropped off their stuff, and went to see Dr. Richard Canfield. He was a kindly older man, and he wore shoes that were a cross between dress shoes and black tennis shoes. Nancy got the impression that he might be close to retiring.

"So then, tell me about Nathaniel," Dr. Canfield asked. Nancy explained about Nathaniel's condition as the doctor wrote on a yellow pad. "Go on..." he encouraged, after she had talked for some time. "And this second pregnancy also resulted in the death... of the baby?"

"Right," said Nancy.

"Now tell me again," he asked, "what the geneticist said about your chances of conceiving a normal child?"

"Based just on pure statistics," Nancy began, "there is twenty-five percent chance of having a normal child, twenty-five percent of having a child who is a carrier, twenty-five percent chance of having a child with extra chromosomal material...."

"And that child would be handicapped as well?"

"Certainly. Severely."

"Go on, then," said Dr. Canfield.

"And there is a twenty-five percent chance of having an infant with Cri du Chat."

Dr. Canfield put down his pen, sat back in his chair and spoke with a fatherly concern. "You've had some pretty major losses. I understand that you are grieving, and this is taking its toll. Still, I think your indecision about whether or not to try to have more children also comes with an emotional cost attached to it. Let me make sure that I understand. You have not yet come to a consensus as to what to do about having more children. Is that true?"

Dave spoke up, sounding a little defensive. "Well, we're still working through those issues."

Nancy offered, "We haven't really decided."

Dr. Canfield paused, looking at both of them closely. "It seems to me," he said, "that it is this very uncertainty that is functioning as a kind of battery drain for you both, but especially for you, Nancy. And I think that this is contributing to your depression."

Nancy nodded in agreement, not caring to argue. Dr. Canfield continued, "Nancy and Dave, listen carefully. You attempted to have children twice since Nathaniel was born, and I think that the Lord has given you His answer. I don't think you should try again, especially given the odds that the child might be handicapped. Nancy, this is what you should do. You should have a tubal ligation. This will go a long way toward ending the anxiety that you both are feeling."

Dr. Canfield offered a few other observations and then led them in a fatherly prayer. Nancy and Dave left. Did Nancy want something to eat? She did. They ate. They went back to the motel. Not much was said. And it was a good thing. Nancy had left the office mad, and she was still angry. Who did that man think he was to tell her what to do? He seemed too ready to play God.

One of the geneticists had already suggested that either Dave or Nancy consider having something done. Dave asked if Nancy wanted to get her tubes tied, and Nancy asked Dave, in return, if he wanted to have a vasectomy. Neither one of them was especially open to a surgical procedure, and their indecision had contributed to this latest pregnancy.

Two weeks later, Nancy suddenly said to Dave, "I've been thinking about it, and I am going to have my tubes tied."

Dave stopped reading the book he was staring down at, rose from his chair, and came over to Nancy. She was thirty-four. This would close the door to the possibility of having more children. It was no small sacrifice. "Are you sure?" he asked. She would still rather he have the vasectomy, but there didn't seem to be any point in having further discussion.

"Yeah, I'm sure."

Nancy went to the doctor's office to make the appointment, but she was apprehensive. She had been to this doctor's office before, and it hadn't been a good experience. When the nurse from A. I. duPont had told Nancy to go "take care of things" because she couldn't be responsible if Nancy miscarried her dead baby at the children's hospital, this office was the place where Nancy came to make an appointment.

When Nancy told the receptionist what she wanted, the lady blandly declared that the doctor didn't do abortions. Even when Nancy explained that the baby had already died, it didn't matter. Indeed, the lady at the desk had made Nancy feel guilty. She was told in no uncertain terms that another doctor would have to do the procedure.

Nancy opened the door, and walked up to the same office lady. "I need to talk to a doctor about doing a tubal ligation."

Nancy ultimately had the operation as an outpatient of Kent General Hospital. Dave drove her to the hospital and then held her hand as she was falling asleep. That was the last thing she remembered.

"Mrs. Norris? It's over," spoke the strange voice of someone who was shaking her.

"What's over?" Nancy said groggily.

"Mrs. Norris, you have to get up now."

"Why? What for?" said Nancy, struggling to discern her surroundings.

"Time to go home."

The nurse helped Nancy into the wheelchair, went down the elevator with her and out the front door. Dave had driven up to the entrance. The nurse locked on the brakes of the wheelchair and opened the car door. Nancy was a little wobbly as she stood and finally settled into the front seat of the car. Dave took her home and helped her into bed and then called for Jackie to come and be with her so she wouldn't be alone. Dave was getting ready to go back to school to teach a class.

Deep sorrow washed over Nancy. Not only would she never have children, but she had put herself through this pain to accomplish that fact. Jackie had come from the school to sit with her. She made some tea for Nancy and then sat on the bed to listen and talk.

After a while, she told Nancy, "I'll be downstairs if you need anything." Nancy slipped into a welcome sleep.

Chapter 18

"You will not take my son!"

"Where is Nathaniel?" Nancy urgently asked the nurse, when she drove into the driveway?

"I don't know," said the nurse, worried. "He just came up missing. He should have been here a couple hours ago."

Because Nancy had not been able to get good cooperation from the bus driver in dropping Nathaniel off at school, she had been getting him dropped off at home. But when school had started again in the fall, this new arrangement had created quite a challenge. Nancy's responsibilities in the reading lab were not complete until 2:45, and Nathaniel got home at 3:20.

Since the Norrises had been able to get four hours of nursing a day through the county, Nancy asked the nurse to be there early, at 3:00 or so, to have plenty of time to get Nathaniel off the bus. But sometimes the nurses were not consistent, particularly if a new nurse was attending him, so Nancy tried to have it double covered.

Yesterday, she came home to find that the nurse hadn't been there on time. The bus driver had threatened her, "Now, listen here, if I have to wait one more time, I am just going to take Nathaniel home with me. You'll just have to come to my house and get him." Nancy thought the lady was bluffing but didn't want to find out.

An hour later, Nathaniel still was not home. Nancy called the school. "Was there some delay in leaving school?"

"No," she replied, "the bus left at the usual time."

"Is it possible to have the telephone number of the supervisor for the bus drivers?"

"Certainly."

Nancy turned to the nurse. "Were you a little late today?"

"Just a couple of minutes. I got here about 3:25."

"Hello, is this the supervisor for buses?" asked Nancy.

The man replied that he was in fact that person. "Can you radio Luci and see where she is with my son?" The man asked for a further explanation and got it.

"She says that she took him home," the man replied evenly, as if this were none of his business. Nancy called the college and quickly explained the situation. "Dave, please come home and take care of this."

Dave didn't get angry very often, and it wasn't Dave's way to explode even when he was. "And you're the supervisor for the bus drivers?" he asked on the phone.

"Yes."

"Is it typical that bus drivers are allowed to take children home?" Dave asked with a sarcasm that the supervisor missed entirely.

"Not typical, no; I would say, no."

"And if something happened to a child who was taken home by a bus driver," Dave asked calmly, "and if the school were sued, who would typically be fired? Would that be the bus driver or the supervisor?"

The man was quiet momentarily, apparently not able to answer legal questions. "Do you want Luci's telephone number?"

"That would be good," said Dave.

"Is this Luci?" Dave asked.

"Yes."

"And do you have my son at your house?"

"I do," came the confident reply.

"How do I get there?" She gave directions and fifteen minutes later Dave was in the kitchen of Luci's house where Nathaniel sat sucking his thumb, both hungry and thirsty. A milquetoast-looking husband was slumped over the kitchen table drinking coffee and eating a sandwich. His posture demonstrated that he didn't want to be part of any conversations. Dave spoke to Luci. "Nathaniel has to have formula every four hours. He is late now and this isn't good for his health. Nathaniel loses fluids quickly when he is not fed. Nathaniel gets hospitalized when he is dehydrated. With his condition, this is dangerous."

"Just make sure that you are there when I come by," said the bus driver, "and everything will be all right."

When Nathaniel was finally home and fed, Nancy asked Dave how it went. He answered, "Not so good. Maybe she's related to the principal of the school or maybe she doesn't need the job. For whatever reason, she wouldn't bend, not one bit, not even when I told her that I would be making a formal complaint to her supervisors."

A few days later, the scenario repeated itself. A student had come to Nancy with some deep personal hurts and had just begun sharing when suddenly Nancy interrupted, "What time is it?"

"Almost a quarter after three."

The nurse was not coming today. The house was four miles away with one stoplight, two stop signs, and a forty-five-mile-an-hour speed limit in between. She stopped by the front office to enlist a friend for support as she rushed out the door to the car.

"Hurry, Rhonda," she appealed, "I need your help." Rhonda wasn't sure what she was getting herself into, but she went with Nancy as she raced out of the parking lot.

"She says she is going to take Nathaniel home with her if I'm late. It's such a hot day and the last time Nathaniel went without fluids for hours." Rhonda listened and watched. Nancy made a quick stop at the first stop sign but didn't bother stopping at the second one. The road curved some but Nancy was still going fifty and even increased her speed when the road straightened out. Nancy was mumbling something about how ridiculous this was that one lady, who should be helping, could cause so much pain and control her life like this. Nancy suddenly burst out, "Rhonda, if she is gone, we'll have no way of contacting the bus to find out where she is."

Approaching the third stop sign, she saw the bus coming in her direction. It had already turned left out of the Norris's driveway and was going to pass her going on the left side of the road with Nathaniel as a prisoner. Nancy laid her hand on the horn, honking steadily, and then screeched the car to a stop. The bus driver was now at the stop sign and looked over at her, nonplussed.

Nancy was beyond talking. She jumped out of the car, frantically waving her arms as she crossed over to where the bus had stopped. Then she let her fists do her talking. She furiously pounded on the glass of the driver's window, screaming at the top of her lungs: "You will not take my son! You will not take my son! Now you turn that bus around and get it back to my house, and you do it right now!" Nancy kept pounding and yelling until the driver put the bus in gear and turned it around.

Nancy never talked about that situation again. Neither did the bus driver. But the bus driver never tried to take Nathaniel home again after that.

That summer, Nancy and Dave received a brochure announcing a gathering of parents of children who had Cri du Chat syndrome. The gathering would take place in Philadelphia in the fall at the Hershey Hotel. Nancy and Dave took Nathaniel. Nancy hoped that she would get to meet someone who had a child on the same level as Nathaniel. Nathaniel was considered "severely mentally retarded," but most of the children at the conference were higher functioning. She did, however, meet a mother whose child was tube fed, but he was not at the conference. The mother showed Nancy a picture of her son, a boy categorized as "profoundly mentally retarded." The child could do little but lay in his crib; he was even more severe than Nathaniel.

One happy outcome was that Nancy got to meet up with the Garwins, a family who had brought their daughter to West Bend three years prior for the picnic she had organized for families of children with Cri du Chat. Soon, Nancy was holding a little girl with Cri du Chat. Nathaniel, who sat next to her in his chair, suddenly started whining

Nancy looked over to see him complaining and then she teased, "Oh, Nathaniel, are you a little jealous?" After he pouted just a bit more, a twelve-year-old girl with Cri du Chat went with Nancy to the changing room and helped her change Nathaniel's diaper. It was good to meet other parents and their children, and to hear from professionals, but it was very disappointing for Nancy that Nathaniel was the most severely challenged child in attendance.

The gastrostomy tube that extended from Nathaniel's stomach had somehow gotten dislodged. This wasn't the first time that it had happened. The tube was supposed to be secure, but time and circumstances had demonstrated that this was not always the case. As soon as Nancy heard Nathaniel crying in his crib and saw the tube that lay beside him, she bundled him into the car and headed to the emergency room. The doctors had explained to her that if the tube came out, she only had minutes to get a new tube put in before the hole in Nathaniel's stomach would start closing. Nancy made it to the emergency room at Kent General in just a few minutes.

Most recently, the doctors had been using a new kind of tube, one that did not require a metal flange to hold it in place but used a balloon inflated with water instead. As the doctor was inserting the tube into Nathaniel's stomach, he said, "You know, Mrs. Norris, according to my chart, this is the third time you have been in here in the last nine months for this procedure. Why don't I just teach you how to put this tube in by yourself?"

"No thanks," said Nancy. "I don't think I could."

"It would save you some trips to the emergency room," coached the doctor.

"Well, maybe then," said Nancy, more bravely than she felt.

The doctor stuck the tube down the hole in Nathaniel's stomach and then pulled it out again. "Now you see," he said, pointing to a certain mark on the tube, "make sure you get the tube in this far." Then the doctor plunged the tube back into the hole in Nathaniel's stomach all the way to that mark. A little blood and some other stuff came out while he was doing this. Nancy momentarily turned her head, feeling faint.

"Now look how the top of this tube branches out. One port is for liquids to enter his stomach. Do you see this second port with the red tip?"

"Yes," said Nancy.

"Okay then. We use this second port to ensure we get the tube to stay in. Let me show you. We're going to take this little plastic syringe and fill it with five cc's of water." He put water into the little syringe while he was talking. "Now just insert the syringe here," he said, indicating the little red port that branched out from the feeding tube. He continued, "This water helps a little balloon inflate in Nathaniel's stomach and holds his tube securely in place." The doctor then readily inserted the syringe into the second port, squirting in the water. "See? Easy as pie."

Less convinced than the doctor, Nancy made no response.

"I'll tell you what," he cajoled. "I will give you a couple of extra tubes and syringes, and if you can do it, then fine. But if you can't, then bring him in, and I will do it for you."

Nancy accepted the supplies with a commitment to give it a try, but she was hoping that the opportunity would not present itself any time soon.

Communications about Nathaniel took place through a spiral notebook kept with Nathaniel's supplies. If Nancy had something to share, she would write it in the notebook. If the school wanted to share something, they would write to her in the same notebook. One day after school Nancy picked up Nathaniel's notebook to see how he had done in school that day. She was immediately alarmed and ran to the phone.

"Kent County Orthopedic School," came the operator.

"I need to speak to the director, please."

"This is the director."

"I need to know what is going on," said Nancy.

"I don't think I understand," replied the director.

"Let me read the entry in Nathaniel's notebook that came home with him today. It says, 'Yesterday, the bus driver reported that Nathaniel was waving his arms so as to cause injury to others and she has begun strapping his arms down going to and from school.'"

"Oh my!" said the director.

"Nathaniel does sometimes wave his hands when he is excited. But it is impossible to think that he will cause injury. His hands must not be tied down!"

The director said she would look into it.

The next day Nancy was waiting for the school bus, expecting a confrontation with Luci. The aide lowered the lift with Nathaniel on it. His arms weren't strapped down. Furthermore, the director of the school had an oversized video camera and was videoing Nathaniel as he was being lowered on the ramp. Another lady from the school was with her, assisting in the procedure. Nancy greeted them.

The director said, "I just thought we would do some videotaping here to see what is going on." Luci pursed her lips. She didn't seem to enjoy having the extra attention on her bus. No one ever mentioned strapping down Nathaniel's arms after that.

Dave was conducting a meeting in the conference room with the teachers from the college. He had come to believe that it was possible for the Bible college to be accredited, and they were mapping out a several-year strategy to work toward that possibility. Suddenly, Janet came through the door of her office into the conference room and motioned to Nancy.

"Can you step into my office for a moment?"

"Certainly," said Nancy, walking into the office with her.

"I just received a call," Janet said. "Nathaniel's tube came out. You need to get home right away." Nancy left in a hurry and drove straight to the house.

When she walked in the door, she saw Anna, a college student who was babysitting for them. Anna was upset. The front of her brand new dress was a mess, maybe even ruined. "I'm so sorry," she apologized in tears. "His tube came out while I was carrying him up the stairs." Nancy consoled Anna as best as she could and then headed upstairs.

"Anna, could you give me a hand?"

"Sure," she replied, not sure about what she was getting herself into.

Nancy opened a package and took out a new tube. Then she tore open a small packet of lubricant and swathed the new tube as the doctor had instructed and began to push the end of the tube through the hole in Nathaniel's stomach. When Nathaniel cried out in pain, she didn't hesitate. "It's gonna be fine. We don't want to go to the emergency room."

"Anna, can you hold the tube right at this level while I get the syringe and put the water in?" Anna looked nervous but she did it. Nancy added five centimeters of fluid to inflate the balloon in

Nathaniel's stomach. Nathaniel didn't look convinced, but it held. Not exactly Nancy Nurse, but close enough.

The Norris household changed for the better when a nurse named Sharon began working for them. A truly caring person, Sharon was never late and was always pleasant. "What if I split my four-hour shift?" asked Sharon. "What if I do two hours in the morning and get Nathaniel on the bus and then do two hours in the afternoon to get Nathaniel off? That way, I can get Nathaniel ready in the morning and give him a bath when he gets off the bus as well."

Nancy was sure that Sharon was heaven-sent. Nathaniel was pleased as well, his routine more certain than ever. Now, rather than training several aides a month and not knowing who was going to show up, Nathaniel would have consistency.

Nathaniel arrived home that afternoon, and the first person he saw at the house was the last person he had seen that morning. "Now, Nathaniel, I am running your bath water," said Sharon, as she wheeled him into the house and carried him up the stairs, stating, "Now, let's get you ready for some fun." Nathaniel's bed also served as a changing table. She laid him down and began to work. Nathaniel's clothes had been changed at least once at school, but he was clearly ready for another change. Sharon pulled off his soiled shirt and pants, saving the diaper for last. Nathaniel began anticipating his bath so much that he started flapping his arms and cooing while Sharon took off his diaper.

"Here we are then, Buddy," Sharon said, lifting him down into his blue plastic bath chair that supported him like he was laid back in a lawn chair. The water was warm enough to feel good and filled the tub enough to allow Nathaniel to feel buoyant. Because of the Velcro strap-on chair, he at once felt free and supported. Sharon then made use of the shampoo and soap that would yield a clean-smelling boy.

For Nathaniel, bath time was not just about getting clean. It was cause for celebration. Most of the nurses that Nathaniel had had in the past suppressed any sort of excitement, but with Sharon, he was empowered to splash. He laughed as he kicked his feet and waved his arms around. In the process, Nathaniel got the wall wet, the floor wet, and perhaps even a few drops on the ceiling. While Nathaniel was getting his daily bath, Sharon was getting a shower. But for her, it didn't matter. The room could easily be wiped down, her own wet clothes would dry soon enough. Such a small investment of time and attention brought such great pleasure.

Once she had gotten him clean and happy, Sharon had other plans for Nathaniel. First, a big fluffy towel. Then talcum powder and a fresh, clean diaper. Next pajamas, and lastly a little bit of rocking in the rocking chair while a drip feed started making his tummy feel full and took away his thirst.

Every single afternoon, Sharon would turn on a cassette tape of Meryl Streep reading *The Velveteen Rabbit*. The introductory music would play, and then the story would begin in earnest. "Once, there was velveteen rabbit...." And this was the cue for Nathaniel to cuddle, and for his eyes to begin closing very slowly.

On the rare occasions when Dave was home at that time of day, he wanted to be informed when the bath was done so he could be the one to rock Nathaniel in the rocking chair.

"Once, there was a velveteen rabbit," began Meryl Streep, and Nathaniel, in fresh pajamas, nuzzled into Dave's shoulder, yawning. Nathaniel smelled of baby shampoo, talcum powder, and fresh clothes. Dave looked down at him as he closed his eyes. This boy was pretty limited. He wouldn't be a Bible quizzer, a football player, or a preacher. He would never win trophies for his dad or make him famous. Dave didn't even know how long this boy would be around. But none of that really mattered. Nathaniel didn't have to do anything to win his father's love. Because this was his son. And that was all that mattered.

Chapter 19

"I thought I told you not to come"

Dave sat behind his mahogany desk, the door to his office closed. Before someone could get to him, they had to pass through another office. His secretary, Barb, sat at her desk, and even though his door was closed, he could hear her on the phone. "No, he's not taking calls right now. Can I take a message?"

Barb kept Dave sane. She knew what needed to be done, even when he forgot to tell her. She actually did most of the administration in his name based on either what he had done in the past or by using her own best judgment, and for that he was thankful.

There were loose ends aplenty as Dave not only taught classes but also was involved in many administrative decisions. Rules were fairly strict at the school, and while he was not on the front line of discipline issues, if things were getting serious, they got bumped up to him. Presently Dave heard Barb say, "You can go right in. He's expecting you."

Dave welcomed Larry and invited him to sit on the love seat while he came around from his desk and sat next to him in the chair. After a couple minutes of chitchat, Dave came around to the main point of the discussion. "So, Larry, how is everything going with you and your girlfriend?"

Larry knew that Dave would not have invited him in for social interchange, and he was quick to head off any questions. "Fine. We're keeping all the social rules," he replied. "I have never been late for curfew once this year." The school had a lot of social rules, and dates were allowed when both homework and the school bills were all up to date.

"Well, that's good, Larry, but there is something I need to ask you about. Someone showed me a local newspaper, and unless the newspaper has gotten it wrong, they have announced that you and your girlfriend have applied for a marriage license. Now I know I could be mistaken, but it is my job to follow up on this sort of thing. So I need to ask, did you and your girlfriend get married?"

Larry thought for a moment, and then apparently decided to explain the situation thoroughly. "Yes," said Larry, "we went ahead and got married, but we never broke any of the social rules."

Dave started to say something, paused, started again, but then was at a total loss for words. A half-hour later, Dave was on the phone with one of the pastors. "Well, I am not sure how it happened either, but this much I do know…."

Nathaniel was sleeping, Dave was on the couch reading a book, and Nancy was just getting in the door. It was 10:30 at night. She was coming home from her class at the University of Delaware. Nancy tossed her purse one way, her books another, and then she plunked herself down on a living room chair. Dave waited for her to say something, but she just stared ahead blankly. After thirty seconds of silence, she said, "Dave, I just can't do it anymore."

Dave put the book down. "What? The U of D class?"

"It's not just the class. I really need to make a change," replied Nancy. "I am caring for Nathaniel, teaching all day in the reading lab, teaching a couple of college classes, going to school, and to top it off, we travel to other churches on weekends. I think I'm done."

The pronouncement seemed final, and Dave took it seriously. "So what's our next step?" he asked. Nancy explained that she was burnt out, that emotionally she was fried. She just needed some margin in her life. She wasn't upset with life or discouraged or angry at anyone in particular, but she had to find a way to recharge.

Nancy decided that she would let the academy know that she wouldn't be coming back to the reading lab in the fall. Also, she wouldn't take any more graduate courses at the University of Delaware; and she was going to cut down to teaching one college class. Dave promised to be more available for Nathaniel. Nancy hoped that was a promise he could keep.

Nancy bought a book entitled, *How to Attract Birds.* Their kitchen window was one solid sheet of glass eight feet across, and from her kitchen window she was fifteen feet from a large wooded area. Following the advice of the book, she had a wire strung from the kitchen window to a tree at the edge of the woods. The book said that sunflower seeds attracted the most variety of birds, and it recommended that the feeder be set out a ways from the house. Gradually the feeder could be moved closer and closer to the house until it was only a few feet away from the window. And that is exactly what she did.

It was morning. Nathaniel was at school, Dave was gone, and the house was quiet. The Bible lay open on the kitchen table while from her cup a rich coffee aroma permeated her breakfast nook. The blue jay that had scared away the smaller birds earlier was gone now, and some of them were beginning to return. "Oh, wow!" she exclaimed suddenly, picking up the binoculars. A dozen feet away, a bird she had never seen was now perched on the fence. It was large and brown with golden wing linings. There were red markings on the back of its head and some kind of a black band across its neck. Because Nancy just had to know what kind of bird it was, that very day she purchased her first book to identify birds. It turned out that what she saw was a yellow-shafted flicker, and Nancy's avocation as a "birder" was born. Each time she saw a new bird, she put a check mark and the date in her book.

Nancy transitioned away from the academy, taught some courses at the college, and continued to involve herself in ministry activities. She and Dave taught at a number of children's camps in the summer and did several weekend trips. Life was still busy; but it was a good kind of busy. Over time, the Norrises each found their own routine, both individually and as a family. Seasons repeated themselves once and again. One day Nancy turned around and Nathaniel was five-years-old, a significant milestone.

Shortly after his fifth birthday, they had to get Nathaniel yet another new wheelchair. It was time for Nathaniel to trade in his Sherman-tank-like red wheelchair for a state-of-the-art blue wheelchair. Doing so allowed Nathaniel to move up from utility to style. Unlike his old chair that sported enough steel to frame a small skyscraper, his new chair had no steel bars. In fact it was ultra-light, consisting of a foamy material wrapped in a glossy, aqua-blue, stain-free, waterproof cover that was form-fitted for Nathaniel. This new chair piece functioned also a car seat. What made it a wheel chairs was that the larger blue piece could also be strapped into a light-weight, state-of-the-art stroller. When it was not needed, the stroller could be folded to the size of a large umbrella. Dave's back thanked him more than once for this development.

Over time, the blue chair had to be lengthened to fit his expanding frame. He was measured in January and the adjustment to his chair took place just in time for his sixth birthday. Friends came over, and the group had a happy time. Nathaniel was living longer than statistics pronounced, and celebration was in order for God's gift of life.

Dave was finishing up his work at college. The seminary he wanted to attend would not accept his Bible school degree, so he worked out a way to do limited residency at the college. They transferred in two years of his previous work, and he filled in the rest of the required credits with CLEP tests, language challenges, and a portfolio, all the while spending as little time on campus as possible. At the college he attended, they gave grades for the CLEP tests, so Dave always had a book in his hand in preparation for one test or another. Dave just had just one more class to do and now spent a lot of his spare time studying vocabulary cards for his GRE test, an admissions test for graduate school. Nathaniel enjoyed sitting on his lap as his father utilized flash cards. "Malevolent; do you know what that means Nathaniel?" Nathaniel laughed and waved his hands excitedly. He didn't really care, but he was glad to be with his dad.

Nancy went to a seminar on "transitions" and was convinced of the need for advocacy for those with handicaps. She joined the Association of Retarded Citizens (ARC) and regularly went to meetings. "Can you watch Nathaniel when the nurse leaves today?" Nancy asked.

"What time do I need to be home?" said Dave.

"If you're here by 5 o'clock, that's soon enough to relieve Sharon."

"Sure."

"Another thing—I need the car. Can you catch a ride back out?" Dave was sure he could as there was always someone going back and forth one direction or another from the Trout house, a hundred yards away.

"So what time will you be home tonight?" he asked.

"I'm not sure. A group of us are going down to the capitol. It depends on what time that piece of legislation on disabilities comes up. I'll call if I'm going to be late."

That spring, they evaluated Dave's work and gave him a full scholarship to seminary. While the scholarship would normally first go to those who were of the same faith tradition as the seminary, apparently they didn't have enough students of that tradition who were eligible, and since the money was earmarked only for a tuition scholarship, it would go unused if no qualified student were available. Indeed, it seemed as if they had more scholarship money available but they could not give it out because it had to go to qualified people. There was only one catch. Dave would be required to go to seminary full-time.

"How are you going to do that?" asked Nancy.

"They have block scheduling, so I could probably do nine hours one full day and then take an evening class," said Dave.

"And Janet is okay with you doing that?" asked Nancy.

"Sure, so long as I can fit in my classes and administrative duties."

Nancy looked a little skeptical, but she could hardly say no to the offer of a full scholarship.

Two days later, Dave's secretary passed through a call from home. "Dave, Nathaniel's temperature is a hundred and three degrees," said Nancy on the phone. He immediately left his office and drove home. The hospital admitted Nathaniel, and he was brought up to pediatrics.

"Nathaniel, it's good to see you!" said the nurse to the sick baby bundled in Dave's arms.

Someone was making up his bed and turned to see the boy being carried in. "Hey Nathaniel, you're back," they said. Indeed, he was.

The next morning Nancy went up to the hospital to see Nathaniel. Something seemed strange as he was furiously sucking his thumb. Nancy immediately went to the nurse's station. "Why hasn't Nathaniel been fed?" The charge nurse did some checking and soon Nathaniel's nurse came into the room to talk to Nancy. "There is a whole bag of formula here to feed Nathaniel, but the pump is off. What's going on?"

"Well, I started his feeding, but the pump kept beeping. I assumed that meant that he was full."

Nancy pulled back the covers to see what was going on. Instead of attaching the feeding sack to the right port, the nurse had attached it to the port that inflated the balloon inside his stomach. It was just a good thing the balloon hadn't burst as his tube would have come out. "Look," said Nancy not too sweetly. She put the connection in the correct port, instructing the nurse how to do the same.

That evening Dave stayed with Nathaniel in the hospital while Nancy went to her meeting. She got to the board meeting of the ARC, of which she had recently become a member. On break, one of the ladies noted to Nancy, "You seem kind of distracted tonight." She was.

Toward the end of the meeting, someone finally asked what she thought of the proposed legislation, trying to draw her out. "I don't have an opinion about that. However, I want to know something on a different subject. What kind of hospital do we have where the nurses can't even service a patient with a g-tube? What kind of hospital is that?"

The outburst was so out of character and so off the subject that people just stared at her. Finally someone asked her to explain and she did. The meeting then awkwardly drifted back to the subject at hand, and Nancy felt a little foolish.

But then, a couple of weeks later, Nancy found out that the hospital was soon to have an in-service on how to care for patients with g-tubes. She was never sure who said what to whom, but someone on the ARC board evidently had more pull than she thought.

"Hello," said Dave picking up the receiver.

"Hey, we've got a new student who arrived in town, and nobody here is sure what to do," said the voice. "Can you come up here and figure this out?"

197

Dave was in old clothes, hadn't shaved, and didn't feel like meeting new people. "Look, just send them to the dorm," said Dave. After all, it was Saturday afternoon.

"But this isn't an eighteen-year-old kid. It's a family."

"Oh, well, I hadn't heard about a family coming into town. I'll be up shortly," he replied, grudgingly.

As Dave pulled up, a slimly built blond man got out of a moving truck. He looked to be in his mid to late-twenties. Beside the truck, a woman, presumably his wife, was walking on the grass with three grade-school girls, stair-step in age. Dave noticed then that she was carrying a baby, an infant boy, as it turned out. The truck apparently contained all of their worldly possessions.

The man introduced himself; his name was Jim. As he talked, Dave remembered a phone conversation that he had had with the man earlier that summer. "That's right," said Dave, "you said you wanted to become a military chaplain."

As Dave recalled, the man had a Master's Degree in Education and was pastoring a church, all the while teaching grade school. Dave was presently curious about why this man had showed up in a moving truck with all his things, arriving at a place sight unseen to enroll in a program that would not specifically address his needs. Dave said, not unkindly, "I thought I told you not to come."

The man answered calmly, "Well, I called several Bible schools, and you were the only ones who even talked to me. So, I took that to be a good sign."

Dave smiled, mumbling to himself, "This has to be the most stubborn man I have ever met in my life." Dave already liked him. Jim saw Dave mumbling and offered further, "The superintendent of education said I needed a little Bible school under my belt before I went to seminary."

Dave just shook his head. "I'll tell you what," he offered. "I've got to go up to a seminary on Monday. Why don't you come with me? I think they may even have some scholarship money left."

On the way up to the seminary, Jim said, "But the superintendent of education said—"

Dave put up a hand to shush the discussion. "I talked to him. I told him I would be supervising you." He said this with a hint of a smile and a twinkle in his eye. Dave figured the man as a possible academic dean for the Bible college. He certainly was the brainy type. It wouldn't hurt him to fill that position for a while as he worked toward his real goal of being a military chaplain.

Every Thursday morning, at 6:00 a.m., Jim and Dave left for Philadelphia and endured nine hours of class at the seminary. Nancy often got up at 5:30 a.m. to make snacks and lunch. She packed drinks into a little cooler and put sandwiches and chips in Superman lunch bags. Dave was gone all day. He didn't return until close to midnight. Somehow Dave had to fit in three more class hours during the week so that he could qualify as full-time. When Dave was home, he was either reading or working on papers. So long as Nathaniel got to sit by Dave, he had no qualms about Dave going to school. Unfortunately, Dave found reading more difficult than memorizing Greek flash cards because Nathaniel enjoyed batting at the pages too much.

Because he loved people, there was no better place in the world for Nathaniel than church. To accommodate growth at the church, services were moved from the cafeteria down to the gym. The good thing about this was that when Nancy needed to leave the service in order to change Nathaniel's diaper, she wasn't far from Dave's office, which doubled as Nancy's own private changing room. As Nathaniel was now much larger and required more than the usual-sized changing table, the privacy was welcome. Because Dave sat on the platform during service, typically he was unavailable to help.

Sometimes Nancy held Nathaniel on her lap so he could get a break from his chair. But most of the time he enjoyed a view of the service from his wheelchair, which made things easier when it was time for offering. The custom of the church was for the congregation to march up to the front and put the offering into a plate. Nancy usually took longer than anyone else to get through the offering line. Between lingering to greet people and people wanting to see Nathaniel, she usually had to rush to sit down as the order of the service changed.

Nancy believed that Nathaniel truly participated in worship. He would get happy on happy songs, and was respectful when slower songs were sung. When there was a message in tongues and a momentary pause before an interpretation, Nathaniel cooed softly in a way that he did not do at other times.

One Sunday morning, Dave was preaching and began raising his voice as he was making a point, only to be interrupted in mid-sentence as Nathaniel abruptly burst out crying so loudly that Dave had to stop speaking right in the middle of his sermon. In front of the entire congregation, he calmly stopped to say to the little boy in the wheelchair halfway back in the congregation, "Now Nathaniel, I'm not mad. Everything is all right." Nathaniel whimpered just briefly, and then he settled down as Dave continued with the message.

Certain pitches of music bothered Nathaniel's ears, and because the PA system was loud at church, Nancy brought earplugs for Nathaniel to dull the sound. Sometimes Nancy wore them herself.

Days could get long, and sometimes Nathaniel required a feeding at church. One night before church Nancy was dumping formula into a large 60 cc syringe when three small children approached. They noticed the formula emptying out of the oversized syringe and going into the tube that led directly into Nathaniel's stomach, three inches from his belly button. "This is how Nathaniel eats," Nancy said warmly.

"Can he taste it?" asked a little boy of about four-years-old.

"No, and that's why I give him a little ice cream to eat at times, so he can taste sweet things."

"I like ice cream," chimed in a five-year-old girl.

"My favorite flavor is chocolate," said the four-year-old boy. Nancy found that children were not intimidated by Nathaniel's tube. Only some adults looked away as she was feeding him.

One day after church, Nancy was wheeling Nathaniel down the hall toward Dave's office. Connie, who was one of Nathaniel's babysitters, came up and kissed Nathaniel directly on the lips. Nathaniel didn't protest, though Nancy would have said something if she had caught it soon enough. While she was digging around in her bag for a "wipe" to get rid of any germs, Nancy looked up to see a man in the Air Force named Dave kiss Nathaniel right on the lips as well. Nancy let out a big whooping laugh. "Do you realize you just kissed Connie on the lips?" Dave didn't care to find out what she meant and passed on down the hall.

Chapter 20

"Just a minute, Budzolla"

Ron had a gift. He could produce the score for brass accompaniment to a song in his head, and then could quickly write out musical notes that captured the instrumentation perfectly. It took him only a couple of hours. Ron had been hired as the director for the twelve to fifteen musicians that backed up the choir. He was working on two things. First, he was getting together the brass backup for the Bible college choir as they prepared to sing at General Conference. Second, he was working on brass accompaniment for choir songs at church.

Unfortunately, Ron discovered that both Jim and Dave played brass instruments and thus he drafted them into the fold of those required to participate in a three to four-hour practice on Friday nights. Rehearsals started late and went even later as Ron attempted to milk out notes above and beyond the normal range of mortals. Gradually crafting a repertoire of enough songs to play regularly for church worship service, Ron rode this momentum to beat brass players into submission so they would not complain about the long practices.

One Friday night, well after midnight, Dave whispered to the trombonist next to him, "How much do you bet that I can get Ron to tell about the guy with one lung?" It was a story Ron seemed to have forgotten that he told weekly. The young man shrugged, apparently fearful of prolonging the practice. "Hey Ron," said Dave, "this lick goes all the way up to a high b-flat. Is there any way we can lower the key just a tad?"

"You know," the director offered, "a couple of years ago I was in Ohio. And there was this guy who played trombone who said that same thing to me. And the thing is…" Dave poked the trombonist next to him as Ron lazily related the tale. "So after a couple of months he was able to hit those notes. Do you know what the most amazing thing was? He only had one lung."

"Don't provoke him any more," said the trombonist next to him. "I have to work in the morning."

Ron flew to Dover on Fridays and flew out on Mondays. Because of the lengthy practices on Friday, he was fairly free on Saturdays, which were generally planned with whatever recreation could be found. If he could come up with enough players, Ron's favorite pastime was a good old game of Monopoly. Joe and Rhonda sometimes made their house available for such an enterprise, and the table was always set with enough markers for a considerable group to try their hand at making a fortune.

One Saturday night, Nathaniel was watching his mom and dad roll the dice. His dad was about to go bankrupt and had lost interest in the game, but Nancy was on a hot streak and had built hotels on the yellow properties. John, who may or may not have been a millionaire in his own right, had significantly less assets in this game. He landed on Ron's property. "Tell you what…," he said to Ron. "Why don't we wait on me paying you? That way, I can get my money from Nancy when she hits my property. That will weaken her significantly."

An evil twinkle flashed in their eyes as the two financial conspirators made their pact. However, Nancy would have none of it. "Just a minute, Budzolla," said Nancy, who was flaring up in indignation. "That is cheating. You take those hotels off your property right now."

Dave realized that it was a good time to find something else to focus on and suddenly determined that Nathaniel was in need of attention. He pulled Nate out of his chair and began playing with him on his lap. "How you doing, Budzolla?" he said teasingly to his son.

"Budzolla" was a family word invented by Nancy for "medium mad" situations. Nathaniel turned into a Budzolla if he had a dirty diaper and spread the contents with his hands while Nancy was trying to change it. Dave was a Budzolla when Nancy had to call him three times for dinner that was getting cold because he was working on something else. Nathaniel enjoyed being held and now actually seemed to be taking an interest in the discussion at the table as he waved his arms and cooed loudly.

"It happens all the time in the business world," said John.

"Looks fair to me," said Ron, innocently.

"It's against the rules," insisted Nancy, standing up from the table. She was now swiftly moving from Budzolla-kind-of-mad to something else entirely.

"I don't think so," said John with a smile.

"Never read it," said Ron.

They were enjoying the response they were getting from provoking in her. She rifled through rules and pounded the table, but the escalated intensity of protest had not yet worked toward solving matters of inter-pretation. "Then I'm calling Parker Brothers!" challenged Nancy.

"Sounds good to me," replied John, smiling. Telephone numbers were consulted, and after a couple of attempts, Nancy reached the corporate office.

"Parker Brothers," came the reasonable response on the other end of the line. Nancy knew immediately she had hit pay dirt and explained how the men in the room were, in fact, cheating her. She concluded her explanation and said, "…so that is why this is totally not fair!"

There was a long pause on the other end of the line. Finally, a verdict was proffered. "Well, I can really sympathize with your position," said the man on the phone, while Nancy quietly mouthed, "Told you so!"

to the cheaters at the table. Then the man continued. "Yeah, I really think you have a good point. But there is only one problem."

"What's that?" said Nancy, suddenly concerned.

"Ma'am, its 10:30 on a Saturday night and nobody is in the office. Actually, I'm a security officer at the guard shack."

One evening the phone rang. The voice identified itself as the general superintendent of their denomination. It even sounded something like him; but Dave had heard this voice before and knew exactly whose voice it was. He was positive that it was his brother Bob playing a joke on him. He was about to say, "Bob, you idiot!" but then thought better of it. He decided to play along and casually asked, "How can I help you?"

The voice responded, "Your grandfather is dying, and I think it is important that you go to see him." Dave was glad he didn't call the voice an idiot. This was clearly not a joke.

"You want me to go see my grandfather?" he asked, now more humbly.

"Yes, I think it would be a good thing if you went and apologized to him."

Dave's grandfather was indeed lying on a hospital bed in St. Paul, Minnesota, and certainly looked as if he did not have long to live. He had a plastic tube looped around his face, providing oxygen directly into his nose. Still, his breathing was shallow, and he was obviously in pain. They said his lungs were retaining fluids. Although he had recovered from such a condition before, there are only so many times a person can bounce back from death's door.

Dave greeted his grandfather; mentioned Nancy and Nathaniel, offered a bit more small talk and finally said, "I'm sorry for the pain I caused you. I am sorry for the hurt." His grandfather paused, waiting for more.

Dave had been in St. Paul the year before. For some months, the church that had been associated with the school was meeting offsite from the Bible college. They now owned another church building. The District Sunday School Department had chosen this church site as a venue for their event since there was plenty of space for breakout sessions. Nancy and Dave were the invited plenary speakers. After they had arrived in St. Paul, he called his father. "Dad, I wanted to stop by and see you." Dave was shocked by the reply.

"No, I don't want you to come."

"Why not?"

"Because you are over there at that church that split away."

Dave was baffled. In the last several years, a lot had changed in his father's life. On the one hand, he had come to find a close personal relationship with the Lord. From what he had heard from others, his new-found faith had given him a measure of peace with himself and with others. On the other hand, his father had made his commitment to the Lord during what had amounted to a very tumultuous time. Based on the best information available to his father, Dave's father had made certain stands in order to demonstrate his family loyalty.

Dave was, in fact, at the church that had split away but explained, "Dad, I'm here for a statewide event. Nancy and I were invited to do seminars for Sunday school teachers."

"But it is held at that church."

"True enough, but the District Sunday School Department has nothing to do with—"

None of that mattered. Dave's dad didn't want to see him.

His grandfather was breathing heavily. He finally lifted a hand and pronounced a blessing. He told Dave never to leave truth and to live for God, and to stand up for what was right. It was more of a priestly blessing than anything personal, but Dave was glad to have received it.

Dave wrote and directed the Christmas program for the academy, weaving in the songs that the children would sing with a story line he had created. On some level, the story was just a little bit bizarre, but he created it that way purposely, attempting to draw in the junior and senior high school boys. The story line was pretty simple. As Dave envisioned it, two high school kids, David and Jenny, in an effort to figure out how to do an authentic Christmas play, were to ask a number of people for information. After encountering a number of skeptics, they would then encounter a mad scientist and her humped-backed assistant Igor. In an effort to try out a newly-built time machine, the mad scientist would send David and Jenny back to Bethlehem at the time of the birth of Christ. In true Wizard of Oz fashion, the characters from the past would look and sound remarkably like the characters from the present. The play had humor, a couple of rap songs, and lines sarcastic enough to keep any junior high kid interested.

Dave worked with the staging and helped the actors with their lines. He drafted several adults as well and had practices with them. "Now Buzz," he said, "I want you to really ham up the part of the liberal minister. Say this: 'Jesus wasn't really born in any sort of miraculous fashion at all. It was the *Sitz im Leben* of the church that caused the Bible to be written that way.'"

"I did say that," complained Buzz.

"I know, Buzz, but it's German. The word '*Sitz*' is pronounced differently than you are saying it. The first 'S' sounds like a 'Z'."

"Like who would know!" responded Buzz.

"And can you give me a bit more of a German accent?" prompted Dave.

"So who are you mad at?" asked Buzz with a smile.

"Just a couple of professors at the seminary. They're heretics."

"And this play is going to stop that?" asked Buzz.

"No," responded Dave, "but I am sure of one thing. It will sure make me feel better."

Christmas vacation was a lazy event at the Norris household as pressures temporarily let up. Nancy and Dave spent time with Nathaniel in front of the fireplace. Unfortunately, as their vacation wound down, they received a phone call reporting that Dave's grandfather was not expected to live through the week. After a second call confirmed that he had passed away, Nancy and Dave flew up to St. Paul for the funeral.

The funeral was held at the Bible college. The large auditorium was filling up with people who had come from far and near to pay their respects. Twenty minutes before the service was to start, Dave peered in from the rear of the auditorium that sloped gently down to where the casket was placed at the front. Pews were filling up. Considerable tension hung in the air. Dave saw hundreds of people from the church that was now meeting in another location, and numbers of people from the school who were intermingling in the congregation. Dozens of ministers had traveled in from various parts of the country.

"Hey Dave," came a familiar voice. It was Jim. He had driven up from West Bend.

"It's good to see you," said Dave, embracing Jim.

Jim offered sympathetically, "I take it you aren't sitting with the family." Dave shrugged. Dave did not see his family in the auditorium. Apparently they were meeting privately as a family unit at some other place in the building. Dave had not been invited.

"You know," Dave offered, "I think that maybe Nancy and I are going to find a place to sit by ourselves. I don't expect people to really understand what is going on here. Some people will probably think I am insulting the family by not sitting with them. Others may think that it is a disgrace that I even showed up at all. Why don't I just meet you after the funeral? You don't want to lose any friends by sitting with us."

Dave and Nancy located themselves on a pew. The funeral was fairly long. A sufficient number of dignitaries were present to honor his grandfather. The former general superintendent had been in a youth group in Columbus, Ohio, which had been headed up by Dave's grandfather. He shared a few funny stories. Otherwise, things were pretty somber.

Nancy and Dave drove to the graveside. "Dust to dust…ashes to ashes," the minister was saying. Dave thought about the family narrative. When Dave's grandfather was a boy, he lost his own father in an industrial accident. The family story included how that little boy sold newspapers in downtown Columbus to put food on the table. Dozens of incidents had been retold in family gatherings about his grandfather's adventures as a businessman as well as important stories about his starting a church in New York City. Those stories hadn't been celebrated nearly enough today.

"We commit this body to the earth awaiting a better day…." Dave recalled some miracles he'd heard reported to him, not by his grandfather but by others for whom his grandfather had prayed. He thought of sermons his grandfather had preached, the annual family Christmas gathering, and classes that his grandfather had taught. Dave remembered all the way back to when he was four or five and would come upstairs from Sunday school into the church auditorium. His grandfather would be in the back of the church, shaking hands with people as they left. Sometimes Dave got a quarter if he hung around.

And on a few occasions, his grandparents would take Dave and his sisters home from church. This was typically accompanied by a treat. His grandpa might stop at the store to buy a half-gallon of peppermint bon-bon ice cream for them. "Remember, Davy. This is the very best ice cream there is." Dave promised that he would remember. And so he did. As the last "amen" was uttered, Dave was thinking about peppermint bon-bon ice cream.

Because there was no meal served at the church after the funeral, groups of people stood in the snow-covered cemetery abiding the ten-degree chill in order to talk and visit. Breath was visible in the cold air as acquaintances were renewed and old friends were found. For thirty minutes people chatted and chattered by the graveside.

At first it was sober. But as is often the case following a funeral, after a required time of solemnity, there is tacit permission to reflect and tell stories. After a few minutes, tales were told and the good old days once again came alive. Teasing and laughter became part of the mix. Over fifty yearbooks confirmed the faithfulness of the deceased to those who had come to train as ministers. And those fifty years of classes had fifty years of stories. "That's not how it happened at all," came one laughing voice. "You were the one who snuck out after curfew."

"She was not my girlfriend. She was never my girlfriend," said an older man, trying to convince a peer of the truth of history. "You were the one who was going after her."

Dave talked with a few people, nodded at others, and then chatted with a couple of friends. He thought of peppermint bon-bon ice cream and of all the other losses that the day represented. After a few more moments of reflection, he asked Nancy if her feet were cold and assented that his were too, thereby deciding to leave. Minnesota snow crunched crisply under their boots as they made their way toward the car that brought them.

The next weekend Nancy and Dave ministered at an inner-city church in Baltimore. Incredible things were happening in the lives of people. But inner-city work is tough. Somebody who has been delivered of crack may do well for a while, but it is a tough struggle.

A middle class churchgoer who gets discouraged will stop reading his or her Bible or may stop praying for a while, but for somebody who comes out of addiction, discouragement can be a death knell. The fall to the bottom is a lot further and a lot quicker.

Nancy did some puppets and Dave spoke. In the most important service they had, the pastor made an appeal for a good offering. Several ushers counted it in front of the pulpit, but apparently it was not enough. Another offering was taken and then another. Finally they had enough. Dave was glad, because his wallet was almost empty.

Nathaniel turned seven. They had to get him another new wheelchair. Nathaniel was now being fitted out at A. I. duPont with yet a bigger chair and larger stroller. The chair was still of the same light-weight shiny blue variety. Since Nancy was by herself for the appointment, she plopped Nathaniel's bigger and better blue chair into the front seat. Nathaniel must have thought that this demonstrated the new order of where he would be sitting, because on Sunday morning, when Dave headed toward the car to drive the family to church, Nathaniel looked longingly toward the front seat. Nancy saw his head turned longingly and she knew immediately what he wanted. "Don't even think about it, Budzolla," she said. "Don't even think about it."

Chapter 21

"What do you think about adopting a child?"

"What would you think about adopting a child?" asked Dave.

"We have a child," said Nancy.

This was one of those difficult conversations to have because there was so much at stake and so many potential ways for misunderstandings to occur. He pressed on. "I know, but I was thinking of maybe looking into adopting another one."

"The adoption process takes forever and going through all the hoops that they require. Plus, the costs are incredible." They had had this same conversation before and had inquired here and there about the possibility of adopting, but this was the point where the conversation usually ended. And it was he who usually ended it. But today was different.

"It wouldn't hurt to check adoption out a little further," said Dave. "We'll take it slow and try to be sensitive to doors that God may open for us."

"Don't get me wrong, I don't mind looking into this," said Nancy feeling threatened by this sudden burst of enthusiasm. When Dave started getting enthusiastic about anything, it was difficult to slow him down. "I think it would be great to adopt a child," she continued. "I'm just not sure it is practical."

He went to see Donna, their banker. She was actually more than just their banker. She attended the same church as they did and had become something of a financial advisor to Dave. He was easygoing about financial issues, so it was important for him to have people in his life who actually thought about money matters in realistic terms.

"So Nancy and I are looking into adopting a child, but it is very expensive. We would probably have to borrow the money to do it."

Donna looked over the brochure that Dave had given her to peruse. A few seconds of silence hung in the air between them before she noted, "This is a half-year's wage for you." Donna knew what he made for a living, and she didn't need to be a math whiz to figure out that this kind of debt might not be a good idea.

She continued, "Look, if I were you and Nancy, I wouldn't go into this kind of debt just to get a child. There is enough expense once they come. Why don't we just pray about it for a while? If it is the Lord's will, someone will supply you with money." Donna was neither flippant nor unfeeling, but she was spiritual, and she was practical. He and Nancy decided to follow her advice.

Nathaniel was once again in the hospital at A. I. duPont. He had been running a high fever and Nancy was able to get him in to see the doctor. Usually Nathaniel's doctor sent Nancy directly to the local hospital, but this time he recommended she head straight to duPont. Once she settled Nathaniel into his room, she went to the cafeteria for lunch.

The food was not too bad and the cost was fairly reasonable. She had just gotten her tray and sat down at a table when Nancy looked across the cafeteria and spotted a friend hurriedly fishing some snacks out of a vending machine and getting ready to exit. "Marion," she called.

Marion looked up and recognized Nancy. "Come up and see me when you can," Marion yelled. "I've got to run. The specialist is coming up to see us in fifteen minutes." Marion gave Nancy her room number and quickly left with snack in hand.

Marion had a daughter by the same name. Her daughter was a couple of years older than Nathaniel—a sweet girl who had significant handicaps and many health issues. Twice before when Nancy had been in the hospital with Nathaniel, Marion was at A. I. duPont at the same time. Because they both faced incredible challenges of providing the very best care for their children, it wasn't long before an important bond had formed between Marion and Nancy.

Nancy stopped at Marion's room on her way back up to be with Nathaniel.

"Where's Dave?" asked Marion.

"Teaching. He'll be coming up tonight."

"Dale is coming in for the weekend," said Marion. "Maybe we can get together."

That night, Dave and Nancy met Dale and Marion at Chilis for supper. Over chips and salsa, Dale explained his delay in getting to A. I. duPont. "I couldn't get out of town because of the big snowfall yesterday," said Dale, who worked for a state university in upstate New York. A great deal of responsibility fell on him in keeping their fleet of trucks operating.

"Are you still singing in those choirs?" asked Dave.

"I had to quit a couple of them for the winter," said Dale.

Marion pulled their attention back to more important issues. "I am not letting them do that procedure tomorrow," she said suddenly.

Dale, attempting to intervene, said, "Honey, they're just trying to find out what is going on. I know it is a little painful for her, but it might help to—"

Interrupting, Marion said, "When the doctor came in today, he told me that he really needed me to sign the release forms for that test. But they have already done three tests and Marion is still suffering from those other tests—no." Marion had a right to doubt what doctors told her. Doctors' poor decisions had on more than one occasion hurt rather than helped their daughter.

"So you didn't sign for tomorrow's procedure, then?" asked Dale, apparently hearing this narrative for the first time.

Marion continued, "I told him 'No way. I don't care how many degrees you have. I have a M-O-M degree, and I know what's best.'"

Continuing, she said, "I will say that the doctors here are so much better than ones back home. I appreciate that. Most things I will allow, particularly if there is a chance to help. But by his own admission, the doctor told me that this test probably wouldn't show anything new. They just want to rule out a couple of possibilities. So there is no way I am going to put Marion through pain for that."

Nancy quickly agreed with Marion, Dale was silent, and Dave seemed to be concentrating awfully hard on his chips and salsa. Perhaps he thought silence was the wisest choice when a mother had made a decision about the care of her child. "Good chips," Dave said.

The next day Nancy arrived early enough for the consult with the attending physician. He said, "Nathaniel's doing pretty well today. If we don't see any further complications, I think we'll probably be able to release him by Tuesday of next week."

"Thanks," said Nancy.

The doctor stroked Nathaniel's head and suggested conversationally, "He does well for someone chronically ill. He is such a happy boy."

Nancy honed in on a term she hadn't ever heard used before to describe Nathaniel. "What do you mean, 'chronically ill?'"

"It's just a term that gets thrown around. Many doctors categorize someone as chronically ill who has five or more hospitalizations a year."

Nancy thought about it momentarily and realized that Nathaniel fit that category. Still, the label did come as a surprise. How odd that living in a state of emergency actually seemed normal.

The following week, the Norrises boarded a plane to Mississippi. They would be in Tupelo for several days to conduct some services at a church there. The church happened to be connected to an orphanage, and seventy-five children from the orphanage were part of the congregation. After the plane took off, Nancy pulled a puppet that looked like the Snuggle Bear from commercials from her bag. She slipped her hand into the puppet, playing with it.

"What are you going to do with that new puppet?" asked Dave.

"I'm not sure yet."

"It doesn't have a mouth," Dave replied, "so you can't do ventriloquism with it."

Nancy made its little arms move. "I thought that maybe I could snuggle people with it," she said, thoughtfully, "but that doesn't seem to be enough."

Strictly speaking, most children at the orphanage were not orphans. Often, the children's stories involved tragic events of some sort. Sometimes abuse, sometimes drugs, and sometimes parents just came up missing. As service began, Nancy noted that all of the children were dressed in their Sunday finest. Lots of time and love had been poured into these kids. Yet even beautiful church clothes could not hide some of the emotional wounds that were still in need of healing.

Nancy decided to wing it with the little puppet she called Snuggles. She brought Snuggles up, and the little bear whispered into Nancy's ear that he wanted to give her a snuggle. Nancy repeated out loud what he whispered: "Oh, so you want to give me a snuggle?" The little bear joyfully shook his head in the affirmative.

"Oh, good!" she said back to Snuggles, as the bear gave her a nice snuggle on her shoulder. Nancy then turned to the audience and said, "Is there anyone here who wants a snuggle?"

Nancy immediately realized her tactical mistake. There was almost a riot as children leaped up and began yelling loudly, "Me!" "Me!" Nancy made a mental note that the puppet should perhaps do this differently in the future. Perhaps the bear could whisper in her ear the identity of a few people in the audience that he wanted to snuggle. That way no one could argue with her, because it was the bear who decided who was to be snuggled. But that strategy would have to wait for another time. Right now she needed to fulfill a commitment. Indeed, little else could happen in the service for the next fifteen minutes while Nancy went down row after row, offering hugs to the children who didn't want to let go of the puppet's grasp. Most came back for seconds.

The pastor had orchestrated the service so that it was actually the children who were taking charge; at least, they did as much as they were able. Children served as ushers and praise singers; some children even made the announcements. At the beginning of the service, a little seven-year-old boy in a suit and tie with black greased down hair brought a big Bible to the pulpit to read the opening Scripture. Unfortunately, whatever Scripture he had intended to read somehow escaped him. The little boy turned the pages of his Bible this way and that for perhaps a full thirty seconds while every one stood, waiting. Dave wondered if perhaps an adult should suggest that he simply read some other verse. However, after a while, the boy came to the place where he evidently wanted to read. He sighed, and then read from Psalm 27, "When my father and my mother forsake me, then the LORD will take me up."

Once or twice a year, Nancy was in charge of the children's program at church on Wednesday nights. During some projects that she and Dave worked on, Nathaniel had a babysitter. However, the nice thing about doing children's church was that Nathaniel, too, could participate. Last fall she had done a western theme. Nathaniel had plenty of bandanas. Nancy was using bandanas instead of bibs, so he already had the beginnings of a western look. He only required a western shirt and a cowboy hat to complete the total transformation. But Nancy couldn't get Nathaniel to keep a cowboy hat on his head for longer than five seconds. He didn't much care for it and was easily able to yank it off.

Nancy decided to introduce Bible quizzing to the children. She used the same verses as they were utilizing for the national program, only she went a lot more slowly than if they had actually been competing. Rather than merely focusing on the rote memorization of verses, she made learning fun.

Because Nathaniel's bedroom had in recent months been decorated with multicolor dinosaurs, Nancy was inspired to utilize a dinosaur theme for the duration of this eight-week curriculum. One day a week, Nathaniel's wall hangings and toys were called upon to double as décor for their Wednesday night program. Nancy and her staff then worked to create a circus-like atmosphere of fun and action. Kids earned "dino-dollars" for learning verses, which they could spend for prizes. There were contests, games, and lots of continuous action.

After the program was over, Dave kept up with the kids who wanted to continue in Bible quizzing. He took Ralph, Jenny, and Chris to a district junior Bible quiz tournament, but because the kids had gone at a slower pace than the others at the tournament, they were soundly trounced. Dave didn't give up. They had a few months to catch up before the state playoffs, and there was still some hope that they could improve enough to place in the competition. He took them to a second tournament, but they didn't seem to be faring any better as a number of highly experienced teams were also competing.

They had beaten one team but the second team rolled over them. Because it was a double elimination tournament, they were only one loss away from heading home early. During the next match they were quizzing against a team who answered question after question, and Dave got desperate to slow the momentum that was working against them. He called a time out and proposed an unusual strategy. "I'll tell you what," he offered the quizzers, "When we get to question ten, contest their answer."

The rules stated that if quizzers felt that something was amiss with either a ruling on a question or with the question itself, they could point out the problem by standing and stating that they would like to contest. After consulting with their coach, either a quizzer or their coach could then take the contest to the judges' table. Dave thought that perhaps if their team contested, even if they didn't win the contest, the deliberation might slow down the quiz a little. Dave's quizzers didn't understand any of this, but they seemed game.

"What if we get the answer?" asked Jenny, who was a bit of a scrapper.

"Then don't contest it."

The quizzers promised that they would contest if they didn't get the answer. Obediently, on question ten, all three quizzers simultaneously stood to their feet, an indication that they wanted to protest something awry. The judges looked up, surprised that all three of these children had simultaneously thought of some error. The captain of Dave's team dutifully came to whisper his protest in Dave's ear, yet not too sure what to tell him. He reported that the team had done what Dave told them and sat down.

Dave nodded his head thoughtfully and began walking down to the judge's bench. He was planning to get right down to the judges, pause dramatically, and then withdraw the contest. But on the way down to the judges' bench, he realized that, indeed, something was not quite right with the question. He had studied the Greek behind the verse and realized that the question assumed something to be true that was not borne out by the original Greek.

He quoted the Greek words to the judges that indicated that the question was amiss, and his protest was granted. But the judges were more than a little suspicious of how it was that all three ten-year-olds knew Greek, and they offered Dave more than a wary eye from then on. Dave's team still lost the quiz, but they had fun doing it.

While junior Bible quizzing was going on, junior and senior high school students participated in senior Bible quizzing. It just so happened that a regional senior Bible quiz tournament would take place at the Bible college the very same weekend as the college graduation.

Dave approached Janet. "We have hundreds of high school kids coming here to the facilities. It looks to me like this has the potential for a great recruiting tool. Why don't we see if the college can put on a drama for their rally service? I am thinking of doing a biblical romance story with a lot of fighting. I mean… it works in the movies…."

"Who do I need to call to get permission?" Janet asked with her usual certainty. A phone call was all it took.

Dave worked with a group of college students to write and produce the biblical drama of Abigail. He had never forgotten a sermon that made the story of Abigail come alive, and he hoped that the drama could do the same. With a little creative license, the drama, set as a romance, told the story of how Abigail's courage caused King David to fall in love with her. The drama had thieves, bad guys, lots of blood and guts. Bart, a student who played the lead role of David, was an incredible songwriter. He wrote some original music that was then orchestrated by Ron.

Dave got a think tank together, and students worked to write, cast, and produce a fully orchestrated full-length musical drama. One student, Harold, took the lion's share of student directing. Mindy and Erica, two other creative minds, added to the mix. Anthony, Janet's son, was incorporated to oversee the fight scenes and lights; and Jeanette, Janet's daughter, was tapped to do costumes. He even recruited a former student, Julie, to fly up from Oklahoma in order to play percussion on borrowed timpani drums.

On paper, it all looked good. Up until a week before the performance, practices had been fairly routine. The biggest technical challenge was a fight scene that included twenty combatants wielding real swords. So far, there had been only one hospitalization for stitches, but no lopped heads. Two days before the performance, however, there was a major meltdown and Dave decided if he lived through this performance, he would never do drama again.

As is often the case, though, the quality of production far exceeded what had happened in the rehearsals. The message of the drama was low key yet powerful; among other things, it challenged teenage girls to live their dreams and be strong in faith, despite life circumstances. Brenda played the lead role. She was not only a good actress, but she was also a great role model. The fight scenes came across pretty much without a hitch. Thieves were dispatched by good guys, and people flew off the platform into the audience in chaotic action while the brass accompaniment pumped out "fight music" from the balcony.

The only issue that developed involved an invited dignitary who had flown in from Ohio for graduation events. As an honored guest, he sat in the first row in the audience. Everything was fine through ninety-nine percent of the performance. Indeed, there was only one time during the drama that fighters with swords almost landed in his lap. Still, no official complaint was registered; at least none that Dave knew of.

The Norrises were going on a little get-away that summer. They were able to do so because of Diana, Nathaniel's first school teacher in Dover. Nathaniel had long ago moved out of Diana's class, yet sometimes Diana took care of Nathaniel through a program of respite care established by the county. It was Friday night. Nancy had filled up the backseat with Nathaniel's things and dropped them off to Diana. There was an IV pole and pump, extra bags for the formula, a small box with formula in it, a bath chair and walker, a whole series of medications with instructions, a bag of diapers and his clothes. All of this was accompanied by a note that allowed Diana to get emergency medical treatment for Nathaniel if he needed it.

After dropping their son off, Nathaniel's parents drove two hours to a motel near Baltimore. Nancy had brought scented candles, potpourri, and special snacks. She was in the process of emptying the contents of the suitcases into the motel drawers when the telephone rang. She picked it up while she continued to unpack. "Hello," she said. There was a pause, and then she said, "Thanks, we'll be there right away."

Nancy hung up and as she started putting things back into the suitcase, Dave looked at her inquisitively but said nothing. She broke the bad news. "Nathaniel spiked a high fever. Diana's taking him to the hospital."

At the end of that summer, Dave received a telephone call from the same orphanage in Mississippi where he and Nancy had conducted services for the children.

"Hello, Steve, good to hear from you," he said. He assumed that Steve was calling to schedule another series of children's service. But he was not.

"Say, Dave, have you ever thought about adopting?" he asked.

He was taken aback, not really sure what to say. "Well, we have given it some thought," he replied.

"Good," said the director. "I need you to think about something. What would you say to adopting a sibling group of three children?"

Chapter 22

"I'd buy them a horse"

Dave was caught completely off guard. The director of the orphanage wanted him to adopt not one but three children. And these children were not infants. "It is two girls and a boy," he said. "You would want to adopt the three of them, as it is always best if siblings can be placed together."

Dave responded, "Well, Steve, let me be frank. The thing that has deterred us from seriously pursuing adoption up to this point is the cost and all the complications associated with it."

"I understand, and you are right to be cautious about costs. The good thing, though, about adopting these children, would be that there wouldn't be the high fees usually associated with adopting an infant, and the whole process would be fairly simple."

"How old are they?" asked Dave.

"The two oldest are the girls. Laura is fourteen, Holly is eleven, and Chad is nine. They are great kids."

"I don't know what to say. It's a big decision. I'll talk this over with Nancy and we'll consider it."

"You do that. There's no rush, and we only want this if it is really the right thing to do."

"Well, if we would want to pursue finding out more, how would we proceed?"

"I'll tell you what. I'll send you pictures of the children. If you decide to move forward, you can correspond with them. Perhaps you could meet them at General Conference in October. Are you going to New Orleans?"

"Yes, we planned on it."

"Great. Well, I will send you those pictures then."

Dave hung up and sought out his wife. When he found her, she saw that his eyes were full of sparkle, the most light she had seen in them in quite some time. Probably Dave thought that Steve's call was God's answer for them and that adoption would allow them to have a more complete family.

Nancy smiled, happy but concerned. She immediately blurted out, "Where would they all sleep?" They had three bedrooms. There was a master bedroom, Nathaniel's, and a guestroom. While the guestroom could readily serve as a bedroom for the girls, she wasn't sure what to do about the boy. Would the boy want to be with Nathaniel? No. That would not be fair to either one of them. Nancy saw immediately that adoption would be difficult given their current circumstance.

"I don't know," said Dave absently. "We'll work it out."

She kept smiling but was even more wary. Her husband seemed to have already adopted the children. A dozen problems composed themselves on the roster of her mind. She thought about clothing, schooling, what it would be like supervising teenagers, how they would get along with Nathaniel. More problems arrived with each new thought, but Dave wasn't ready to hear her list. He was saying, "Well, Steve did call us. And Nancy, we have been praying about it, so I think it would be foolish to dismiss this out of hand. Let's get some more information on it, okay?"

There was, of course, an elephant in the room. One she couldn't talk about. It was the unspoken issue: she couldn't have children. She couldn't give Dave a family, so was it right for her to deny him children that she herself couldn't provide? Smiling, she said, "Yeah, let's think about it."

Dave was in his last full year of seminary and was working on his thesis. Along with the thesis, he was doing one class at the seminary and an independent study. For his other class, he had signed up for a course at Temple University. His school had a reciprocity agreement with Temple, and although Dave was a little intimidated about taking a class that was being offered on a doctoral level, he was also comforted by the fact that it was listed as a foundations course. Since Dave had just started being tutored in Hebrew, he decided that a foundation course in Old Testament genre might be basic enough to be within his reach. But he wasn't sure. He would have to go to the first class at Temple to see if it seemed too difficult. If the class was beyond him, he would drop it and replace it with a course at the seminary.

When Dave walked into the classroom, there were eight other students all seated around a table. They were nice enough. Someone explained that the class was conducted as a seminar. The professor was a Dr. Wright who soon came walking through the door, engaged in conversation with one of his doctoral students. He had the syllabi in hand and readily passed them around the table of students. Along with the books assigned as required reading for the class, a long list of suggested reading accompanied this bibliography. Dave wasn't sure if the suggested reading was merely suggested or if, in fact, he was expected to read this list of books as well. As the professor talked, it seemed to be the latter.

This was all very strange, not like any class he had ever been in before. All the students knew each other and joked easily. Further, they all seemed to be working on some sort of on-going projects related to this or that subject that was well over Dave's head. Some were even continuing work from other semesters in this class in a way that Dave couldn't quite understand. After class he talked to the professor.

"Dr. Wright, I am not sure whether to take this class or not. I thought I was getting into something basic because the course was listed as 'Foundations of Hebrew Bible.'"

Dr. Wright laughed. "That is just the nomenclature at Temple for a doctoral course."

Dave continued. "I am trying to understand the syllabus. There are no tests, no response papers, and no reports on the reading. So the only thing that is really important in this class is the paper?"

"Look," said Dr. Wright, "this is a seminar class, so as soon as we begin our discussion, it will become immediately apparent to me whether you have comprehended the reading."

"Help me understand on what level the paper should be written," Dave said.

"My philosophy is that if you are saying something that has been said before, why bother? I am looking for original research."

"I'm not sure I can do this," said Dave.

"Sure you can," returned Dr. Wright. "I'll help you."

Nancy looked out the front door and saw Wayne, pulling weeds, a hundred yards away. Others regularly attended to the yard work, but if Wayne saw something amiss, he would fix it, whether he was in work clothes or a suit. Although he was in work clothes and was down on his knees pulling up some offending weeds, this work did appear to be an impulsive act, given that the car door stood open on his vehicle, and the engine was still running. She decided to catch him before he left to go work on some other project.

"Hey there!" she offered in greeting as she walked over to where he was. Wayne kept working but seemed in the mood to talk. He greeted her, smiled, and continued yanking up the offending growth of random green sprouts that did not belong.

"I was wondering what you would think about three extra kids on the property," Nancy said easily. Although most people found it hard to talk to Wayne, Nancy had no problem speaking to him. In fact, it was a whole lot easier for her to talk to him than to Janet. Further, Nancy had some kind of unique ability to talk him out of supplies and prizes for contests, something nobody else would even try to do.

For Wayne, every day was occupied by fourteen hours of building and working. He got the church to volunteer to bring ingredients, and then he would bake pies to sell back to the very people who donated the materials. Recently, he had taken over cooking for the college and somehow fit this between his other activities. If emergencies arose, he conscripted whoever was around to help.

Wayne was a true entrepreneur. Raised poor and understanding the need to make his own way in the world, he didn't think much about leisure, either for himself or for others. He had no use for slackers or time wasters. One day, Nancy and Dave had been riding with him in the car when Wayne saw a jogger. "He should at least put a plow behind him and pull. Then something productive would come from all that effort."

Nancy had a very specific issue about which she wanted Wayne's blessing. She was concerned that the property might be thrown off balance by the addition of what would soon be three teenagers. Wayne had built three upscale homes on connected acreage, had turned the barn into a beautiful home, and there were not merely children on the larger compound but grandchildren as well. "So, we're looking into the possibility of adopting," she concluded and waited for a response.

Wayne pulled a few more weeds, threw them in a pile and then got into his car. He shut the door that had stood open for fifteen minutes while the engine ran. He put the car in drive, rolled down the power window, and said simply, "I'd buy them a horse so they could ride." Then he drove off. Nancy walked away from the conversation uneasy. If Dave was so excited about the possibility and if Wayne had been so kind, what in the world was wrong with her?

Dave was pretty nervous as he entered the classroom at Temple to present his paper. The pattern of the class was that someone would present a paper and another student would take the lead in critiquing it. Others would then follow with their critique. A man named Jim was assigned to begin the critique of Dave's work. Only then would others around the table join in putting their two cents worth, and of course, the professor had the last word.

Dave had found a research topic that seemed to offer an opportunity for original work. But it was tough. He put all of his other work on hold while he dug into this topic. His subject was from the Book of I Enoch, an obscure text compiled from various Enochic traditions. At issue was the date of writing of a certain section of the Book of I Enoch not found in the Dead Sea Scrolls. The reason this problem was so controversial was because of the way in which the material seemed to interface with the New Testament.

Dave proposed that this section of Enoch, sometimes called the "Similitudes," could be dated based upon a particular historical trajectory; specifically, the way that "wisdom" was dealt with in the text. Whereas in Proverbs, wisdom was spoken of metaphorically, by the time of the writing of this section in the Enochic tradition, "wisdom" had arguably been hypostatized. That is, it had actually become a "person"; in I Enoch chapter 42, wisdom was actually treated as God's consort.

Dave was hoping that the table of doctoral students would be impressed with his scholarship, originality, and the significance of his work. They were not. After three hours of critique, he was left battered, bruised, and mauled. As the clock ran down, he felt himself bleeding all over the floor. Finally, the professor offered a dozen suggestions as to how his paper could be rescued, and Dave was sent out to do it all over again.

Only one thing saved Dave from total misery. As Dave left the room and began walking down the hall, he was greeted by Grant, a Ph.D. student who had at one time attended the same seminary where Dave was currently enrolled. He offered this consolation: "Don't worry about it. You just went through a rite of passage, that's all. And I will say this. Not too many people from seminary could even begin to tackle the kind of research that you have been doing."

At the General Conference in New Orleans, Nancy and Dave spent some time with the children that they were considering to adopt. They met them in the booth area, talked awkwardly for a couple of minutes, and then headed out for some burgers at McDonalds nearby. Dave was working hard to make a connection. He was animated, asking questions, genuinely interested in drawing out the children. He didn't want them to feel like puppies in the window of a pet store, but it was all very awkward as to what the children should even call them and that sort of thing. Everything had to be negotiated just to have a conversation.

Dave was in a take-charge mode and was doing so handily. As the conversation continued, Nancy warmed to the children. She had a soft spot for Chad, who was nine. He hadn't yet warmed to Dave, but Dave was making some progress with the girls. Maybe she and Dave had to divide and conquer. Maybe. Maybe the kids had "getting to know you" jitters. Maybe. In any case, Dave plowed ahead. He promised to write them all and explained that they would be able to meet at Nancy's parents for Thanksgiving.

Dave talked to Steve some more on the phone. "We're on a limited income," he explained to Steve. "These kids have beautiful clothes. I am a little concerned that they have an appetite for nice things, things which we will certainly not be able to buy them."

"Let me tell you my philosophy," returned Steve. "We do give kids things that are nice because we don't want them to return to some of the places where they came from. We want them to see that there is a better way to go than where they have come from, but it really doesn't matter what you can supply them with materially. What is important is a good home, and I know you can give them that.

"While it is true that children at the orphanage generally dream of 'Cinderella' kinds of adoptions where everything becomes a perfect world, no dream is ever met by reality. The adjustment that has to take place is all a part of the process, and it is a process in which there are no shortcuts. Still, these are wonderful kids. We just have to work through these things together. What is most important is that the children get established in a 'forever family.'"

It was the day before Thanksgiving. Nancy and Dave were greeted at the door by Nancy's dad, the retired Reverend James Abshire. "Hello there," he boomed in a voice that resonated welcome. Only that week, someone had asked him, "Did anyone tell you that you look like Senator Moynihan?"

"Yes, I have been told that," he responded in a dignified tone.

Nathaniel wasn't with them. They thought it better to leave him home. After they embraced, Nancy showed her mom the pictures of the kids. "Oh, they're beautiful," said her mom, genuinely happy.

Nancy and Dave had always been comfortable with Nancy's mom and dad. In fact, early in their marriage, for two years they had used their home in Chicago as their base for evangelizing. Never was there a time when they were not welcomed with open arms or made to feel a burden. Their home was a safe place to meet the kids. Further, because it was only two hours away from Tupelo, it was convenient for an orphanage staff member to drop them off on her way home for the holidays.

Later that afternoon, the doorbell rang. The lady from the orphanage had arrived with the children in tow. "Oh," said Nancy's mom in bubbling welcome, "You're as pretty as your pictures!" She pronounced the name of each child warmly. "So glad you are here." The lady from the orphanage left and there were the usual questions about likes and dislikes, school, church, but the children seemed to tire of this fairly quickly, and then came the challenge of what to do next. Nancy took the girls out to shop for a few last minute Thanksgiving items for the next day. While she was at the grocery store, Dave tried to interest Chad in some books. Neither event went over well.

Nancy stopped at a department store and Holly tried on dresses. Laura didn't see anything she liked and was indifferent to the whole enterprise. Supper at home was a little forced, and when Nancy got in bed that night, she announced, "I am bushed."

"It's hard," returned Dave. "We're just getting to know each other."

Thanksgiving morning was a little slow and finally Nancy's sister Cathy showed up from the motel where she was staying with her two daughters, Chrissy and Angela. Another sister, Jan, arrived with her little ones from across town. Their presence livened things up a little. Thanksgiving dinner was followed by a ball game in the backyard and table games that night. Nancy got into bed noting, "That was exhausting."

"It was a big day, but I think it was good," returned Dave.

"Chad sassed you."

"Yeah, he did. He said, 'You're not my father.' He was testing me to see if I would discipline him."

"Which you didn't," Nancy noted, a little agitated.

"It's tough when you have a big group."

"The kids laughed when my dad was saying grace."

"Well, they are not used to him. That's kids for you."

The next day brought on activities over at the hotel. Cathy had brought some games and the kids enjoying playing in the pool with Cathy's children. It was a long and busy day. That night, Nancy got into bed and was about to speak. "Don't say it. You're tired. So am I. Let's not talk about it."

On Sunday morning, there were pictures and hugs and good-byes as the children got ready to leave to go back to Tupelo. Nancy's dad prayed a blessing on them as the orphanage lady joined the circle. But the door to their house was no sooner shut than Nancy's mom announced abruptly, "I need to talk to you both in the other room right away." Dave turned, noting her urgency, and both he and Nancy followed her. She closed the door and then blurted out, "I have to say my piece right away. You simply cannot take those kids."

Dave was impressed. In all the years he had known this family, he couldn't remember a time when any advice had ever been issued to him and certainly nothing this direct. She continued, "I know you are parents of Nathaniel and that he can be hard to care for at times. But you have never really parented children who are going to talk back to you and disobey you and for whom you would have to work quite hard to establish discipline. I think you kids are wonderful, but you are not up to this challenge."

"I am not saying that you lack ability. You minister to hundreds of people all the time. You're in charge of a lot of things. But these children have already lived their formative years. They are already raised. You won't be able to really influence them that much. If I were you, I would really think about this."

Dave responded warmly. "Thank you for sharing with us things we should know. Nancy and I are still considering what to do, and your opinion means a lot to us. I do not take lightly anything you say."

"Well, what do you think?" asked Dave on the road back to Delaware.

Perhaps for the first time Nancy thought Dave might be open to listen. "I think my mom is right."

Back in Dover, Diana, Nathaniel's first school teacher, had just finished eating left-over turkey with her family for their Sunday dinner. Nathaniel had been with Diana for a couple of days now, and he was enjoying himself in family room, comfortably seated in a bean bag chair. The same group had gathered only three days before for Thanksgiving dinner, and Nathaniel had enjoyed that day as well. The room cheered as the Philadelphia Eagles scored on the big screen, and Nathaniel made happy sounds in response. Someone had found him a helium balloon, and he was attempting to see how many ways he could bite into it.

Chapter 23

"Mom, there's a gun in the restroom"

Nancy chatted easily with her friend, Rhonda, while at the same time wheeling Nathaniel through Dover Mall. The halls echoed with people hurrying into this or that store, and traffic flowed readily in each direction. Presently a lady coming from another direction veered over and began talking, not to Nancy, but to Nathaniel. Nancy didn't recognize her, but the lady didn't seem to care. Bending over his wheelchair, she said, "Well, hello there Nathaniel! Good to see you out and about." Nathaniel waved his hands in excited greeting and though Nancy was happy that Nathaniel was being appreciated, she wasn't quite sure how to account for this unexpected familiarity. Seeing her questioning look, the lady merely said, "Oh, we know Nathaniel from church… when Diana brings him." The lady then got up, waved good-bye, and walked on.

"Who was that!" challenged Rhonda defensively.

"Sometimes Nathaniel's school teacher does respite care for him when we go away on weekends. Of course, they take him to church with their families. I think Nathaniel has been to more churches in this city than we have."

Rhonda nodded, turning to see that no stranger was accosting her two children who were in tow. Eric was age seven and Elizabeth five. Nancy and Rhonda had brought them to the mall for a specific purpose. They were not there to shop. Tonight, they had come for a birthday party, Nathaniel's eighth birthday party to be exact. Nancy remarked, "I really think this is going to be better this year. No muss and fuss of cleanup at the house."

Rhonda agreed dutifully as they made their way into the McDonalds at the mall. A little area had been set up for Nathaniel's party. Nancy continued, "I mean we practically have this whole back area to ourselves. I know it's not totally private, but at least they do all the work for us." Another half-dozen children began straggling in along with their families. Ryan showed up, as did a couple more boys named Nathaniel and a few other families. Each child found playthings and color crayons at the tables and before long were working on their happy meals.

Presently their private party was interrupted as a tall, dark-haired man made his way through the tables on his way back to the restroom. He wore a dark brown jacket that steeled him from February in Delaware. Games were being served up as the man wove his way back out through the birthday gathering, but he didn't seem to notice the children as he made his way out the exit. Two minutes later, Eric tapped his mother on the shoulder and said, "Mom, there's a gun in the restroom." Rhonda became wide-eyed while Nancy immediately acted.

Nancy knocked on the side door used by staff members to get into the McDonald's kitchen. No one answered. She went around front and asked for the manager, who met her in back. "There's a gun in the men's restroom," she said urgently and went back to her seat. Cake was being served as the manager slipped through quietly and exited with a rifle in his hand. "Well, I guess we won't be coming here next year," Nancy said to Rhonda apologetically.

"I wonder," said Nancy later on the phone to Rhonda, "if that man was going to do some horrible thing, and perhaps he saw my Nathaniel and it softened his heart." Rhonda wisely agreed with Nancy that this could be a possibility. Nancy knew better than to offer these same theories to Dave. At times, he could be so unreasonable while Rhonda was always so much more sensible.

As springtime approached, Dave was almost always gone. He was working on his thesis and even had to stay over at the seminary on some weekends in order to complete it. He came home one Sunday night and Nancy announced to him as he came through the door, "We're going out on a date this Friday night."

"I can't," said Dave. "I am way behind. I was supposed to have my thesis half-done by the end of last semester but I spent all my time on that paper for Temple. Now I am drowning."

"All the more reason to go out," noted Nancy. "It's arranged. Connie will babysit. We can go to that Italian restaurant downtown. We'll get some pizza. Come on," she offered, snuggling up to him, "we need to keep the romance alive."

Dave ultimately warmed to the suggestion of keeping the romance alive and thought that it would, after all, be a good idea. He even seemed to relax some on the way to the restaurant. They found a remote corner booth. Soft music was playing and because there were only a few people around, the restaurant seemed even cozier. Nancy snuggled closely as they waited for their salads. It had turned dark outside, but there was something wrong with the ambiance. Suddenly Nancy realized what it was. The room was simply too bright.

Fortunately, at the same time she discovered the problem, a solution presented itself. "Dave," she whispered in conspiratorial tone. "Do you see that dimmer on the wall behind you?" He did. "Well now, my hunka-bunka burning love, why don't you turn that dimmer down just a little?"

Dave gave her a sideways glance, leaned over and whispered softly into her ear, "How about if I don't?"

That was the problem with Dave. He just had no sense of adventure. Those cold Minnesota winters he suffered as a child had somehow gotten into his blood. She leaned over again and with a saccharine sweet plea intoned, "Please...."

Once more he returned the favor, whispering softly into her ear. He engagingly pronounced, "Noooo...."

Nancy could see that he was not going to be cooperative and decided that it was time to take matters into her own hands. She leaned past him and turned down the dimmer herself. Immediately, the overhead lights darkened and the candle on their table danced more brightly from within its glass enclosure. The effect was multiplied throughout the restaurant where soft candlelight on every table romanced the patrons. A lady at another table smiled appreciatively at the gesture.

But very soon Nancy heard loud angry chatter booming out from the kitchen as four people poured through the door into the restaurant, two of them with chef hats on. The verbal hubbub between themselves continued as they came over en masse to the booth where Nancy and Dave sat. One of them turned the dimmer back up to its original position and the restaurant went back to its original bright light. While she was never sure how she did it, somehow Nancy had turned the lights out in the kitchen.

When they returned to the house it was dark and cold. Connie was missing. So was Nathaniel. Dave looked into the fireplace that had been roaring when they left but there was no fire. This was curious. There was always a fire. The fireplace had an insert and blower. It was what they used to heat the home. Dave felled trees from the woods behind the house with a chain saw borrowed from Robert, the dorm supervisor. Dave wasn't too good with it and sometimes didn't have time to split the logs, but this was generally remedied with some help from college students. But there was no fire. No lights. No Connie and no Nathaniel.

The phone rang. It was Jeanette, Wayne and Janet's daughter, calling from her house in front. "I saw you pull up. You missed all the excitement."

"All the excitement?" said Nancy.

"Yes, the fire trucks and hoses and water. It's all cleaned up, but you had a chimney fire with fire shooting straight out the top of the chimney."

"Really? Where is Nathaniel?" asked Nancy.

"Over at Mom and Dad's with Connie."

They collected Connie and Nathaniel along with advice that had been passed on from the fire chief: "Don't use green wood, get the chimney cleaned more, and don't make such big fires."

Dave should have graduated in May, but the registrar made a mistake and told him it would be okay to take a class that she decided later would not count toward graduation. One class short, he decided to just do an independent study over the summer and graduate the following May. That was fine with Nancy, though she had been looking forward to the summer being free of classes. Dave was home most of the summer in any case.

In the morning he spent time with this year's set of junior quizzers. The one who needed the most encouragement to study was Sue's son Eric. Dave tended to bribe him with McDonalds and lots of attention. Kevin was also on the team. When Eric and Kevin got together, the hyperactivity quotient in the room was on the dangerous side. They weren't bad boys, but they simply could not sit still. Christine anchored the quiz team and because she was light years ahead of them in maturity, provided a needed balance.

National playoffs were at the headquarters building in August, and Dave coped with the laughing, giggling, and horseplay on the trip to St. Louis. This was his second year to take a Dover team to the national playoffs. He got them a fast-food fix after they dropped off their luggage; then they headed to the playoffs. A minister friend was leaving the denomination's headquarters building with a group of other suited gentlemen when he saw Dave entering the building with his charges. "What's this?" he said, pointing to Dave's casual clothes.

"Well," said Dave in turn, "I have diplomatic immunity because I am here with junior quizzing. Besides," he said, pointing to his sunglasses, "I am incognito."

When Dave walked through the door, Kevin and Eric were already at work. Kevin was doing a rap song rhyme-time about how good the acoustics were in the lobby. As Kevin was tap dancing the rhythm in conjunction with the rap he was making up, Eric was leaping over the thick velour cord draped regally between the brass poles. "This must be three and a half feet high," Eric announced loudly as he jumped— the very moment that the general superintendant walked through the lobby. Dave really wanted to control the boys. He sincerely wanted to model accountability to them. His ideal was that he would demonstrate steel and velvet as he formed the next generation. However, at that moment, Dave could only think of one strategy that might work seemed like the beginning of a crisis. He turned and walked back outside as if he had never seen these unruly boys before in his life. Dave was never sure what might have been inside the building that day. Perhaps nothing. Still, although Dave was never sure whether it was a coincidence or not, the next year they moved the junior quizzing finals from the headquarters building to a hotel.

"Nancy, you need to get more age-appropriate toys for Nathaniel," said Cathy, Nancy's sister, when she visited her in Washington D. C.

"What do you mean?" asked Nancy.

"Come on. He's eight-and-a-half-years-old. He's too old for that rattle."

"But he likes the noise it makes, and he can transfer it from one hand to another." A couple years earlier, Cathy was the one who had suggested that Nancy replace Nathaniel's bibs with bandanas. The bandanas certainly had been effective in catching the dribble just as nicely. Otherwise, he drooled until his shirt was soaked. Nathaniel went through quite a few bandanas during the course of the day, but they were better than bibs.

"How about one of those plastic sticks that makes noise when you swing it?"

"I don't know what you mean, but I'll check into it," said Nancy.

Just that week, Nancy headed to her annual IEP review, the meeting where the school planned the goals for Nathaniel for the following year. She went dutifully, but the meetings all ended up the same. Every year, the goals were the same as the previous year. Nathaniel had made very little progress. Although Nathaniel was at six to eight months socially, physically he was much lower. He didn't turn over, couldn't crawl, and he didn't communicate verbally. At least that is what they said.

Nancy was more certain that he did communicate, even though he didn't talk. He had little sounds that he made in the morning when he was awake and wanted attention. If there was no one to come and pick him up right away, the noises would increase in volume and intensity. He had happy sounds, complaining noises, and noises just to say he was part of a conversation. Nancy was sure that he said "Mama" several times. It happened when he was in pain. She told Dave, but he remained skeptical.

"Mrs. Norris," said one of the teachers from school. "We have good news and bad news." Several teachers, an occupational therapist, physical therapist, and others all sat around the table reviewing the previous year and laying out plans for the current school year.

"What is it?" said Nancy.

"Well, we are trying to teach Nathaniel stimulus/response; that is, we are trying to show him that if he does a certain thing, a particular result will follow. We put headphones on Nathaniel, and we have three buttons that Nathaniel can hit for music. One button gives him classical music, one button gives him country music, and one button gives him rock music. The good news is that Nathaniel loves music. The bad news is that he only likes rock music."

Nancy functioned fairly well in emergencies. When Nathaniel had to be admitted to A. I. duPont Hospital, she started bringing decorations and potpourri, and sometimes she even brought puppets to help encourage other patients. But she was no supermom. In fact, she was under so much stress most of the time, that at any given moment, the daily routine might suddenly become overwhelming. Particularly when challenge quickly followed challenge, Nancy could feel herself sinking. When this happened, sometimes Dave was there for her, but sometimes he was not.

It was that time of year when Nathaniel was supposed to go up to A. I. duPont on successive days for a series of tests. She asked Dave if he could take him one day. He could not. Nor was there any other help available. By the third day she was exhausted both physically and emotionally.

"Are you sure you can't go with me today?"

"Nancy, I have classes. In fact, I have to hurry to catch a ride so you can have the car."

"Could you just for once get a substitute?"

"Nancy, it's my job!"

"And what am I? Chopped liver?" she snapped. With that he was out the door as the car picking him up for the day drove into the driveway. He didn't say "I love you," as he walked out the door. He always said "I love you." She hadn't said "I love you" either. She was now alone in the house looking at a full day of caring for Nathaniel and his needs. Today, those needs seemed like a whole lot to carry.

She had wanted to talk to Dave about her loneliness and how hard it was, but he was just too busy to listen. Fall was a hard time for her anyway. She couldn't put her finger on why, but this time of year she took a dip emotionally.

Nancy started to cry. She cried as she packed diapers into Nathaniel's bag. She cried as she put his formula in a giant syringe. Nathaniel was heavier today as she carried him in his blue chair and put him in the front seat of the car. She played Christian music in the car as they went, but today it didn't speak to her at all.

The trip to the hospital took an hour. They had another twenty-five minutes to go when Nathaniel started crying. She didn't know why he was crying, whether he was wet, hungry, or in pain. It didn't matter. She didn't have the patience for it. "Shush, Nathaniel. Please shush." He didn't. He just grew louder. And cried longer. For ten minutes he cried, but she didn't have time to stop and hold him.

Most days it was enough that Nathaniel was alive, that he was not in the hospital, and that he had already lived longer than some of the statistics from the books pronounced. But today was not one of those days. Suddenly, Nancy felt absolutely overwhelmed, engulfed in a feeling of hopelessness. Then something occurred to her as she began to notice bridge abutments that they passed. She said, "You know, Nathaniel, maybe Daddy would just be better off without us." She wondered how quickly she would have to slam into the abutment to make certain that it would all be over so that Dave could get on with doing things for the Lord without her and Nathaniel as a bother. She was going about sixty. Tears streamed down her face. But she kept driving.

Nancy struggled to get Nathaniel out of the car. She lifted his car seat into a kind of stroller, strapping the two pieces together to function as Nathaniel's wheelchair. Immediately after getting inside the building, Nancy headed to the changing room where she lifted Nathaniel up onto a larger Formica table. Nathaniel was heavier than a fifty-pound sack of potatoes and was just as much dead weight. Nancy got him changed and put back into the chair. She opened a can of formula and poured it into a syringe so that Nathaniel could get a dump feeding to keep him hydrated. She was late for her first appointment, and she spilled some formula and had to wipe it up. Finally, she stood wearily to determine what section of the hospital she had to go to find the gastrointestinologist. She had never felt so alone. It was like everyone in the world had abandoned her.

Then something unexpected happened. She heard someone calling her name from across the busy lobby. But it really couldn't be, because she had been up there for two whole days and had not seen anyone who knew her. Yet once again she heard the voice. There *was* someone calling to her. She turned to see a lady whom she had met only briefly. She was from the church pastored by Wayne and Janet in North East, Maryland, thirty miles away. The lady crossed the lobby and was coming toward her.

245

Nancy didn't really know her, but she was glad for the welcoming voice. Someone who knew her name. Someone who wanted to know why she was there. And because of the warmth she showed her son, Nancy felt supported in her own care for Nathaniel.

It is impossible to identify ahead of time those unique moments when simple kindness turns into a priceless gift. And the people who give that kindness can never quite understand the value of what has been bestowed. However, at that moment, this warmth did not at all feel coincidental. Nancy was remembered, and not just by a human companion. These few simple gestures reminded her, when she needed to be reminded, that she did not struggle alone.

It was the gift of love to her son. It was the gift of words. It was a gift of a warm embrace. She still had the same burden of the day ahead of her, but ever so slowly Nancy felt her loneliness begin to lift.

Chapter 24
"You sided with others... that's why..."

Nancy tied a Mylar helium balloon to Nathaniel's chair as she worked around the kitchen. He immediately began to bat at the string with his right hand. If after considerable and repeated effort he could get the ribbon that suspended it wound around his hand, he would then pull the balloon down, wrestle with it, lick it, and try to bite it. After ten or fifteen minutes he would then have silver from the balloon all over his face. Nathaniel had succeeded with phase one and two and presently held the balloon in his hands. One side was silver and the other side had a cartoon character pronouncing, "Happy Birthday."

"Not now," said Nancy in mock rebuke. "You want to look nice when the kids come over for your party tonight." She unwound the string from his hand while Nathaniel laughed at his own ingenuity.

Nancy was putting nine candles on the cake when the phone rang in the other room, and Dave, who was sitting in front of the fireplace, picked it up. "Hello," he said.

"Dave, this is Joanne." It was unusual to have his sister call him. Joanne was the youngest of four sisters, a full nine years younger than him. Dave wondered if something was wrong.

"I called to tell you about Dad," said Joanne.

"Oh?"

"Yeah," she continued. "You know he has always been in pretty good health. He never missed work, no matter what. Well, this past December when he retired, he thought he was fighting off a bad cold, but when they admitted him to the hospital for pneumonia, they discovered that his lungs were full of cancer."

Dave was stunned. "So, it's pretty bad, then?"

"Very bad. They don't give him much hope."

"So, is he in the hospital?"

"Yeah." There was a pause.

"Would it be okay if I came up to see him?"

"Dave, you know how things are around here. I think it would be better if you didn't." Joanne wasn't vindictive. She had never been unkind to him. She had no agenda. Dave accepted what she said.

"So what's the prognosis?" Dave asked, wanting more details.

"Well, they are going to try a couple of things, but it sounds like they are probably only giving him months to live, maybe weeks."

"I'm sorry. But thanks for calling."

They received the call in April. Dave's dad would probably live only another day or two. Dave and Nancy flew up to St. Paul and immediately went to the hospital. His oldest sister Barb was still flying in from Ohio, but his sister Pat, eleven months his senior, had been in town for a couple of days with her kids. They were staying with an aunt. Linda, three years younger, stood in the waiting room with her husband Tony. Joanne was also in the waiting room. Bob, Dave's younger brother by six years, was in the hospital room with David Sr. A couple of little nephews and nieces roamed freely in the waiting area. As in all family tragedies, tension hung in the air. Presently Bob came out to the waiting room, solemn.

"Not much longer," he said to Dave. They stood silent for a time, and then Bob offered, "Hey look, Dave, I've got to tell you something. You know Dad never had a will. Well, someone has a lawyer in there, helping Dad make out a will."

"Yeah."

"Yeah, well… uh… I don't know how to tell you this. But when the lawyer asked Dad if he wanted everything to be equally divided among his six children, Dad told the lawyer, 'I only have five children.'"

Dave stood, staring, not quite able to receive this. Bob continued talking—attempting to explain the sequence of events that had led to this—but Dave had already lost focus. The conversation had just moved from reality to unreality. Finally, Dave looked up just as Bob was saying, "And so that's how it happened."

A little while later, Dave and Bob went down to the room to see their dad. He was lying on his side, and because he was so hot, he had his shirt off.

Dave said, "Hey Dad, Nancy and I flew in this afternoon. We just got in a little bit ago."

His dad acknowledged his greeting. Dave continued, "Dad, I am sorry for any thing that I have done to hurt you. I want you to forgive me."

"Apology accepted. All is forgiven."

It seemed a relief for Dave's dad to hear and say those words, the last words Dave would hear from him. David Sr. died that night.

The next night, the evening before the funeral, the family house bulged with siblings and children of siblings. Dave sought out his sister Pat. Hers was the opinion that mattered to him. For Dave, Pat was the spiritual and moral leader of the family, and he needed to see if she understood. But she did not. Things had been said, accusations had swirled. She began to share what was reported. Some of what she'd heard was partly true, some not at all. But Pat wasn't listening, not tonight. "The point is," she offered, "you sided with others against your grandfather. That's why Dad wouldn't talk to you."

Dave challenged, "Pat, I wasn't siding with anyone." She looked at him disbelievingly, challenging him to explain. Dave had kept a file—a record of events that would arguably justify himself. He had placed it safely in his desk drawer in his office. After a time, though, the file seemed to rest heavy in the drawer. It contained nothing of a legal nature. He was just hoarding hurts. One day, he threw it away and felt better for it.

Pat stood waiting. "It simply is not true," Dave offered once more without any justification. Even to him the protest sounded weak. He and Pat had always been close. She never wavered from her faith in Christ. She was his mentor. He remembered times when she chided him for laziness or not being spiritual enough, but she was also his greatest promoter and helper. She and Dave had been leaders together in the youth group. He never remembered a time when they were not on the same page when it came to any moral issue.

There had been the usual sparring previously that night when Dave came into the family home, the teasing about him renting a nice car and his not staying with family. Family values dictated that one did not spend money unnecessarily. This sort of teasing was routine, but the banter and sarcastic remarks cut more deeply tonight. When Dave ushered Nancy out the door to the car, he knew he left condemned in his sister's eyes, and most certainly in the eyes of his other siblings.

"I'm not sure if I'm going to be able to make it," said Dave as he was driving to the church for the funeral the next day. Read me something from the Bible, something from the Psalms.

Nancy tried to find the psalm that matched the date of the month and read, pausing only when she came to verse ten. Finally, she choked out the words, "When my father and my mother forsake me, then the LORD will take me up." Tears flowed down her cheeks and Dave sobbed heavily, still driving toward the church.

Dave was used to feeling wanted and needed. He was not used to stares, mumbled whispers, or innuendos. Today, supporters were few. Jim came from West Bend and stood with him, even though Dave knew it would cost him some friendships.

Dave wasn't sure what he felt for his dad. He would have to sort it all out later. Now, he just felt numb. Anecdotes were shared and nuanced references were made, and politicizing things spilled out, even at the funeral. One man said of Dave's dad, "Dave knew who he could trust." It was a purposeful barb. Dave simply wanted to leave.

Dave had known some significant inner hurt when Nathaniel was born, but today he felt like there were elephants walking across his chest. He had the sensation of drowning, going down for the last time. And just when he thought he couldn't take any more, something additional would be said. He never wanted to see his family again. Any of them.

Some time after they had returned home, Dave noticed a book on his nightstand called *The Blessing*. Nancy had put it there. Dave was usually reading several books at once, so Nancy knew that all she had to do was lay a book out and it was guaranteed to be read. He casually picked it up and began scanning the chapters. Fifteen minutes later he read to her excitedly. "Nance, listen to this...." She turned as he explained the biblical concept of a blessing, something he hadn't really considered before. "It's like this book was written just for me." Nancy listened attentively and went back to her magazine. Dave always did better when he discovered things for himself. "And look at this chapter; it explains what to do if you were not blessed by significant people in your life." He read some more, and then presently offered, "I never thought of it before, but I see that my dad was never able to bless me." He read on and suddenly blurted out, "He couldn't say 'I love you.' Maybe when I was little... I don't remember. No, I don't think so. And he couldn't say, 'I'm proud of you.'" Dave sat and stared... just reflecting. "Did I ever tell you that my dad didn't come to my high school graduation?"

"No."

"I spoke—and another time, John, my quiz coach, did everything in his power to get my dad to say, 'I'm proud of you.' I was standing there, and he says to my dad, 'You know, your son is a pretty good Bible quizzer.' He paused and waited. Finally, when my dad knew he had to say something, he said, 'Yeah, I just wish he would clean his room a bit more.'"

Dave read on in the chapter. "Oh, wow. It says here that a lack of blessing is a generational problem—that's true. My grandfather couldn't bless my dad. But my grandfather couldn't give that kind of personal blessing because he never got one. He didn't get a blessing from his dad because his dad was killed when he was little. It's hard to pass on what you don't receive. It's funny. My grandfather was an incredible minister, he was always doing great things, and still, personally, he was not able to give out that kind of personal affirmation. Dave read some more... and then offered soberly, "You know, I am just like them."

Nancy countered, "No you're not."

"But I am. They gave conditional blessings... if you pleased them they offered material blessings, but if you didn't, then...."

"You wouldn't disinherit your son," remarked Nancy.

"It's all a matter of degree. You know, Nancy, I really don't have time for people who aren't doing right. I give conditional blessings all the time." He turned and smiled at her. This time she didn't argue with him. She smiled back. Dave stared thoughtfully, and then offered, "I wonder what it would be like to bless people unconditionally? I wonder if I could start doing that?"

Dave needed to travel that summer and had told Nancy so. He had a specific idea of what he wanted to do. Dave resurrected a drama he had written in Wisconsin on the life of Joseph. Earlier that year, a group from the college performed the "Dare to Dream" drama for a children's rally, utilizing a cast of thirty. After they performed it, Dave reported to Nancy, "I want to travel with a half dozen kids. I could do this same drama in churches. I'll just bring the lead actors."

"Where will you get the rest of the cast?"

"From the church where we would perform."

"Well, how will they know what to do?"

"I don't know. I suppose we could go a day early and have a dress rehearsal. We could bring the costumes with us."

"But how will that work?"

"I'm not sure yet, but I think it will be good. I need to do this." Dave had that look in his eye, the one where it was difficult to argue. She agreed, even though he would be gone for weeks.

The summer would also provide Dave some time to begin journaling in an attempt to work through his issues with his family. Before he left for tour, he had talked with Nancy about some of the things that were said and done at the funeral. He named different things, saying, "Perhaps they really didn't mean it."

Nancy answered sharply, "They meant to hurt you. They said what they meant. Deal with it." So Dave attempted to own hurt and bring offenses to the surface so he could work through forgiveness. He didn't get as far very far in the process that was just so painful. While his heart told him he wasn't making progress, his head reminded him that he was at least using the words of forgiveness and blessing in his prayers. He didn't think he meant these words and told God so, but at least he was saying them.

Dave called every few days to give a progress report. "So how did last night's performance go?" asked Nancy.

"Great," said Dave, not coughing up too many details. Nancy was curious how they were able to pull off coming to a church, having a dress rehearsal with brand new actors one day and then doing the performance the next day.

"So how do you do this, anyway?" she asked. "I mean, how does a youth group learn a play in one practice?"

Dave happily charted out the strategy. "Well, the actors never really know what is going to happen until they see it being performed in the play. We only practice the lines that they need to know for sure. Joel gets the guys who are going to be Joseph's brothers and works with them. Michael gets with the slave trader and others and teaches them lines. Colin sets up the backdrops. Brenda and Shanna work with the girls, while Shane works with the ending."

"So what do you do while all this is going on?"

"Unless there is a crisis, I am having coffee with the pastor."

Nancy laughed. "Is there a crisis often?"

"There haven't been too many so far. And Nance—I am getting pretty close to the kids."

"I'm glad."

"Every week when I give them their allowance, I write them a blessing letter. I affirm their gifts and dreams, and tell them how special they are."

"Why don't you just tell them out loud."

"I'm working up to it."

"So what state are you in now?"

"Southern Minnesota. We're performing at the church where my sister Joanne and her husband are working."

"And that's good?"

"Really good. Hey, my sister Pat called."

"And that's good?"

"It's sorta good."

"Oh, tell me about it."

"Well, she's mad because this weekend I'm going to Robert's church in St. Paul. I said, 'Look, that's the church I grew up in. I've got a boatload of friends I haven't talked to in six years in order to keep peace in the family, but that didn't work very well, did it? How much more disinherited can I get?'"

"What did she say to that?"

"We agreed to disagree. She's bringing some of her kids to the play tonight, driving three hours to get here. Maybe there can be some healing."

After a few weeks, Dave returned home. Nancy listened to some funny stories from tour, but she could tell Dave had something else on his mind. Eventually, he shared it. He began, "Nancy, I've got to tell you something."

"Alright."

"Well, in the story of Joseph, Joseph gets betrayed by his brothers, sold as a slave, framed by Potiphar's wife, and then winds up saving the nation. He reconciles with his brothers at the end."

"Right...."

"At the end, Colin gets out of the character of Joseph and tells a story about a little boy who had asthma and couldn't run and play with his friends outside or participate in athletics. He takes five minutes to tell it, but the little boy eventually overcomes obstacles and competes in races, eventually winning a medal in an international race. Then he pulls the medal out and says, 'I was that little boy.' Anyway, he makes an appeal for children and young people to believe in the dreams that God gives them."

"I saw Colin give that appeal in Dover," Nancy reminded Dave.

"Well, anyway, I've been praying for kids all summer to believe in their dreams, and I've been a little convicted by not believing in my own."

"Are you talking about you doing a doctoral program?"

"Yeah. I know I said we can't afford it, and that it really wouldn't work with all the administrative things I have to do at the college, but I would at least like to send out the applications and see if someone would give me money. I mean, I don't know if this is just my idea or if it is maybe a dream that God has for me. But I think I need to at least give it a try."

"Hmmm... we are going to have to talk more. Let's just think about it for now."

255

Chapter 25

"Code blue! Code blue!"

"**S**haron's church is getting rid of a chair that goes up and down stairs," said Nancy.

"Pretty smart chair," returned Dave in what Nancy deemed to be some sort of sarcastic retort. He had been back from tour for a week, and though she had missed him, she thought that the tour had done him some good. He seemed more at peace with himself.

"No," said Sharon. "It's an electric chair."

"I take it your church isn't against capital punishment?" teased Dave.

"It's electric. It plugs in. It is a chair that rides a track. When you press one button, it glides up the stairs, and when you press the other, it comes back down."

"Oh," said Dave. "Now I get it." If she were someone else, Dave wouldn't have persecuted her. But it was Sharon. She was more than just their nurse. She had loved Nathaniel for years, and most of the time that they lived in Dover she had dutifully come by in the morning and afternoon to care for him. Nancy and Dave had also had occasion to celebrate Sharon's children. Getting updates, going to a child's play, a daughter's wedding—these were all experiences in Sharon's family that Nancy and Dave had felt privileged to share.

Sharon continued, "I don't know if it could be adjusted to the stairs here, but it probably could." Sharon was very petite. And Nathaniel was no small chunk of change. A ride up the stairs to his bedroom would save her back considerably.

"Do you know anyone handy who can put it in?" Sharon asked.

"'Joe Electrician' at your service," said Dave, and Nancy just laughed. If people were building something or doing work that required a skill, they generally tried to keep Dave away from the project. When they built the new dorm on the campus, he had been rightfully assigned to dump truck duty, just to keep him as far away from the building and power tools as possible.

"Yeah, so Nathaniel's fifty-five pounds," Dave told Glenn. "And I've got this 'electric chair' a church will give me, but I just don't know if it's going to work."

"Would it fit in a pick up truck?" asked Glenn.

"I think the track would hang over, but your truck would work."

"You can borrow my truck then."

"Well, that's the least of my issues."

"What do you mean?"

Dave explained his lack of skills, and Glenn, who was talented all the way around, said he would see what he could do to help. Whether he had expertise or not, Dave couldn't say for sure, but he certainly knew more than Dave did. So while Dave held this or that thing in place, Glenn lined up the tracks, drilled things in and then wired them up.

First the chair was sent up and down the stairs by itself, and then Sharon rode in the chair, testing how effective it would be for its intended purpose. Finally Sharon did a test run up the stairs with Nathaniel in her arms. He loved it. His arms were flailing and he was making happy noises all the way up.

Dave smiled. "I'm telling you, Sharon, in Nathaniel's book, Disney World has nothing on that chair. Thank you for telling us about it. And Glenn, thanks for making this happen."

Dave was coming to understand that ministry was more than he had been making it. It involved blessing people, something that he wasn't doing enough. The problem was that his roles didn't seem to readily complement his opportunity to bless others. He was the disciplinarian for the school. His classes were based on grades. If someone did well, they passed. If not, they flunked; it was their problem, not his. But maybe it was his problem. As Dave worked on his syllabi, he tried to figure out ways, where it would be natural to write blessings to his students. He would have to think about it a bit more. Perhaps he could offer more on graded papers.

The first day of class arrived and Dave presented his syllabus. He said something new, and he wasn't even sure if he believed it. He wanted to believe it. "And so the most important thing to me is that everyone in this class is successful. If you are successful, then I am successful. And if you fail this class, then that means that I have failed." Dave was beginning to believe what he saying, but his head was working hard to catch up with his heart.

Nancy taught "The Role of a Minister's Wife" as an elective in college. Jim had tried to get her to change the course to "Women in Ministry" but she refused. She had a specified curriculum that she wanted to teach that mirrored some of her own life experiences. "If someone else wants to teach that other course, fine. But not me." She insisted, "I'm a minister's wife!" Jim let it go.

Nancy's teaching style was inspirational and innovative. Students never knew what the class would bring. Because Nancy always had trouble sitting still in school, she made sure her class always had plenty of activities and her students always had permission to talk. Nancy's philosophy was that learning could absolutely take place in hubbub. There should be a lot of laughing in class and a lot of crying. One of Dave's friends had dubbed Nancy's class the "color and cry" class. But Nancy didn't merely have students. She had heart friends.

An official from the Home Missions Division had called Dave from St. Louis and wanted him to be on a committee to create more emphasis on church planting in Bible colleges. He was gone for three days and Nancy picked him up at the airport. "How was it?" asked Nancy, after she got her welcome kiss.

"Terrible," said Dave. "They put us in this cheesy little hotel right by the headquarters building. The blanket had a cigarette hole and the shower nozzle came up only slightly higher than my navel. And the water was cold."

"Sounds like fun. Anything else come of it?"

"Well, they want me to write a book of some sort."

"You must have talked too much."

Dave smiled sheepishly. She knew she was right. "So what about that new book you said you were going to write this fall, the allegory about Jesus? Haven't you already started on it?"

"Well, I'll just have to put it on hold until this other book is finished."

"The man in demand," she offered with more than a little edge. She was hoping that while Dave wasn't in school there might be a bit more time for her and Nathaniel.

Dave had his secretary send out ten applications to graduate schools all over the country. He didn't explain why he would be applying to schools in California, Texas, Chicago, Indiana, Philadelphia, and New Jersey. Dave knew that Barb was discreet. And she never asked if he was planning to leave or why he was sending away the applications for doctoral programs.

Several years earlier, a doctor at A. I. duPont first pointed out the problem. Nathaniel had curvature of the spine, and it was a problem that was getting worse with each passing year. "We need to put a rod in his back," the doctor had said.

"Sounds like major surgery," replied Nancy.

"It is."

"Then we'll wait," said Nancy. They had waited several years. Now, the doctor said that if they waited longer, it would be very difficult to correct. So they scheduled the surgery. The morning of the surgery, the surgeon told Nancy and Dave how long they could expect the procedure to take, the length of time in recovery, his time in the ICU, and how long Nathaniel would have to stay in the hospital. He sounded confident, and so they signed the papers.

Nothing went according to plan. Nathaniel was a lot longer in surgery and a lot longer in recovery. Then they took him up to Intensive Care. He didn't look well. In fact, Nancy was afraid of how poorly he looked and was upset with herself for being so casual about the whole operation. Because Nathaniel was often in the hospital, they hadn't even requested that the church pray for his surgery. Her thinking had been that if they put in a prayer request every time something was going on with Nathaniel, the church would never stop hearing about him.

Because Nathaniel might be in the ICU for several days, Dave stayed at home and commuted to the hospital while Nancy stayed in Wilmington at the newly opened Ronald McDonald House, a place created for parents to stay while their children were in the hospital at A. I. duPont.

"How is he?" said Dave, entering the room where Nancy sat uneasily on a chair.

"The same," offered Nancy. The suite where she had been staying was very nice. Because it was Friday, Dave had driven up to spend the weekend.

"They have supper downstairs," Nancy explained. "It's provided by one of the local restaurants."

"That's nice," replied Dave. After he polished off some lasagna from Olive Garden, they headed over to the Intensive Care Unit.

A person could not simply walk into this section of the hospital unbidden. As doctors approached this wing of the hospital, even they had to hit some code keys along the wall in order for a buzzer to signal the door to open. Dave went over to the intercom and pressed the button while Nancy looked through the panels of glass in the door and waited to be invited in. She could see a nurses' station and then a bit further down the hall, the door to Nathaniel's room.

"Mr. and Mrs. Norris, to see Nathaniel," Dave announced loudly. The door buzzed and Nancy pressed down the latch and pushed open one of the large double doors. They nodded to the nurse and walked into the single room where Nathaniel lay on the hospital bed. His eyelids were drooping half-open. Nathaniel's face was ashen. Leads were secured to his chest. Methodic beeps accompanied by squiggly lines on a screen announced Nathaniel's heartbeats. A nurse came and went but said little. The doctor who was on call that morning had been a rather taciturn lady. She was hardly a fount of information. No news was forthcoming, no new prognosis, no plan for the future. The beeping continued as Nancy held Nathaniel's hand.

"I thought he was only supposed to be in the intensive care unit for a day after the surgery," said Dave.

"Well, doctors don't know everything," said Nancy.

"Yeah, but Nance... he's been in ICU for about four days and nobody is talking. He is just not getting any better."

"We shouldn't have had this surgery," said Nancy, a tear rolling down her cheek.

"We've put it off for two years. He needed to have that rod put in."

"But they said it wouldn't be a problem."

"I know."

The atmosphere was so thick with waiting. After forty-five minutes, Nancy and Dave left to get something to drink. They entered the parents' lounge where a vending machine was located. Nobody else was there.

"He doesn't look good," said Dave, flatly.

"Yeah, but he'll get better," said Nancy, too energetically.

Dave continued, "Do you remember that little booklet that Dr. Hermann gave us on Cri du Chat babies? Nathaniel was in the category of those missing that critical part of chromosome number five; still, Nathaniel has done very well, hasn't he?"

"Dave, he's gonna get better. He just is!"

"I know, but I was just thinking that—"

"Code blue! Code blue!" The speaker announced loudly. "Doctor, STAT. Intensive Care Unit." There was commotion in the hall as a flurry of people flew by the doorway down to the double doors.

"What's code blue?" asked Dave to Nancy.

She didn't bother responding but charged out the door behind the commotion, rushing toward the double doors of the emergency room. Several personnel were already entering inside. The last man restrained her. "You can't go in there, Ma'am."

"Yes, but my son…." The door shut in her face. Two more doctor-type people were jogging down the hall toward the door. Nancy looked through the glass and saw that in fact, the commotion was entering Nathaniel's room.

"That's my son! That's my son!" she yelled at the guy who was pressing the code to get into the unit. He had a strained look on his face but ignored her plea. "Out of the way, Ma'am. Please! Let us do our job."

Nancy hurried back to the parent's lounge. "Dave, it's Nathaniel! It's Nathaniel. They won't let us in."

Dave dialed the church in Dover. It was Friday night. There was choir practice. They needed help praying right away! Thankfully someone answered.

Nancy paced and prayed. Dave sat with his head in his hands. He didn't talk. He didn't say a word. "Jesus… Jesus… Jesus…" Nancy whispered. Whatever Dave was doing, he wasn't doing it audibly. He just sat and stared at the floor.

Because the emergency was handled by whatever doctors were handy, if there had been some set procedure to talk to parents, none of them seemed to know it. Nancy never really knew if and when the crisis was over. After a while clumps of medical people walked out of ICU, but all of them ignored them. And after a couple of hours, Nancy and Dave were allowed in by the nurse to see Nathaniel, but no one was present to officially debrief the distraught mom and dad. This upset Dave as much as anything else. Nathaniel looked worse by far than they had seen him the last time. "What crazy doctor ordered this stupid operation in the first place," Dave complained angrily to no one in particular, the closest Nancy ever heard him get to swearing.

Slowly but surely, Nathaniel got better. The leaves had turned golden when he went into the hospital and by the time he got out, they had lost their prettiness. Though he seemed sore and cried a lot, he did come home. The weeks that Nancy had spent in Ronald McDonald House were over, and she was home too.

Dave was on the couch looking at the fireplace, a stack of letters on the coffee table. Nancy looked down at them. They were from various universities—responses to his applications for the doctoral program. "Will anybody give you money?" she asked.

"Some of these programs will."

"Which is the best one?" she asked, just a little fearful of what might happen next.

"Well, I'd like to go to Temple," he said. "That way, I could still teach here at the college."

"How would that work?" asked Nancy.

"Well, I have a plan, but I'm just not sure that Janet will like it."

"Have you talked to her about it?"

"I see her tomorrow."

"So you don't think she will approve it?"

"I think she'll probably tell me that if I want to do a doctoral program, I won't have time to do what really needs to be done here."

"And she would have a point, wouldn't she?" said Nancy.

"We'll just have to see what happens," said Dave.

Chapter 26

"See, Nathaniel—she dedicated this book to you"

Dave buckled his seatbelt for the take off. The wheels shuddered just a second or two and then they were aloft. He was going to Jamaica. He had been to the villa on several occasions for staff retreats, but this trip was different. Very different. He wouldn't be staying long, less than forty-eight hours. The scary thing was that his future would be determined by what happened in these next forty-eight hours. Jim, academic dean and fellow student in seminary, sat next to him. He, too, had life issues that would be decided in this short window of time.

The warm tropical air rolled into the plane as soon as the flight attendant opened the door. Dave and Jim threaded through the taxis to get to the car that picked them up and brought them to the villa. They would not be staying at Janet's villa that night. They were down the hill, at the villa of that guy who owned the limo company. The next morning they came up for the big meeting. Dave was meeting the board of the college. They had already been meeting for several days, so he was late on their agenda.

Dave read from a prepared text of five single-spaced pages. Most of it was an argument for advanced education. Only toward the end did he begin to explain what he wanted to do. "And so, I have been accepted by several schools around the country, and in some cases I have opportunity for scholarship money. Several universities are within driving distance of other Bible colleges, so it would be possible to supplement my income by teaching at one of these schools. I have been in discussion with one or two schools, so that possibility does exist. That is not my preference, however. I would like to continue teaching here and do my doctoral work at Temple. The only issue involved is whether it would be possible for me to take a cut in pay and altogether drop my administrative responsibilities. I would still teach a full complement of classes. Now if you look at the next page...."

Janet was born a dreamer. While she had lots of big plans of her own, she was also good at being able to facilitate the goals of others. That had been the joy of working with her. But when Dave tried to approach her about making this change, she was hesitant to talk about it. She said that he should take his case to the board. So, here he was. Jim was also here to ask permission to go on to a Ph.D. at the University of Delaware, both of them, hat in hand. "So, are there any questions?" Dave asked upon completion.

One of the men on the board was a lawyer, and in Perry Mason fashion, he began to seek for a flaw, a mitigating circumstance, some way to convict the accused. He began, "Yes, I have ethical concerns with you contacting other schools while in the employ of this institution. When and where did such conversations take place?"

Dave was rescued from this rabbit trail by James, another board member with a bit more sense. He asked several practical questions as to what this request might include, teased out possible implications, and asked for Dave's suggestions as to what adjustments would be required administratively. Finally, he offered, "The board has been working on a financial plan to alleviate debt and to plan for the future. My question to you is whether you would be willing to wait a year or two before you begin your doctoral program?"

Dave thought for a moment and then responded, "Well, my acceptance in these schools is for next fall. This is February, and schools are looking to lock in students for specific slots. So, deadlines are a factor. Also, in all due respect, I have never known of a Bible college that did not have on-going financial concerns. I do not question your sincerity on this point, only your ability to significantly alter the financial picture in one, two, or even ten years."

Dave was sent out of the room while deliberation took place. If Dave were home he would be having some of Nathaniel's birthday cake celebrating the big one-zero, number ten. Instead, he was waiting to find out what his future would hold. Twenty minutes of waiting passed, but ultimately, the board decided that if Dave would wait one year to make the administrative shift, they would actually pay for a class in the fall and spring so he could at least begin his work at Temple part-time. Dave agreed.

Nancy came home from teaching her child evangelism class to find Dave laboring over his manuscript. He had finished that other book on church planting and was working on this allegory about Jesus Christ, a commander who became a private. Nancy didn't particularly like the violence in the book or the meanness of Dave's sergeant character. She had tried a couple of times to read the manuscript, but she would always wind up putting it down. "I'm telling you once and for all, David Norris, if there is no romance in your book, I'm not reading it!"

Dave smiled and suddenly got an idea. He added a nurse named Hope. Romance would blossom in the book after all. Then, maybe Nancy would read it. As he progressed through yet another draft, he received some help with the book from others. Lisa did some editing. Dawn helped with layout and did a nice job with the design. Denise helped him find a picture that he could use for a cover. Some good friends would be printing the book. He was all set. Well, almost.

It wasn't enough to write a book. The problem was that Dave didn't have a ready way to market his book. Then Dave got another idea. He would perform the book as a play, traveling with it during the summer. Dave asked Ed if he would help him with the script and the directing of the play. Ed was incredibly creative. He even had an idea for special effects and lighting. Tammy wrote some original music for the play and recorded it to be used as a background effect. Before long they were in business and began full-fledged practices.

Nancy came into the house one day while Dave sat the desk, wadded up paper surrounding him. "What are you doing?" she asked.

"I'm writing blessing letters to my students," said Dave.

"It looks more like your making paper wads and throwing them on the floor," said Nancy.

"Well, there are a couple of letters that I am having trouble writing," Dave replied.

"Oh?"

"Yeah, I start writing good stuff, and then I start yelling at them in the letter, that sort of thing."

"Why?"

"Because they are carnal and irresponsible."

Nancy laughed. "So much for blessing unconditionally."

"Like I said, I'm working on this. I know that I have a problem."

Nancy smiled and went in the other room. She thought it wiser not to say anything.

Because of Nathaniel's spinal fusion, it was hard for him to sit comfortably in his wheelchair for a long period of time. And because he was getting bigger and was harder to lift, Dave stopped sitting on the platform at church and began sitting next to Nancy and Nathaniel so he could hold Nathaniel from time to time. Nathaniel enjoyed the additional attention and happily left his chair to sit on Dave's lap.

It was Sunday morning, and church had already started when they made it into the sanctuary. There was room on the front seats, so Dave rolled Nathaniel to his favorite spot. Nancy got out the earplugs as they were pretty close to the speaker. She put some first in Nathaniel's ears and then put hers in as well.

They had only decided to bring Nathaniel at the last minute. He was having bowel issues and was in a little bit of pain. For several days, Nathaniel hadn't had a stool. So yesterday, Nancy had supplied the necessary medical motivation for things to get moving. But, there were no results. All day Saturday nothing had occurred. And because life must go on, they brought him to church.

While the congregation was singing and Nathaniel was sitting on his lap, Dave began having a warm feeling. And it wasn't from the song. It was his leg. Dave looked down, and from the top of his leg down to his ankle, his blue suit pants had turned brown. Because this was more than he could clean up in his office, he leaned over and whispered to Nancy.

"What?" she said.

Dave signaled to her to take her earplugs out and then said, "Say Nance, I think you should probably think about getting your own ride home. Nathaniel and I have to step out. I suspect we won't be back."

Dave's military book was really an allegory about Jesus. It came out in the spring, and they would tour with it that summer. For Nancy, the thing that made the most sense about the play was the romance. She was glad that the evil sergeant got his just desserts in the end. She was happy that the Commander received due homage. However, the most important part was when the students who played the lead characters, Hope and Butch, got together, ending the play in an embrace. A student named Lisa played Hope and another student named Ed played Butch, and so convincing was their performance that Nancy was sure that they would make a great couple. Dave tried to convince her it was just a play. He did not know if she ever accepted this.

Dave had already left with his summer drama tour. He had collected as many uniforms and boots as he could find. Like the previous year, he was going to pick up actors along the way. In this case, the actors played the parts of soldiers. Ironically, these volunteer actors would not have ever seen a full practice. Consequently, during the play they would stand in formation and get pushed around, yelled at, and even shot at but would never even understand what the play was about until the very end (just the sort of chaos that Dave loved).

Nathaniel sat on the couch with Nancy having some alone time with mom. "Nathaniel, look here," pulling her son onto her lap. "Let's read something." Nathaniel made happy noises and waved his hands excitedly as Nancy opened the newly-printed school yearbook. "And look here, Nathaniel—here's a picture of you. Lisa is the editor. See, Nathaniel—she dedicated this book to you." Nathaniel continued to wave his arms. "And here is what it says: 'Even though he was born with Cri du Chat syndrome and has endured numerous operations to correct various physical anomalies, he still smiles and laughs while others who've suffered less, long ago turned sour.'"

Nathaniel was beating the page with his rattle, wanting a little more action. "Let me finish," said Nancy. "I'll turn the page in a second. It says, 'It has been said that real strength is born out of weakness—that you and God can take any situation and succeed. Nathaniel is living proof of this, and it is for this reason that we dedicate the 1993 yearbook to him.'" Nathaniel wasn't impressed. He had learned how to turn pages and had finally caught the page, flipping it over. He laughed at his own success.

Dave started his class at Temple in the fall and was somehow able to balance everything else at school. One Sunday night in October, after Nancy and Dave had finished speaking at the church in North East, Maryland, someone called down from the office upstairs. "Hey, on your way home, stop off at the Dover church for a meeting."

When they got into the cafeteria, there was a big surprise. The church had raised money for them to go to Israel with a tour group headed up by Wayne and Janet. The trip went through Rome and stopped at all the major sites in Israel. They would stay at five-star hotels and have all the best food. Nancy and Dave didn't know what to say, but they were thankful to be going.

They went during the first part of November. They saw the Golan Heights and sat on the Mount of Beatitudes. On a boat on the Sea of Galilee, Dave was drinking a diet coke. He looked down at the bottle, amazed to be reading the letters in Hebrew. Dave had studied pointed Hebrew, where the markings under the consonants indicate what the vowels are. But when he got to Israel, everything was written consonantally, without the points, and this created a bit of difficulty for him as he tried to sound out the words. Dave was working out the ingredients on the back of a coke bottle. "Let's see, "koph, resh, mem, lamed… I wonder what that could mean?" Dave sounded out different possibilities, "Careemeel… coromol…."

Suddenly Denise, in the seat in front of him announced, "Caramel."

"Yes," said Dave. That's exactly right. Denise went further and began listing the other ingredients. Dave went through them and was amazed to see that she had it exactly right. "Denise, are you studying Hebrew? You're amazing!"

"Well, actually," she pointed out, "the English is on the other side."

They traveled to Jerusalem to spend a couple of days in a nice hotel. The next day the bus would take them to Masada. It was night. Dave was reading over the itinerary while Nancy was doing something out on the balcony. Because of the tension in Israel, giant searchlights in Jerusalem beamed across the sky. Suddenly, the beam caught Nancy in her nightgown. She screamed and came rushing back into the room, a handful of laundry in her hands.

"What are you doing?" demanded Dave. "Well," said Nancy, "you know that I packed light for this trip, which in itself is a miracle. Tonight, I washed out a few unmentionables and was hanging them over the balcony railing when the spotlight hit me. Maybe I'll just hang them over the lamp shades instead."

In February, Dave got a call from his former pastor, Robert. "Hey, how'd you like to go to Russia?"

"What do you mean?"

"Well, they have a short-term Bible school, and I was wondering if you would consider teaching Old Testament Survey. Our church will pay your plane fare."

"It sounds interesting. When is it?"

"This April."

"Sure, I'd love to," said Dave.

Nancy and Dave were making plans for the fall. They were going to move out of their house and closer to Philadelphia. Dave would no longer do administrate work and had stacked his classes so he would only actually have to be at the college two days a week. Because he was taking a cut in pay, there were a few things still to work out. A church in Newark offered the possibility that he could come on staff part-time and have a limited number of responsibilities. Dave was pretty sure he was going to take him up on this offer.

But in March, a pastor called from suburban Philadelphia and asked Dave to take the pastorate of that church. This seemed to be more than just coincidental. This church could supply income and yet because it of its relatively small size, Dave assumed that he could invest the limited amount of time required to oversee it.

Nancy and Dave had been to the church before. It was a fairly new church, one that met in a rented office building, but it was nicely decorated. The potential was exciting, yet there did seem to be a lot of loose ends. The church wasn't incorporated, and the pastor didn't want an election. When Dave met with him and suggested that maybe the whole thing could be delayed just a bit, the pastor offered, "I'm leaving in two weeks, whether you take the church or not."

So, rather than being voted in as pastor, Dave was appointed to serve in the office. And the day that the transition was supposed to take place, neither he nor the previous pastor was there to make it official. The outgoing pastor was on his way to Florida, and the incoming pastor was on a plane, half-way across the world.

Dave heard his name being called. "Mr. Dave Norris, please go to Gate 32." It was the voice on the loudspeaker that woke him up. He must have dozed off and drowsily tried to recall where he actually was. He remembered that he was on a stopover in Finland. He hurriedly made his way toward the gate. He personally didn't know anyone in Leningrad, his final destination, and he surely didn't know anyone in Helsinki.

When he boarded the plane, Dave looked at his watch and figured out the time difference in America. Right now someone else would be speaking on his first Sunday as the new pastor of a church he knew very little about.

Dave went over his teaching slides. One of the students in Dover was Russian, and he had translated Dave's material for him. After he passed through customs in Russia, Dave met Dmitri, who insisted on dropping Dave off at a fine hotel with the presumption that Dave would be paying for it. This was a surprise to Dave, who looked anxiously at what the hotel room was going to cost him. He had thought he was going to be staying with people in the church.

Soon Dave began a marathon of teaching, thirty hours in all. He grew to love the people who were there for training. Between classes they sang, they talked, and they truly enjoyed fellowship. Dave spoke at a four-hour church service along with a number of other people. They must have sung twenty songs, all of which were loaded with verses. People had spent a long time commuting to church from around the city, and they weren't ready to leave any time soon.

On a free afternoon, the interpreter took Dave to a store to buy souvenirs. She pointed out the drug dealers, easily recognizable. They were the people driving nice cars and wearing nice clothes. After shopping, she took Dave to the front of a long line of people standing in a queue. As he paid for the few gifts for people back home, he asked her, "Why did they automatically allow me to go to the front of the line?" asked Dave.

"You're an American. They want your dollars."

"How do they know I am an American?" Dave asked. The interpreter just rolled her eyes and laughed. Dave bought a few things, conscious that he would have to somehow pay off his credit card, but not really sure how he would do it.

The church in Leningrad where Dave was teaching had been given a significant plot of ground by the Russian government. Prior to the fall of communism, the building site had been slated to become a museum for atheism. It was in a prominent area. Dave walked over to see a construction crew of about a couple of dozen men working on the foundations of a church facility that looked to be the size of a civic center.

Dave recognized one of the men who seemed to be a kind of construction boss. He was a man from church. There were other men working at the construction site who apparently had also seen Dave at church. They waved but knew little English.

The construction boss came over to Dave, speaking loudly in a thick accent, inches from his face. "This is to glory of God," he said, pointing to the cement foundations. He continued, "Big building. It is good. You send us money." Dave smiled, slightly nodding his head to acknowledge that he understood what was spoken.

While in Russia, Dave had trouble getting used to how people at church greeted each other. They took the Bible seriously and greeted one another with a holy kiss—right on the lips. Dave knew that the Bible offered this admonition in the epistles of Paul, so he didn't really have an excuse, but this was one time when his greatest desire was to remain unbiblical and just greet folks with a holy handshake. The whole time he was there, Dave was pretty successful at stiff-arming people. He was hoping that people wouldn't take offense. Dave particularly tried to keep the men from kissing him on the lips. At the last service, though, a rather large grandma caught him off guard when he wasn't looking. Her lips seemed to cover the entire lower half of his face. As fulfilling as the teaching sessions were, Dave was ready to go home.

Chapter 27

"What will you do when you can't lift him anymore?"

When his dad got home from Russia, life began to look very different for Nathaniel. His routine changed in noticeable ways. First, instead of a seven-minute car ride to church, the trip to church in King of Prussia, Pennsylvania, took closer to two hours, and because there was a Sunday morning and Sunday evening service at Nathaniel's new church, the afternoon was spent at a motel in King of Prussia.

His home life got busier as well. While Nathaniel knew that his parents were gone a lot, he could not have understood that they were looking for a new place to live and that this summer in the eleventh year of his life would be his last summer in his born-again barn. Soon he would leave behind his bedroom, but not his bed. He would be moving from the country to the city. Whereas Amish children now played in the road in front of his residence, his new home would be on an upper floor of an apartment that overlooked a turnpike.

Nancy had mixed emotions about the move. They had been living rent-free at a nice place for eight years. By comparison, the cost of rent in the Philadelphia metro area seemed enormous. Dave was taking a considerable pay cut and then was expecting to navigate a graduate program where tuition was hundreds of dollars a credit hour. The folks at their new church had been very welcoming, but it was a big step into the unknown. A big step indeed.

After the Bible college graduation in May, Dave got a summer job working second shift as a security guard at a vegetable processing plant. His paycheck helped some with income, and it gave him an additional chance to study. For his doctoral program, there was certainly a lot to learn. Not only would he have to become more proficient in biblical languages, but he would eventually have to translate German and French—no small challenge. Boxes of vocabulary cards and books made their way with him to the guard shack, a random pile of work scattered here and there on an old desk stained by years of neglect and cigarette burns.

Dave's security job had a regular pattern. Hispanic workers gained entrance to the second shift of the factory by showing him their badges. For the most part, they could not understand anything Dave said, but he matched the pictures on each badge with the faces that presented themselves and then sent them through the gate. Every so often, he toured the grounds with a flashlight, but the rest of the time was his, and he used it to shuffle books and vocabulary back and forth across his desk. Still, eight hours can get really long in this kind of effort; five or six hours of self-inflicted language study can weary even the most enthusiastic soul. During the emptiness of the evening hours, Dave began to reflect on his life.

As he thought back over the years, hurts and offenses seemed to accumulate and Dave began to feel sorry for himself. First, he journaled. Then he wrote a letter to his sister Pat, telling her how he felt—how unfair everything had been. Even as he penned it, he doubted that he would ever send the letter, but it helped him sort through his feelings.

After that, Dave did what people often do when feeling sorry for themselves; he blamed God for his woes. He complained and called it prayer. He was forty-years-old and didn't own a house. He had followed God's leading and had been shortchanged in life. He didn't know how he would get rent money. He was going to spend the next six years in school and anticipated drowning in debt. If only God would have prevented his father from disinheriting him, he wouldn't be in this mess. With the anger came tears—tears that he had held back by being too busy to mourn. Tears banished through his denial of circumstances. Tears that now came because he dared to feel hurt.

It's a funny thing about God. One can never predict how He will speak. In that guard shack, no lightning struck Dave for his rage. In fact, He didn't even sense God's anger. Instead, what Dave felt was genuine compassion. Though the touch was not human, it was just as real nonetheless. God felt his hurt, his losses, and the lack of his father's blessing. Then Dave heard the Lord whisper, "I will be your inheritance." He didn't know what His words meant exactly, but in the stillness of the night, in a guard shack on a vegetable plant in the middle of rural Delaware, Dave felt a peace settle over him.

In July, Nancy and Dave had been asked to speak at a children's camp in Buckeye Lake, Ohio. This was the third time they had been there. Thirteen years earlier, when the theme of the camp had been 'flying,' a helicopter flew Nancy and Dave over Buckeye Lake and then landed on the campground in front of three hundred kids that stood waving at them. Another year, Dave spoke the first several nights of that camp without Nancy because Nathaniel was sick. Now, at this camp, they worked in tandem with puppets and skits. The camp theme was 'news,' so they had editors and reporters, skits and lessons, and actors and acting based on a curriculum Dave had written some years back when he lived in Wisconsin.

The last night of camp, the auditorium was full. Parents had driven from here and there to pick up their children after the service. Dave performed a skit, incorporating the theme from the curriculum into a play he had written about the prodigal son. He involved children and the camp staff as the prodigal tried to get a job at the newspaper. However, since the lad had no qualifications, the young man ultimately ended up in the hog pen. Finally, after a change of heart, the prodigal son headed home to his father. Dave's character ultimately experienced a joyful reunion.

As Dave finished, Nancy caught the audience by surprise. She walked out dressed as a mime. Sporting a black outfit and a white face with all the accents, she reenacted the entire story of the prodigal son without saying a word. Because this mime act was so unexpected, and because Nancy was so animated, hundreds of people sat in hushed silence as she reenacted the biblical story of reconciliation between family members.

Dave found out earlier in the week that his sister Pat would be in the audience that night. She had travelled from southwestern Minnesota with three of her six children. She said she was coming to Ohio to visit her best friend Cheryl, and that while there, she wanted to visit with him and Nancy. The next morning they sat with Pat and three of her children, two girls and a boy.

"So you are out seeing Ohio," said Dave, acknowledging the hundreds of miles they had driven from southwestern Minnesota.

"Yeah, Bill took the other three children to California to see his mom," replied Pat. She went on to explain how that trip was organized, how things were back in their hometown and church, and then changed subjects. "Dave, I've been in remission from cancer for over two years, but during these last years I have thought through a lot of things. I have been thinking about what is really important in life."

"Yeah," replied Dave. "You started this conversation at Jessie's funeral."

Only eight weeks earlier, Dave had seen Pat when they both had traveled to St. Paul for his grandmother's funeral. They called their grandmother "Jessie," using her first name, but there was no disrespect intended. None of the grandchildren ever called her "grandma" because she had said that "grandma" made her feel old. Whether Jessie ever felt old or not, she did not say, but she was in her nineties when she died.

"Well, anyway," said Pat, "like I was saying in St. Paul, I decided to do some things that I have put off for a long time. I haven't seen Cheryl in years, and she was my best friend in Bible college. It's just that I've been so busy with raising the kids that we just never got together. And I wanted to see you as well."

Pat continued, "Look, Dave, I'm sorry for the things that happened... and I want you to know that you are important to me. All of this taking of sides and accepting or rejecting people based on what side they take on issues is simply wrong. I love you, no matter what happens."

"Thanks, Pat, that means a lot, and I love you too."

Pat continued, "Dave, I'm not in charge of a lot of things, but I've taken out an insurance policy. And if the cancer comes back, they don't offer much hope. I've instructed Bill to send you a tithe of the amount he gets from the insurance and...."

"Pat, you're not going to get cancer again. You're going to be fine."

At the end of August, Dave and Nancy borrowed a truck from "Classic Interiors," a furniture business that Janet owned. With a little help, they packed up their worldly goods and transported them to Philadelphia. Rhonda and Joe helped as did Jim and Judy. Fred, the loadmaster, saw that everything in the truck was in good order and secured. Finally, the Norrises pulled out of the driveway for the very last time, heading from country living to the "D" building, one of seven buildings in a larger complex of apartments that towered into the sky in King of Prussia, Pennsylvania. At one time, these apartments had been considered upscale luxury apartments with a doorman and all kinds of extra services. However, that had been some time ago, and as the buildings aged, most of the amenities had disappeared. Still, the Norrises were close to the church and their large apartment had the square footage of a small house.

Twenty people from the new church arrived to help them get settled in. In conveyor belt fashion, boxes and furniture were passed hand-over-hand until they filled the elevator. Once filled, the door closed and the elevator arose eight stories to the floor where they would be living. By the time the elevator descended, the next load was ready to ascend.

The Norrises picked their three-bedroom/three-bath apartment for a good reason. For some time now, girls from the Bible college had lived with them to help care for Nathaniel. In the last couple of years, at one time or another, Heidi, Jenny, and Debbie all took turns providing help to the Norris household. Now a young lady from a local college would be staying in the third bedroom of their apartment, a bedroom that had its own bath.

A week or two after they had moved, the mail started coming in a fairly steady fashion, having been forwarded by the Dover post office. When Dave opened a bundle of mail bound with a large rubber band, he noticed an official letter from a lawyer. He opened it and noted that it pronounced him an heir to his grandmother's estate. He wasn't sure how this was possible. Inside the letter he was surprised to find a large check, enough for a down payment on a house if he and Nancy should choose to buy one. While they had a year's lease on their apartment, this gift would certainly be a blessing down the road.

That summer, Nathaniel had moved from a car to a van. Richard, who had helped the Norrises get cars from auctions, found them a van with a lift. The van was old but functional, and it was needed. Because Nathaniel was sixty-five pounds, he had become quite a burden for Nancy to lift in and out of the car. At first, Nathaniel wasn't really sure what he thought about this new vehicle. While the lift was a plus, and he could travel without ever leaving his wheelchair, the view had been much better from the car. Apparently assessing that this new seating arrangement was something of a demotion, he was a little pouty on his first ride. He soon got over it.

Dave didn't pay bills and didn't worry about them. He hadn't actually worried about them in some time. That is not to say that he always had enough money. It just meant that he left the worrying to someone else. Some years earlier, when he bounced a check to the church in Dover, Rhonda, who was the bookkeeper, made a suggestion. She said, "Why don't you let me handle your checkbook. I'll pay your bills, and you can worry about other stuff."

Dave thanked her and told her he appreciated the offer, but that he couldn't impose. But issues continued because Dave wasn't taking time to balance his checkbook and was only guessing as to its balance. Over time, Nancy and Dave became closer to Rhonda and her husband Joe. So, after a second bounced check, Dave accepted Rhonda's offer, and she had been paying their bills for years.

Because both Rhonda and her husband were accountants, this was no great stretch for her. So when Dave took the pastorate of the church, he understood that not only would he have to get the church incorporated; he knew he would have to have good books as well. Because Rhonda and her husband had started a business helping churches, and she was already doing this sort of work at a couple of other churches, she was the obvious choice to help him.

"Look, Rhonda," Dave said, "if you would do the books of the church, I would be forever grateful. I would be happy for the church to pay you to be its business manager. Just make sure the bills are paid and the documents are in order for the board and the business meetings. And don't bother me with details."

Dave taught two days a week down in Dover. On one of those days, Nancy also accompanied him on the all-day trip. Church services were on both Wednesday and Sunday. Dave took two classes at Temple. One class required him to read a book a week as well as write original papers. Another class challenged him to do exegetical work beyond what he had ever done before. As to teaching classes in Dover, Dave could survive with minimal class preparation because he had taught these same college classes in the past. Routine business concerns were taken care of by Rhonda, and church services were accomplished only by the help of the Lord.

Because the nursing program that their new county provided ended up being abysmal, Nancy was glad for the college girl they had living with them. Unfortunately, they had a different idea of what her responsibilities should include. Nancy made requests, but they were ignored. Then she made stronger requests, and these too were rebuffed. The girl complained that between school and work she had very little time to help. Yet, she was getting room and board. Then a big argument occurred. Nathaniel, ever sensitive to moods and words, started crying as things got louder. It was clear that something would have to change.

Nathaniel had to have another stomach surgery, called a pylorplasty, to improve his digestion. Though they were apprehensive, the Norrises knew it had to be done. When Nathaniel came out of surgery, he was crying. And he kept crying all through the day and night. No one seemed to know what to do. The Norrises stayed all night with their crying boy.

Finally, the next morning, the lead physician overseeing all his care came up to see Nathaniel. As he examined the crying boy, he was suddenly alarmed. "What in the world?" said Dr. Miller. Then the doctor pulled a certain way while doing something with Nathaniel's shoulder. "There," he said with a certain authority. "I've just popped Nathaniel's shoulder back in joint." A few minutes later, the crying ceased.

"Now why didn't somebody else see that?" Nancy asked Dave. He didn't know, but he was thankful that Dr. Miller had come.

Nathaniel went home but was not yet fully recovered. Though he received good care at the hospital, it was certainly better having him at home. Nancy made the half-hour commutes to A. I. duPont for follow-up. Yet, his condition worried Nancy, and she had a difficult time sleeping through the night.

Then she had an idea. Because she had finally been granted eight hours of nursing help a week from the county, she decided to use it all in one night so she could finally get a good night's sleep. She asked a nurse to come at 11:00 p.m. and to stay the night.

In the morning, when Nancy went into Nathaniel's room to see how he was, she found him whiny and wet and found his nurse asleep in the rocking chair. Nancy woke the nurse and asked for her help to get him ready for his doctor's appointments at A. I. duPont. After the nurse left, Nancy noticed that the nurse's hair was on her boy's brush.

After she arrived at A. I. duPont, it took Nancy ten minutes to get Nathaniel down from the van. Even though the van was a blessing, the lift itself could be temperamental. Sometimes the switch had to be coaxed along. She finally wheeled him to the front door, but before checking in, Nancy took Nathaniel to the changing room. She struggled, lifting him to the changing table. After getting a clean diaper and settling him back in the wheelchair, Nathaniel began whining. Nancy felt his brow. It was warm.

Before the first of three appointments, Nancy tried to soothe Nathaniel during their half-hour wait. Then Nathaniel fussed the whole time that they ran a test. She had a second appointment, and then waited to have a routine visit with their social worker. During her wait, Nathaniel seemed uncomfortable, so Nancy lifted him unto the changing table. But as she did she strained something in her back. Nathaniel went from whining to crying. By the time the social worker walked into the room, Nancy was crying too.

"What's wrong?" asked the social worker.

"What's wrong!" replied Nancy, erupting. "Last night I got in a fight with this college girl who was supposed to be helping but is not; then I talk to my husband to intervene and he would not. He tells me he has no emotional energy to deal with it. The nurse uses my son's hairbrush. The lift on our van won't work. And now I hurt my back!"

Whether the social worker understood everything that Nancy said was doubtful, but she couldn't miss the tone of her voice. Nor would she misunderstand the tears that coursed down Nancy's cheeks. She patted Nancy's arm and spoke soothing words. After Nancy settled down, the social worker asked, "Mrs. Norris, have you ever thought about putting Nathaniel in a home?"

"Absolutely not!" came her swift reply.

"He is getting bigger, isn't he?"

"Yes," Nancy said defensively.

"Well, there may come a point when you have to decide some things. What will you do when you can't lift him anymore?"

"I'm pretty close to that now."

"Do you know what the average waiting time is to get a child placed in a home?"

"No."

"Almost five years. I want you to think about something. Get Nathaniel on a waiting list. Then you will have options if the time comes when there is an opening; at least you will have a choice."

"I don't know," said Nancy.

"Well, at least think about it."

Nancy and Dave went to their county office where such things were handled. They waited in a rather dingy waiting room until they were called and then they explained to the lady who handled such things that they would like to be placed on this waiting list that someone had told them about. Dave had on a suit and Nancy was well dressed. "I see," said the lady. "And there are two parents in the home?"

"Yes."

"And there is no financial hardship?"

"No."

"And there are no other extenuating circumstances?" Nancy and Dave looked at each other, deflated. They shook their heads, not able to think of a circumstance that might qualify them.

"I'll tell you what," she offered. "Here is a list of homes in the Philadelphia area. Visit them and see what your preference is. If you find one you like, you can try to get on a waiting list, but I have to say, Mr. and Mrs. Norris, the odds are that it will be a long time before anyone will even look at you."

While in one way such news was discouraging, in another way it was also comforting. Nancy and Dave were relieved that they would not have to make any decision about Nathaniel until some future time. Because they would just as soon forestall any decision as long as possible, what the social worker gave them was the gift of time.

Chapter 28

" 'Didn't you hear the alarm?' yelled the fireman"

As the leaves blushed red and turned gold, Nathaniel eased into his autumn routine. Mornings in the city were much faster paced. Instead of waiting for the school bus on a tree-shaded driveway across from an Amish school house, Nathaniel anticipated the arrival of his bus in the glass lobby of building "D."

Still, there were at least some advantages to this new school experience. Montgomery County Intermediate Unit where Nathaniel went to school was, appropriately enough, in Norristown, Pennsylvania. Nathaniel loved his school teacher. Carol was an attractive lady with long blond hair who took special interest in Nathaniel. In Dover, after Nathaniel had been promoted out of Diana's class, some of his teachers were more caring than others. But now Nathaniel was in a situation where he was given attention throughout the day.

When he lived in Dover, there had been way too much drama related to his trips on the bus. Now, his morning bus trips to school were considerably more peaceful. Nathaniel's wheelchair was locked in right up next to Dawn, his bus driver, and he seemed to think that he owned the bus and the school. Dawn was actually happy about life and liked the children she picked up, factors that made riding to and from school a pleasant experience. One day, Dawn accidentally drove past the school, and Nathaniel began waving his arms and making noises. Whether it was coincidental or not, she was never sure, but Dawn laughed when she realized that

Nathaniel had possibly signaled her to turn around and head back. "Worried about missing our school teacher, are we?" teased Dawn as she turned around and headed into the driveway of the school.

The paperwork came through and the lady at the social services agency told Nancy and Dave that they were now approved to visit some residential homes to see if they could find one where Nathaniel would be put on a waiting list. However, visiting homes was difficult. They visited several homes in Philadelphia where the person who gave them a tour seemed competent while the help did not. After a few too many of these tours, Dave said he would not look again; so Nancy opted to wait until the spring of the year before exploring further possibilities.

Dave was looking for a place to have special services and visited an older Presbyterian church in Bridgeport to talk with the pastor. His name was Don, and he was interested that Dave was in graduate school and in what he was studying. Don not only taught at a local college on the side, but he was also involved in numerous other activities, including that of providing a weekly political commentary on a cable television station. When he found out that Dave's congregation normally met in a rented storefront, he suggested that Dave do more than rent the Presbyterian Church for special services. "Why don't you come and have services in our building? We won't even charge you for rent."

"That is awfully kind of you," said Dave.

Dave's church congregation moved into the Presbyterian church building, and they changed to a Sunday afternoon service. While Dave insisted that they pay at least something for rent, the token amount they paid was inconsequential. Further, Dave didn't have to worry about maintenance, upkeep, or improvements on a building. Their church was even allowed to post a sign indicating that their church was meeting in the building. Don and Dave soon became fast friends, meeting for lunch almost every Friday to talk theology.

It was spring. Nancy's sister Cathy called from Maryland, wondering if Nancy had done anything about getting Nathaniel on a waiting list. "He's turned twelve," she noted. "And if it is going to take you years before he is eligible to actually be accepted, you should really look to sign him up for someplace soon."

"Well, it's really hard," said Nancy. "We don't like the places we've visited, and Dave doesn't even want to visit any more." Cathy had a passion for children with special needs, having worked in the school system for years with them. She had a foster daughter named Maggie with special needs as well. And Cathy had another quality about her. When she saw a task that needed to be done, she would not be easily deterred by circumstances. "Nancy, how is your back?" she asked.

"They are talking about putting in a lift to get him from the bed to the bathroom."

"Nancy, are you telling me that there is absolutely no place you would even consider looking after Nathaniel?"

"We did hear about a place called Ridge Crest forty-five minutes north of here that is supposed to be good, but I don't know. It is in Sellersville, Pennsylvania."

"Let's go visit," said Cathy.

"Alright, I'll make the call."

When the lady answered the telephone, Nancy requested, "I'd like to make an appointment to visit your facilities."

"There is no need," said the lady, introducing herself as Patty. "You are welcome anytime."

Her response was definitely unusual, because most places that Nancy visited carefully crafted their schedules as to when visitors could see their operations. Patty continued, "Any one of our staff can help you, but if I'm here, I'd be glad to give you a tour and tell you about our place." Again, Nancy found it remarkable that she, as a visitor, was not being "handled" but welcomed.

Because of Cathy's background, Nancy knew that she would know what to look for when they toured the facilities. "I love this place," said Cathy, after they had been shown around. "A number of the kids are PMR, but there is an incredible feeling of warmth and caring here."

When Cathy used the acronym 'PMR,' she meant that some of the infants and children were capable of doing nothing more than lying in a crib. She was right. But she was also right about something else: the love that they felt in the building. The notes on the bulletin board demonstrated that the staff genuinely encouraged one another. Each room was decorated with a different theme; the staff did this decorating on their own time. Administrators doted over a picture of Nancy's son. Patty explained that yes, there was a long waiting list, but if they ever did have an opening, they would love for Nathaniel to come.

On the way back to the house, Cathy offered, "If Nathaniel ever did go to a home, this should be the one."

Dave finally took ownership of the conflict in the home and asked a family in the church if the college student that was living with them could stay with them for the duration of the school year. Even though Nancy never found a nurse who clicked with Nathaniel and genuinely cared for him since their move, she somehow made it through the school year.

It was Memorial Day, and the holiday seemed to call for some sort of special recognition. They began looking for a parade. Dave scanned the local newspapers. Any number of adjoining communities stretched for twenty miles towards Philadelphia, and it seemed likely that they would find something in one of these municipalities.

"It says here that this town has a parade," said Dave pointing to the paper.

"That was at nine this morning."

"Okay… here," he said pointing again. "Let's go down Route 30.

It looks like there is a neighborhood parade just south of there."

"What's a neighborhood parade?"

"I have no idea, but let's find out."

So they drove to the neighborhood, and they parked the van where kids were gathering in the street. A fire engine stood by, ready to lead the parade, but there were no brass bands, floats, or dancing majorettes, only dozens of mothers and children dressed up in patriotic outfits who were either walking or would be pushed in strollers. Nancy and Dave set up with Nathaniel by the curb to watch the proceedings.

Just then a voice crackled over the radio in the fire truck, and the firemen swiftly put on their gear. Two minutes later their siren was on and the truck was gone. Given that the official status of the parade seemed to have changed, Nancy decided that they should do more than simply watch the parade. "Come on, you're both dressed in red white and blue," she said to Dave and Nathaniel. Of course they were, for she had dressed both her boys that way.

He wasn't really enthusiastic about it, but soon Dave joined Nancy and dozens of strollers who began parading in earnest. The merry band walked for three blocks to the delight of an occasional onlooker, and then seemed to disband for lack of interest or perhaps because they were finished. Nancy and Nathaniel were very pleased with themselves. Dave remained grumpy but compliant. They had a good day.

The good thing about living in King of Prussia was that it had everything. Within blocks of the house was the largest mall on the East Coast. Across the street from the apartment complex where the Norrises lived were a couple of little shopping centers and a grocery store. The real challenge in King of Prussia was not a lack of opportunity for shopping; it was figuring out the back roads in town so as to avoid as much congestion as possible.

Nancy was at the grocery store when she heard the sirens. She didn't think anything of it. But when she approached the guard at the entrance to their apartment complex, she could see the fire engines up ahead. "What's going on?" she asked.

"There's a fire in one of the high-rise apartments," he stated.

"Which one?"

"Uh… I think it is 'D' building."

"Oh, no!" said Nancy, alarmed. "That's our building, and my husband never listens to those fire alarms. They go off almost every week, and he simply ignores them. He says that those alarms are just a bother. He won't know it's real!"

"Well, I don't know what to say about that," said the guard.

"Nathaniel is up there with Dave!" cried Nancy "They're on the eighth floor. I need to get up there right away."

The guard didn't know Dave or Nathaniel and nonchalantly said, "Sorry, it's all blocked off. Maybe if you parked down the hill, you could walk up."

Dave sat reading while the alarm went off. He was mumbling something to himself about getting some earplugs to block out the incessant noise when he heard someone knocking on doors down the hall. The knocking got closer until he heard it on his own door. A fireman stood staring at him in the open door.

"Didn't you hear the fire alarm?" yelled the fireman.

"Yes." Dave didn't bother explaining the multiple false alarms.

"Please leave. There's a fire in the electrical system. Don't take the elevators. You'll have to go down the stairs." Dave picked up Nathaniel and joined a stream of people padding their way down eight flights of darkened stairs, illuminated only by a dim emergency light.

Nancy was frantic with worry. Finally she saw them; both Nathaniel and Dave were relaxing on a blanket that had apparently been provided by a Good Samaritan and looking for all the world as if they were on a picnic. If Nancy hadn't been so relieved that she found them, she might have been mad at them for looking so relaxed. No! She was mad at them for being relaxed while she was getting sick with worry.

Dave saw Nancy coming and though he didn't know exactly why she looked so distressed, he stood to comfort her. As they embraced she sobbed, and after a bit she was able to say, "I didn't think you would believe the fire alarm."

"A fireman helped me believe," said Dave as held her.

"Did they let you down the elevator?" Nancy asked.

"No. And let me tell you, I didn't realize how big Nathaniel was getting until I carried him down eight flights of stairs."

"That's it," said Nancy. "We're moving."

"It would be a good time," said Dave.

"Why?"

"Things are a little 'iffy' in Dover. Now that Wayne and Janet's son is pastoring the church, the future of the college is a little in doubt."

"So what are you saying? Is the Bible college where we teach closing?"

"I don't think so. It is probably just a rumor, but we'd better buy a house while we can. Our payment on a little three-bedroom house would probably be about what we're paying for our apartment. But if the school were to close, I doubt whether we'd be able to get a loan."

"Nathaniel needs surgery, and he needs it now," said the doctor at A. I. duPont.

"Perhaps we could wait a bit more," negotiated Nancy.

The doctor understood her reluctance, but he tried to impress on her the need for the surgery. "Mrs. Norris, I told you that we needed to do this surgery two years ago. Nathaniel is twelve, and his legs are tightening up even more."

"I don't understand why this is happening," said Nancy. "They do therapy on his legs,"

"He's not using them," said the doctor easily. "It's normal for this to happen. And the surgery is not a big deal. We'll just cut the muscles, lengthening them so that Nathaniel can sit more freely in his chair."

"Why don't we schedule it for some time after the first of the year?" Nancy said finally, not wanting the surgery, but not wanting to be irresponsible either.

"Shall we say January, then?"

"Okay," said Nancy, writing the date into her pocket calendar.

Dave's sister Pat called. "Dave," she said resigned, "the cancer has returned."

There was a pause, and then Dave said, "I'm so sorry." Only prayer could help now.

They moved to their three-bedroom ranch the latter part of October, and they didn't have far to go. Although it was almost a mile away on the side roads, as the crow flies it was only three blocks. Church folks, along with a number of students from the Bible college, came by to help with the transition. Dave drove the U-haul truck to the back of the high rise unit, and the same furniture that had ridden up the elevator to the eighth floor a year earlier rode its way back down. Pizza was served to the helpers as the furniture and possessions began to be stowed away in their new location.

Their new house was located in an older neighborhood. Most of the homes had been built in the boom after World War II. While there were younger families in the subdivision, the neighborhood seemed to have more than its share of retired veterans. Frank was a retired Navy man who lived behind them and told them that if they ever needed anything, he was there to help.

The first day that Nathaniel was dropped off at the house, Nancy met another neighbor. As the bus pulled away from the driveway where Nathaniel was dropped off, Nancy realized that they were going to have a problem. They had a large front step, and Dave wasn't there to lift the chair. So as she struggled to get Nathaniel's wheelchair up the front step, she met Jack, a World War II veteran who had lost his arm in the war. The fact that he so quickly came to their aid with Nathaniel touched Nancy deeply.

The week before the Norrises actually moved into the house, Nancy received another call from A. I. duPont. They had a cancellation in the surgery schedule, and they wanted to take Nathaniel in for the operation to lengthen his leg muscles. They wanted to schedule the surgery three days after they moved into their house.

"What do you think?" she asked Dave.

"The doctors are recommending that we do this now?" he asked.

Nancy nodded. "Yes. They say we are already late doing this operation, but Dave, the last two surgeries that Nathaniel had didn't turn out so well."

"I think we'd better go ahead," he said.

They had said it was routine, but Nancy had the feeling it would not be. And she was right. When the surgeon finally came into the waiting room, he was shaking his head. "There were complications," he said.

"What?" said Dave, forgoing formalities.

"He went into shock."

"Will he be all right?" Dave asked.

"We're doing the best we can," said the surgeon. "We'll keep you informed." Things were touch and go throughout the night, but as the morning broke things started looking better.

"Are you going to stay overnight?" Nancy asked Dave on the second evening.

"I can't. I have to prepare for my Chinese Buddhism class at Temple in the morning. I really can't afford to miss. I am really struggling with this one."

The next afternoon Dave showed up, and Nancy looked glum. Dave kissed her. "So, is Nate the Skate doing any better?" he asked, smiling.

"He's out of ICU."

"Is he still crying?"

"Not so much," said Nancy.

"Then why so glum?"

"Dave, I have to tell you something," said Nancy. "Sit down."

Now Dave was worried. "What is it?"

"Dave, they called from Ridge Crest. They have an opening for Nathaniel."

"No. That can't be," said Dave. "It was supposed to take years. No, that's just not right... when would they want him?"

"As soon as he is well enough to come there."

"But he would get to come home first... spend a bit more time... be in his new home and...."

Nancy was shaking her head. "No. They have a slot open. We need to take it or leave it."

"Who did you talk to?" asked Dave stalling for time.

"Patty. She said that we were only forty-five minutes away and that we could come up every day, whenever we wanted. They have no visiting hours and they have an open-door policy."

"She was really nice," said Dave blandly. He had met her on a second visit after Nancy told him about the place.

"The whole staff is nice," said Nancy.

"Very accommodating," droned Dave.

"Right," said Nancy, matching his tone.

"And it's not that far," said Dave in a complaining voice that trailed off.

Dave stared at the wall. Nobody said anything for a couple of minutes. They wouldn't even look at each other. Neither wanted to speak first.

Finally, Dave offered gravely, "I think we've got to do it."

Chapter 29

"Thanks for raising me"

Two more weeks passed before Nathaniel fully recovered from the surgery. On the morning of November 17, the Norrises drove Nathaniel from the hospital to the Ridge Crest Home. They didn't take the van to Ridge Crest because the home had plenty of wheelchairs already. Nathaniel rode in the passenger's seat of the car while his mom sat in the backseat. She tried to talk to Nathaniel but felt too guilty to say much.

The staff made over Nathaniel like he was the president taking office, and they were gentle with Dave and Nancy. Nancy and Dave had no plans once they arrived, and they settled the few things they brought into Nathaniel's room. But the pain they felt was almost physical. They didn't know anyone who had ever put their child in a home. This was not something real parents did.

"You're only forty-five minutes away," consoled Patty, as they were getting ready to leave Ridge Crest that day. It is a good thing that Nancy was able to acknowledge her words, because Dave couldn't speak at all. Nathaniel was eyeing his dad suspiciously after he kissed him goodbye and had prayed for him. As Dave turned the corner to go into the hallway, floods of tears coursed down his cheeks. Dave opened Nancy's car door and got into the driver's side with the keys in his hand. But they wouldn't be leaving any time soon; both Nancy and Dave kept heaving with sobs of uncontrollable sadness.

The next day Nancy and Dave drove up in the van to Ridge Crest to see their son. It was Saturday, and they found Nathaniel in the playroom in the middle of kids. The staff was busily interacting with all the children. Although Nancy felt their genuine concern for the children, she didn't want to spend time in the larger room. Today, she needed private time with Nathaniel.

Dave put Nathaniel in a wheelchair and wheeled him down the hall to his room. Nancy announced, "Nathaniel, I brought your rocking chair." She sat while Dave handed the boy to her and she began to rock with him. She didn't know what she would have done if Nathaniel had snubbed her. But he didn't. Nathaniel put his hand on her face and licked her, making happy noises.

Nancy and Dave went up to see him after church on Sunday. On Monday, Nancy went up by herself because Dave had class. Weekdays, Dave was unable to make the trip with her, but she came as often as she could. Jerry was one of the workers there who loved Nathaniel. He was always giving him special attention, as was Reesha, whose body was full of tattoos and piercings. Her hair was spiked and colored in unusual ways. Nathaniel loved to see her coming, and he would coo happily when she tickled and played with him. Nancy always tried to stop and see Trish on the way out. She was so kind and gentle that Nancy felt like she was leaving Nathaniel with friends.

After they returned home from their Saturday night Christmas program, Dave called to see how his sister Pat was doing. He usually talked to her husband Bill. The report was never good. Bill's jogging partner was the doctor overseeing Pat's care. The message was always the same. He was doing all he could for her, but at this point, there wasn't much that could be done. The cancer had spread and the tumor had enlarged. While the calendar charted her decline toward the inevitable, Dave always asked the same question: "Does she want us to come?"

The answer was always the same: "Not yet."

This time it was different. That morning, the family physician told Bill, "Look, Bill, I know that Pat doesn't want a lot of extra fuss. But if her family wants to see her before she passes, they'd better come now."

Nancy and Dave made the trip in two days. They arrived on a Monday night, checked into a motel, and then went to the house. Pat was in bed, obviously in a lot of pain, but she was lucid. As Nancy and Dave talked with her, Becca, Pat's second-born daughter who was in her sophomore year of high school, reported in to her mother. She seemed to be some sort of assistant mom, the second in command. Pat gave a few instructions as to when bedtime was for Tim and John, the two youngest boys.

"Are John's blue pants washed for school?" They were. "Is Jessie picking up Joe from hockey practice?" She was. "What time is Deborah coming home?" It was clear that Pat was still very much in charge of the household and had not in any sense relinquished oversight of her six children, the three older girls or the three youngest boys.

Pat had always said she wanted six children. Dave never knew why that was such an important number. Maybe it was because there were six children in her own family growing up.

Pat's siblings began arriving the next day, and because of the busyness of the household, they stayed in the same chain hotel as Nancy and Dave. Bill and Pat pastored in the town of Worthington, and they knew lots of people in the community. As people arrived the manager asked, "You're with the Roos family?", and if the answer was yes, he offered a significant discount on the rooms.

Pat wanted private time with each of her siblings. When Dave came in, she gave him some old letters and notes she had written and received. She had taken time to compile what was meaningful to her. Included among the stack were some letters written during their teenage years and some of Pat's personal notes that were more journals than observations. Pat's journals began with reflection and broke easily into prayer.

On Wednesday night, when Barb came in from Ohio and Pat had a full complement of siblings present, she called a conference, insisting that everyone make a circle around her bed. In their family system, although it was Barb who was firstborn and two years senior to Pat, it was Pat who often took charge. And as Dave was next in line at a year younger than she, sometimes she would tell Dave what to do and then he would tell everyone else. Or she would just tell them all herself.

Pat spoke solemnly. "There are a lot of things that are important in life. And some things are worth fighting for, but some are not. In fact, it's a shame when we do. We need to come together as a family, not make an issue of small things, and pray for each other. Dave, you pray." They held hands as commanded and Dave prayed.

That's the way Pat was. She wasn't trying to usurp the firstborn spot from her older sister, but she couldn't help taking charge.

"Dave, I wrote a letter a couple of weeks ago. I need to read it to my family."

"What does it say, Pat?"

"I need to tell them good-bye."

"I'll tell you what. I'll see if the kids can write letters in response, saying good-bye to you, at least the older ones."

Thursday night Nancy and Dave were at the house when Pat called her own family together. Pat was helped into a living room chair where she sat supported by pillows. Her face demonstrated the cost of this exertion, but she masked the pain as best she could. She carried a letter with her. When everyone was in place, Pat read the letter, one that pronounced a blessing and instructions to each one of her children, from the oldest to the youngest, and then she shared her love for her husband. In turn, each child responded in order, beginning with the oldest.

Jessie, a senior in high school, read her letter to her mom. She recalled Pat's bravery in the face of cancer, offering, "Almost three years after the cancer went into remission, it came back. Mom, you've gotten out of bed every morning, suited up the boys for hockey practice and games, you got them there, cheered them on and then brought them back home again. Mom, you didn't have to do this. Becca or Jessie could have done it, but you didn't want us to sacrifice the activities we were involved in."

"Mom, you've never complained about being sick. Your face is pale or flushed, you've lost your hair and your eyebrows, eyelashes, and you have circles under your eyes because you're so tired. I know that you've been scared, but not for yourself. You just want to see your six children be all they can be."

Tears started flowing around the room as Jessie continued. She told of her love for her mother and of several experiences they shared together. Jessie recalled playing a duet with her mother of the song "On Christ the Solid Rock I Stand." Jessie noted about the audience, "They had no idea what the song meant, but you did, and you meant it, and they knew it."

Becca read her letter next. It began: "You are the best mom that I could ever have. In the past sixteen years, you have always been there for me. I remember all the stories about how when I was a baby everyone wanted to hold me, but I would only let you hold me. I knew that you were my mommy." Becca continued to talk about her toddler years, grade school, and church. She wrote, "Every time I sat at the piano, you always sang along. And when I got to the end of the song, you said, 'play that song again.' I hated playing the organ at church. After the first time, I said that I would never play it again. It was too complicated. But you were there, rooting for me." Becca continued, reminding her mother of what had happened earlier that year when she got her driver's license. "The first time I drove the car by myself, you kept reminding me about my seatbelt, and then as I looked back as I drove down the street, you were there at the door, still watching over me." After a few more paragraphs, Becca ended her letter, "Whatever happens, I know that it is God's plan, and we're going to make it. I LOVE YOU, MOM!"

In her letter, Becca told of a dream that she experienced some time back. In it, her mom was sick but that sickness brought all of her siblings together. Dave winced just a little bit when Becca said that. He didn't want these children to believe that God had caused this tragedy just to bring the family together. He would have to think about how he could best communicate this to them.

After Becca and her mom embraced, fourteen-year-old Deborah read a poem that she had written. The last lines read,

"I know if you leave, I'll see you again someday
I'm looking forward to that day
Because in heaven—everything will be okay."

The boys didn't have letters, but Joe, age twelve, easily offered a sincere and extemporaneous speech. Like the letters from the girls, he listed specific things that his mom had done for him. He ended by saying, "Thank you for being an encourager. Whenever I needed something, you were there to help me. I will always love you."

John, age eight, was no less sincere. "You helped me practice the piano. You always helped me make my bed. You loved me very much. You're the best mom I'll ever have."

Finally, Timothy, age six, came over and spoke to his mom before he embraced her. Timothy offered, "Thanks for taking me to hockey. I love you very much. Thanks for raising me."

Earlier in the week, Pat had asked Dave to be one of two speakers at her funeral. He said he would, though he was still praying for her healing. On Friday, Dave came in to see Pat. "Hey Pat, I've been working on the details of the funeral like you said. We'll still take a miracle if God so chooses, but if He doesn't, I wanted to get your approval on this sermon I wrote."

Pat wanted to hear the sermon, so Dave read it out loud. She thought it was good, but like the older sister she was, she offered a few suggestions. Finally she said, "And Dave, read the letter that I wrote to the family." He said he would.

Pat had refused to go into the hospital because it was an admission that she was no longer in charge of the household. On Saturday morning, she needed to go. As they were getting ready to get her out of bed, she suddenly stopped due to the noise coming from the living room. She yelled, "John, what video are you boys watching?" The response was not appropriate and Pat called out, "We will not be watching Power Rangers in this house. Take it out, now." Dave could hear the sound of obedience from the other room.

Pat died on Sunday morning, Christmas Eve. The funeral was Wednesday. Their church sanctuary could not hold the number that came, so a signal from a camera in the sanctuary allowed it to be displayed on a large screen in the fellowship hall. Robert, who had been Pat and Dave's pastor in St. Paul, played his trumpet and was the first speaker. Then Bruce and Sharon, neighboring pastors, sang, "I Want to See You There," a song written by a mother who was apparently dying. It offered a charge to her children that she wanted to meet them once again in heaven. Then a lady from the church sang "The Lord's Prayer" in Spanish.

Dave stood to speak. "I don't have to wonder what Pat would say to you if she were here. As you may know, she planned this funeral in great detail. Pat asked me to speak, so I read to her the sermon I had prepared. She made some corrections, and I offer it to you now." Dave read his text from Matthew 13, where a farmer's field was visited by an enemy who planted weeds along with the crop. When the crop came up, the man's field hands were aghast that the weeds were present and asked how it could it happened. The answer was the title of Dave's message: "An Enemy Has Done This."

"We ask how a mother who was not yet finished raising her children could be taken from us. There are no easy answers. But we live in a fallen world. Lucifer, who had been the friend of God, chose to become God's enemy. Satan's seed of rebellion produced the tares of Adam's transgression, the thorns of human suffering, the sweat of pain, grief, and death."

"There are those who would use this tragedy to assert that faith is futile, to advance skepticism, or to attack a lifestyle of faith. It wasn't because of anything that she or anyone else did that my sister died. To ascribe this tragedy either to some human failing or to the Lord that she loved would be an incredible tragedy."

"It takes better than average vision to see the eternal, to evaluate things from heaven's eyes. Though many people have gathered together here today, there are no heads of state, no ambassadors, no presidents or kings. From any sort of measurement of human fame or renown, this was an ordinary life."

"But God has a different measuring stick, a different way of sorting things out. From a human perspective, this is a tragedy today of a life cut short, of a task unfinished. But from heaven's point of view, there is the absolute of a mission accomplished. While I don't pretend to understand God's purposes, this I do know—Pat embraced the eternal."

Dave continued, "If you allow me, I will include a personal letter that Pat shared with her family, shortly before she died."

Dave began, "Dear Family…" And then Dave read the letter, first reading the greeting of love Pat offered her family, and then reading the specific blessing for each family member in order.

"Jessie," Pat wrote, "The Lord has blessed you with many talents. I hope and pray that you are diligent in using those talents for whatever work He has for you to do." Then Pat added a couple of paragraphs of further direction. She ended with the statement, "God bless you as you graduate from high school and venture out into life. I love you, Jessie."

Sixteen-year-old Becca was next. She was offered considerable praise by her mother, followed by some advice. "You want to be in anything and everything. Pick the things that are most important to you and pass on some other things. Put the Lord first and He will bless you. I love you, Becca."

To fourteen-year-old Deborah, Pat offered, "From the time you were little you have related well to people, whether young or old." Pat then praised Deborah for her gifts, gave her advice about schooling, and concluded with "Use your enthusiasm for the Lord. I love you, Deborah."

Not everyone could see the children as they were called out by their mother's letter in the service. While the overflow crowd that filled the fellowship hall could see Dave, their larger view was limited. Dave continued, now reading Pat's blessing on the boys.

"Joe, your dad and I wanted a son. I prayed for you for several years." Pat then retold the story of why her eldest boy was named Joseph. She recounted the biblical narrative of Joseph and how he resisted temptation and ultimately fulfilled his dream. Even though Joseph had been betrayed by his brothers, "Joseph had a heart of forgiveness. God put him as second in command in all of Egypt and restored to him his family. I hope and pray that you will be like Joseph in the Bible."

Pat's family sat in the first few rows on the right side of the sanctuary. Handkerchiefs were employed to wipe away tears. Joe listened as the letter addressing him ended, "I love you, Joe."

It was difficult to know what eight-year-old John was thinking when the letter continued, "John, you were a cuddly baby, and I still think of you as a cuddler. You are a deep thinker." Pat went on to explain to John his gifts and talents and expressed her blessing and desire that he would utilize those gifts effectively. She ended by encouraging John that God will "show you in His word and speak to your heart. I love you, John."

And then to the youngest, Pat wrote, "Tim, you are my sweet boy." Pat then praised Tim for his skating and for how he wanted to be on the Lord's side. She closed, "I love you, Tim."

Bill listened as the words of his wife from a few days earlier were once again repeated again. "Bill, I have loved you these twenty years of marriage and have been faithful to you. I would have loved to celebrate fifty or seventy-five years of marriage. There is pain in separation. I pray that the Lord gives you wisdom to be a good father. Time helps the pain, but you will always feel the loss. But there is hope in Jesus that we will be together again."

"I love all of you.

Mom (Pat)"

Pat had said that she wanted the funeral procession to go around the lake that was the pride of the town. Their family's house was on the lake; they knew a lot of their neighbors, and Bill often jogged the path around the lake. So it was that a long procession of cars circled the lake in an indirect route to the cemetery, and, as was typical in a small town, cars pulled over to let the procession pass. "Who died?" asked one man. "I haven't seen that many cars since the mayor's wife died."

When Nancy and Dave arrived at the graveside, the snow-covered ground was filled with people as the committal was offered. Becca began leading the family in hymns. Others joined in. Even after things were supposed to be over, one hymn led to another. No one wanted to say their last good-bye.

When Nancy and Dave returned to Philadelphia, they immediately went to see Nathaniel. He was in the middle of finger painting with a staff member who was helping him to rub both hands around in blue goop. Nathaniel was laughing at the blue paint and at the staff member as well as the squishiness of the texture between his fingers.

Nancy was an impatient spectator while her boy was being cleaned up. Finally she got to hold him. He waved his hands in delight to see her. He licked her face in a welcome kiss.

Nancy and Dave took Nathaniel to church. Because the church was well over seventy-five-years-old, there was no elevator, even though the sanctuary was on the second floor. There was, however, one of those chairs that rode a track up stairs. This was especially interesting as the stairs curved around and ascended twenty feet to the second floor.

Nancy rode in the chair while Nathaniel sat in her lap. "Okay, press the button," she said, as Andrew, age six, gave it the official push. The chair chugged its way to the top, where Joey lifted Nathaniel from his mom and sat him in the wheelchair. Joey had moved to Philadelphia from the Midwest to attend a military academy. He was on "leave" for the weekend, and supplied the necessary muscle power to make things happen. As soon as Nathaniel got situated in his wheelchair, Jeanette, a lady from the church, came over to talk to him. "Do you remember me?" she said, leaning down to Nathaniel as if he had been gone for years. He reached out and grabbed her arm. Jeanette cried. Nancy did too.

Chapter 30

"This is aspiration pneumonia"

After church, Nathaniel caught a ride back to the Ridge Crest Home with a family from the church who lived out near Sellersville, the town where Ridge Crest was located. Because the Norrises kept a spare wheelchair at home, and because the residence where Nathaniel stayed had wheelchairs aplenty, Nathaniel was travelling light. He merely needed to be buckled in the back seat along with the rest of the boys from the large family who were now pulling away from the curb. Nathaniel looked out the window to see Nancy waving good-bye to him and the boys who would provide an action packed forty-five minute ride back to the Ridge Crest Home. A call later that night confirmed that Nathaniel had made it just fine.

When Nancy arrived at Ridge Crest the next day, she headed straight to the room Nathaniel shared with another boy. Motivated by her sister Cathy, the sports decorations Nancy had collected for his half of the room were now almost complete. Cathy had complained, "Nancy, a teenager should not have his room decorated with stuffed dinosaurs!" Consequently, the Philadelphia Eagles were displayed prominently as a backdrop. Nathaniel also had a Buffalo Bills bedspread, a team about which Nancy knew little except that she liked the team colors.

As Nancy entered the room, she saw that Nathaniel was not there although his roommate was. His crib was situated by the door, and even though a humidifier was providing him with a steady stream of moist air, his breathing was still raspy. "Hey there, Justin," Nancy said sympathetically to the little boy lying there. "Not feeling well enough to join your friends in the playroom?"

As Nancy was stroking his hair, a nurse popped her head in the room to check on the infant. "How's my little Justin?" she said warmly. The nurse breathed on her stethoscope to warm it up before placing it on the little boy's chest. While on the one hand, all the children in Ridge Crest Home were medically fragile and technologically dependent, on the other hand, every one of those lives was precious.

As Nancy turned to leave, Justin gifted her with a little smile. Moments later, Nancy discovered Nathaniel in the playroom resting comfortably on an oversized wedge. He was perusing the half-dozen small children and infants who were placed on chairs, in walkers, on giant bean bags, or on the couch. Music played from a tape recorder, a children's video played on a monitor, and some kind of noisy toy was talking back to a child from the opposite side of the room. Staff members appeared here and there dispensing medications.

There didn't seem to be clearly drawn lines as to which staff member was overseeing which resident. Every child was likely to be greeted, teased, or to have their hair tousled by anyone who might be passing by. Reesha came over to give Nathaniel his meds, and without any inhibition whatsoever, she pulled up his shirt, blew raspberry sounds on his stomach and got Nathaniel laughing hysterically. Then shortly after Nathaniel had taken his meds, Jerry came by on the way to somewhere else and crouched low enough to talk face-to-face with Nathaniel. "Hey! How's the little guy? I hear you are going to be a teenager next month: the big one-three. Are there gonna be girls at the party?"

After Nancy had returned home that night, the phone rang. It was Patty from Ridge Crest. "Say, Nancy, I just wanted you to know that Nathaniel spiked a pretty high fever, and he's starting to get other symptoms as well. It looks like pneumonia. We're watching him pretty closely, and we may keep him here for awhile longer, but more than likely we're going to take him over to the hospital."

"Is there a hospital there in Sellersville, or is it someplace else?" Nancy asked, concerned.

"Oh, it's right next door. The name is Grand View Hospital. Don't worry. They do a fine job."

The next morning, Nancy went up to the hospital and stayed the day. It was small and the staff was kind. She asked the doctor for the prognosis. "Well," the doctor reported, "his lungs are pretty junky. Unless it gets worse, he'll stay right there. Otherwise—"

"What do you mean, 'if it gets worse?'"

"Well, you see they're delivering him oxygen through these nasal prongs that loop around under his nose. And do you see that little line attached to his finger?"

"Yes," Nancy said.

What we're doing is checking the level of oxygen in his blood, and if that level goes too low he would need to have oxygen delivered to him more aggressively. For that we would need to take him down to CHOP."

"Excuse me?"

"Sorry," he said laughing. "CHOP stands for the Children's Hospital of Philadelphia."

"Why would you take him there?"

"We wouldn't normally. That is, unless his oxygen level gets dangerously low. Then we would take him there to push some oxygen into those lungs of his. But don't worry, we'll keep an eye on it."

The next morning the phone rang again. "This is Nancy calling from Ridge Crest Home. I just got a call from Grand View Hospital that they are just now medevaccing Nathaniel to CHOP."

"Medevaccing?" asked Nancy.

"Yes, they took him by helicopter." She then gave them directions to the hospital. Nancy and Dave packed a few things and within a half-hour they were headed to downtown Philadelphia. They parked in the garage but had to walk quite a ways before they got to the hospital. Passing a parking lot attendant, they asked if there might be a closer parking lot.

"'Youse' are parents of a child who has been admitted?" asked the man loudly with a strong Philadelphia accent.

"Yes," said Nancy.

"Okay," he said, gesturing confidently with his hands. "I'll tell you what you do. You get you arm bands, see?"

They didn't. "Then you get to park in the special lot." Dave thanked him. He'd figure it out later. Downtown Philadelphia had a personality all its own.

Nancy and Dave located the ICU where Nathaniel was being treated. After gaining entrance, they found his bed. There was a machine that someone referred to as a bi-pap. A mask was strapped tightly to his face, and they were forcing air into Nathaniel's lungs. Although he looked ashen, his eyes lit up when Nathaniel saw his mom.

Dave stayed until 9:00 p.m. but then went home. He had some reading to do for a class at Temple, and he had to drive to Dover to teach his first class by 8:00 a.m. the next morning. Nancy stayed the night in a room provided for parents and was in the room with Nathaniel early the next day.

Nathaniel remained in ICU the whole day. Patty visited from Ridge Crest, and Dave stopped by that night with some more clothes and supplies so that Nancy could be comfortable for the long haul. On the third day, Nathaniel was moved to a regular room, and on the fifth day he was well enough to be released to the care of Ridge Crest.

Jerry came in the room to get him. "Looking mighty good there, Buddy," he said to Nathaniel as he placed him in a wheelchair and started toward the car, but not before Nathaniel's mother kissed her boy good-bye.

Nathaniel did better through the rest of the month of January, working toward his thirteenth birthday without another hitch. He enjoyed visits from his parents, went to church twice, and participated in all the action at Ridge Crest, including the daily routine of the school program.

Nancy and Dave fit in their visits with church activities, classes in Dover, and Dave's Temple classes. Dave spoke twice a week at church and besides this tried to keep the teenagers from church busy. To this end Dave started a senior Bible quiz team for his church that included several teenagers. Gracie and Sabrina were on the team. The captain was Joey from the military academy. Dave also had two more quizzers, B. J. and Cassandra, who were combining with them from a new church in Philadelphia. Practices were sporadic, particularly with Joey, who was largely restricted to the campus of the military school he attended, only rarely getting a "leave" for the weekend.

On a Friday night at the end of January, Nancy and Dave were going on a date. They would be going with Joe and Rhonda to hear the Philadelphia Symphony Orchestra, an excursion made possible by shuffling numerous activities into their proper places. Because Dave's team was competing the next day at a Bible quiz tournament in New Jersey, Joey was staying at their house for the weekend, having gotten leave from the military academy until Sunday night.

Joe and Rhonda's teenage son, Eric, rode in with them in the car as they came to pick up the Norrises, but as they neared the Norris's driveway, Dave was backing out and seemed to be heading someplace. Joey, who was in the front seat beside Dave, yelled out the window to the approaching car, "We're going to get the pizza. We'll be right back!"

As he drove off, Dave saw Eric get out of the back seat of the car carrying study materials for Bible quizzing. Although Eric quizzed for a different team, he and Joey were planning to study together tonight while the Norrises went out with Joe and Rhonda. Dave thought that he had better give marching orders to the young man who sat beside him. "You and Eric make sure to study when we leave," said Dave. "No goofing off."

"We've got this tournament in the bag," said Joey, confident and ever aggressive. For Joey, all of life was a contest. He continued, "We'll roast them and toast them."

"The only thing I want you roasting and toasting," said Dave, "is your review session."

"Huyah," said Joey, no doubt in some sort of flashback from earlier that day when he had to salute and march around with just the correct dose of military enthusiasm.

Joey was doing well. He was bold about his faith in a place where it was tough to be bold. Anybody in need of healing would be immediately prayed for. God had already done some miracles at the school, and Joey was expecting more, but the pressure on him was relentless.

As soon as Joey and Dave returned with the "Supremes," Nancy yelled, "Dinner is served." A pizza and a half later, Joe and Rhonda were driving the Norrises downtown in their car.

As Joe wove his way through traffic on I-76 and they made their way to the heart of Philadelphia, Rhonda stated, "I read the program and they're featuring a duet with two pianos in the first half."

Joe parked the car with twenty-five minutes to spare. Nancy slid on her leather gloves and wound her scarf tighter against the Philadelphia cold as the foursome fell into a flow of concertgoers headed toward the front entrance. The crowd of fur coats, mink stoles, and gray heads made their way past steaming grates populated by homeless people. Nancy felt a little guilty. Dave had gotten season tickets for a half-dozen performances, and though it was clearly an unnecessary financial indulgence, the concerts were one thing that helped them forget life's burdens. For Dave, though, tonight's performance would not be particularly effective in this regard.

Dave had received the news earlier that week which spelled out the crisis—the Bible school where he was teaching would be closing in three months. He was one of only a few people who had any inkling. Rhonda knew more than she was telling. Dave knew more than he would tell Nancy. Nancy would find out soon enough.

As Dave looked around at the audience for the concert, he suddenly turned to Joe and asked, "Is it just me, or are we the youngest people in this whole building?"

The official announcement that the school was closing came in March. Within a couple of weeks, Bible colleges in Indiana and Missouri had made overtures for Dave to join their staff, but the reality was that because he was right in the middle of his doctoral program, it didn't make any sense to leave Temple now. Still, it was nice to be wanted.

The general atmosphere at the Bible college in Dover was gloomy. Grief hung in the air. Good-byes were really tough because defeat was not something anyone wanted to own. It was important to encourage and support graduates, teachers, and staff. Dave penned letters of affirmation and delivered those letters personally to staff members with whom he had been especially close. He spent a little time with Barb, his secretary for a number of years. Dave thanked her for her loyalty and resourcefulness, for keeping everything together even as well as helped him through school. "If it wasn't for you, I never would have made it," he shared.

Dave entered an inner office. He asked, "Are you ready?"

"Raring to go," said Jim.

As they got in the car, they continued an ongoing conversation. Because they had already complained and grieved about the loss of the school, they reflected on other things, particularly their long trips to seminary together. Dave offered, "Hey Jim, I want to thank you for all the times that you allowed me to complain about Vince." Vince was one seminary professor that Dave had a hard time stomaching. Dave then added, "That heretic!"

"I still like him," said Jim, defensively. "He was a much better teacher in my ministry classes."

Dave and Jim were never too far from some sort of playful sparring. Although Jim was academic dean, that didn't mean he was always able to command the total attention of the faculty. At one of the first faculty meetings that he conducted, he was greeted by a table full of teachers wearing party glasses that made their eyes look cross-eyed. The glasses had been Nancy's contribution to liven up the meeting. For Jim, this was "the beginning of sorrows."

After their meal, Dave's tone became serious. "Jim, I know you are going to move to St. Louis to teach, and I will still be in Philadelphia, but I want to make a covenant with you."

Jim looked surprised but let Dave continue.

"In the Bible when Jonathan had to leave David because of difficult circumstances, he made a covenant with him. And he gave him a gift. I don't have anything of value, but I want to give you the book that has been the most significant to me the last couple of years." Dave handed Jim his Hebrew Bible in which he had written in the front. "Jim, I want to make several promises to you. First, I will never purposely hurt you, never compete with you or come against you in any way. Second, I know that you and I don't have much in the way of resources, but I want you to know that if there is ever any way I can help you in a time of personal need, you have only to ask, and I will do everything that I can. And third, if your children have a need, I want to be a help to them as well. I know neither of us has much, but I promise to make myself available to you whenever and however you need me."

Parents and friends filled the large playroom at Ridge Crest to see the end-of-the-year school program. The room was brimming with activity, and the program had a Hawaiian theme. Each child was dressed up as some Hawaiian object, a fruit, plant, or a bird.

Nathaniel was the one exception. He was dressed up as the tour guide. That meant that he had on a borrowed tropical shirt from one of the boys in church and wore a special hat. One of the teachers held his hand and helped him push the tape recorder to deliver the narration at the appropriate time. With a musical background, the narration described a particular fruit or bird while the parents "oohed" and "aahed" over the child dressed as the featured object.

Nathaniel wound up at CHOP later that week, and when Nancy got the call, she headed right down to see him. "This is aspiration pneumonia," the doctor said to her.

"What are you saying?" asked Nancy.

"Well, the contents of his stomach are getting into his lungs. Once that happens, everything starts to go downhill."

"But I thought that this wasn't supposed to happen," said Nancy. "With the operation to close his stomach, he should be—"

"Look, Mrs. Norris," said the doctor gravely, "we've got some major issues going on here, and one way or another, we are going to have to deal with them."

In June, Dave took a guard job with a company that serviced Lockheed Martin. The main building was tall and housed acres and acres of floor space. Another ten warehouse-style buildings were scattered across the huge complex. Dave could be posted in any number of areas.

While the typical job of a guard was to check the badges of employees, his favorite job was to "guard" a satellite that Lockheed was building. It wasn't as if someone were going to steal it. It was housed in an enclosed room declared to be a static-free zone. Dave's job was simply to make sure no one came in without the proper lab coat and latex gloves. Since Dave could count on one hand the total number of people that might even enter the room during his eight-hour shift, this job afforded a wonderful opportunity for study.

Study time was always less fruitful when Dave had to work at other guard stations where too much time might be required to check badges. If it was true that some guards were "wannabe cops," it was also true that the engineers who worked at Lockheed had little respect for guards generally and sometimes displayed this disregard through their greeting. "How's it going, Bub?" was a phrase Dave heard more times than he could count.

"Fine," he said with a smile, waiting for the traffic to clear so he could get back to his book. One of the men who had entered the building was curious and turned back to the guard station before proceeding.

"What you reading there, Bub?"

Dave wasn't sure how to give a quick answer. He offered tentatively, "It's about a debate on the existence of the so-called wisdom school during the time of Antiochus Epiphanes."

"Right then. Have a good day, Bub."

Nathaniel was back at Ridge Crest again, and Nancy and Dave were taking some pictures of him in the playroom. When Nancy held him on her lap, he was so long that Nancy felt like she was holding a little man. Jerry came in and watched Dave take a picture.

"So how was the Phillies game last night?" Dave asked Jerry when he saw him coming in the door. There was a group from Ridge Crest that had attended, and Dave thought Jerry and his girlfriend had gone.

"Oh it was great!" he said, but I didn't get to go. "But other staff members took him, and Nathaniel really enjoyed it."

"Did the Phillies win?" asked Dave, trying to lighten the mood.

"Yeah," said Jerry. "Three to one—say I've got to ask you something. If you guys move to Indianapolis, can I adopt Nathaniel?"

Nancy and Dave looked at each other in surprise. Then it occurred to Dave what was going on. Jerry had heard them talking about possibly moving to Indiana or St. Louis to teach. They had never seriously considered it, but even if they had, they would have never left without Nathaniel. But apparently Jerry didn't know this. He had decided that if they moved and left their boy here, he wanted to adopt him. It was really nice that someone cared that much. Dave smiled warmly in response. "Thanks, Jerry. That means a lot. It really does. But, uh, we're not going to be moving."

Chapter 31

"You'll leave my arms and go into the arms of Jesus"

Nathaniel once again had been admitted to the children's hospital. Although he was there for several days, he still hadn't yet gotten out of the ICU. Nancy had been there all day. Dave arrived in time for dinner. As they ate, they began to talk about a trip that they had both planned on making. "We'll cancel my ticket, but you should go," said Dave.

"I just can't go," said Nancy. "Nathaniel needs me."

"Your parents need you too," said Dave, "and it's only right that you go to honor them. Look, I've got the weekend off work, and I can get Pete to take care of service." Pete was Dave's assistant pastor. "I'll stay with Nathaniel, but you have to go and be a part of this. It's important."

So Nancy left the next day and flew down to Tennessee for her parents' fiftieth wedding anniversary celebration. There were speeches and presents and restaurants. It was good that she had not missed the special occasion. She called several times while she was there, and Nathaniel was doing fine.

"How's my boy?" she asked as Dave but the phone to Nathaniel's ear. Nancy couldn't hear his familiar coos as he was too busy having air whooshed into his lungs and not able to speak. But he could hear her at least. Three days after Nancy returned home from Tennessee, he was well enough to go back to Ridge Crest.

A few days after getting back into his routine at Ridge Crest, Nathaniel had another episode of aspiration pneumonia and was taken back to CHOP again. Dave came from work, and was just entering Nathaniel's room when Nancy signaled that she wanted to go down to the lounge area. Dave obliged. She was clearly upset and had something on her mind. She signaled for him to sit down, obviously not wanting to chitchat. "Dave, this is the third time in the last eight weeks that Nathaniel has been taken in an emergency down here to CHOP. Twice, Nathaniel was medevacced by helicopter."

"I know. Poor little guy.

Nancy continued, "The doctor tried to talk to me today. And this is very serious. He has been thinking a lot about Nathaniel and how his condition is degenerating. He thinks that maybe we should just let Nathaniel stay up by Ridge Crest next time."

"In Grand View Hospital?"

"Yes."

"But they don't have the means to keep him alive. He couldn't make it."

"That was his point. The doctor said that in a way... well... in a way, we are prolonging Nathaniel's suffering by continually bringing him down here."

This kind of talk slapped Dave upside the head, and he wasn't prepared for it. He said urgently, "So what then? We just let him die?" He shook his head vehemently. "No way!" Nancy paused but Dave continued to vent. "Stupid doctor," said Dave. "I thought they were here to help, not kill people."

But then Nancy continued. "Dave, the doctor says that we aren't solving anything by just trying to treat the pneumonia when it occurs. This is not getting at the cause. It is not doing any good. So, if we insist on treating Nathaniel down here at CHOP, he says we should operate and do surgery on his lungs, and he also wants Nathaniel to have a tracheotomy."

Dave winced but then said immediately, "Well then, let's do it. It's better than us letting him die!"

"Better how?" said Nancy, crying. She put her finger on Dave's Adam's apple and pressed. "How would you like it? How would you like it to have a 'trach'? And do you really think he could survive another surgery if he was operated on again?"

Dave found something interesting on the floor to look at, but he said nothing at all.

After a long time of silence, Nancy said, "I've been reading some books this afternoon on death and dying and—"

"Let's not talk about this right now, Nancy. I just want to see Nathaniel."

The next morning, Dave was at work at his usual time, 5:30 in the morning. He was in a building where there weren't too many people entering, so as a guard checking badges, he didn't have much to do but sit at his desk and study. Only, today, he wouldn't be doing any studying. Today he would be asking himself some very serious questions and forcing himself to think about some things he had thus far refused to address. When he arrived at work that morning, he was absolutely certain that it was best to aggressively treat Nathaniel. One thing was certain. His boy should live.

As the day wore on, he began to reflect on all Nathaniel had suffered. He recalled the doctor who first examined Nathaniel at Ridge Crest and saw his scars. The doctor observed, "It looks like this little fellow has been through a war." When he made that observation, Dave had been offended. While his boy had suffered a lot, he lived and loved a lot too. Life could not be reduced to some sort of quota of operations. Although it was true that he was suffering, Nathaniel needed to live. That would be best.

Finally, Dave asked the question, "Best for whom?" Only an occasional entrance of a worker showing her badge interrupted Dave's thoughts. So Dave had time. He did a lot of crying and praying during those eight hours, and finally his shift was over.

After changing at the house, he headed to the hospital. When they got a moment alone, Dave said, "Nancy, I've been thinking about this… and praying about this… and I agree with you. Let's decide together that when Nathaniel gets better from this episode and goes back up to Ridge Crest, we won't bring him back down to the Children's Hospital any more, but we'll just let him go." Nancy and Dave held hands and cried.

But Nathaniel never made it back to Ridge Crest. When they moved him from ICU to a regular room, and he was just getting ready to leave the hospital, he had another relapse. Dave was at work. The phone rang and it was Nancy. She said, "Dave, you need to get down here right away so we can confer with the doctor. He wants us to choose between an operation and letting Nathaniel go."

Dr. Shears met with Nancy and Dave. Rhonda was there too. He noted, "So the bronchoscopy demonstrated the malformed breathing passage. If you advise us to, we can do the surgery. As I suggested earlier, the tracheotomy won't solve the problem, but there are other things that we can do…." Dave glazed over. He already knew what they had decided. He just wasn't sure how to get the courage to speak it.

"Dr. Shears, you said that we had the option to defer any further treatment."

"Yes, I did."

"And you wanted us to make a plan."

"Yes."

"We've already decided that this is what we want to do, and we understand the implications of that decision. We have decided against any further aggressive treatment for Nathaniel's condition. We don't want any more operations, and we no longer want the oxygen forced into his lungs. If that means we are letting him go, then we are willing to do that."

The doctor paused and then said, "I would never have said anything if you chose to do the operation, but I will tell you, I think you are making the right decision."

Dave then asked, "Uh... um... would it be possible to get a private room so Nancy and I could... stay with Nathaniel during this last little bit."

"I don't know for sure. I'll see what I can do.

The nurse took the mask off Nathaniel's face. The oxymeter showed an immediate increase of Nathaniel's heart rate and breathing. The alarm bell went off. The respiratory attendant turned it off, sheepish. Still, Nathaniel was breathing and was stable.

They moved Nathaniel to a private room. He was supplied oxygen through a nasal prong, but now, oxygen was no longer being forced into his lungs. Nancy and Dave stayed the night. The next day, Dave called relatives and told them that Nathaniel didn't have long to live. Nancy's sister, Cathy, would be coming with her daughter Chrissy. Nancy called Ridge Crest and talked to Patty. That was a hard call to make. As she was about to hang up, she remembered something else. "And say, Patty, the first meeting of the parent's support group that I was starting was supposed to be September 7."

"Don't worry about it," said Patty. "I'll call and cancel."

Dave talked to Don about Nathaniel. "Don, I am in the process of making plans for the funeral, and I was hoping it would be all right if we could use the church for a dinner. It's not part of our usual schedule but—"

"Dave, we'll do anything we can do to help. Just tell us what to do."

Dave explained that he had already stopped by a funeral home near the church and was looking into working with them. Earlier that day, Dave went by Valley Forge, a cemetery near their house.

He was put off by the man with expensive clothes who drove him around in his Porsche to look at grave plots. But he really had no choice in the matter. On the phone, Don offered, "Let me see what I can do."

Awhile later Don called back. "Dave, I just got off the phone with a good friend of mine, Frank Videon. He is a funeral director. Do you know that cemetery you visited?"

"Yes," said Dave.

"Well, he has a burial plot there that another church wasn't using. He will donate that to you. And he'll do the funeral and won't charge you for his services." What Don knew but did not say was that Dave didn't have money for this funeral. He had never been able to get insurance on Nathaniel and certainly didn't have any money in savings.

"Thanks, Don," was all Dave could say.

Nancy and Dave were in the room with Nathaniel that night, not sure he would make it until morning. They didn't get much sleep. Nathaniel's breathing was shallow.

Rhonda came up Saturday morning and told Nancy and Dave to go get some breakfast. She would watch Nathaniel.

Shortly after they left, Nathaniel started gurgling as if he would die shortly. Rhonda asked the nurse, "Is it getting close?"

The nurse replied, "Yes, it's getting near."

Rhonda held the boy's hand, saying, "You've got to hold on till your parents get back, Nathaniel." Unexpectedly, he squeezed her hand.

Nancy and Dave came back and sat with Nathaniel. They were not alone. Cathy and her daughter Chrissy were in the room as was James, a pastor friend from Newark, Delaware. As Nancy began rocking Nathaniel in a rocker similar to the one at home, Rhonda turned on Nathaniel's tape recorder with all his music. When she turned it on, they were singing, "Swing low, sweet chariot, coming for to carry me home...." She rushed to turn it off.

Nancy stopped her. "No, it's good. Let it play." And then Nancy began to reminisce as she rocked her boy. "Nathaniel, do you remember the time that you went with us to a children's camp in Connecticut? Joy watched you, and we stayed in an old folk's home, and your dad kept getting lost on the way home because he wouldn't look at a map and...."

"Watch it there," said Dave easily.

"And when Jean was babysitting you, she took you to prison to meet that guy and his heart softened... you had your own prison ministry." The rocking chair continued its rhythm as Nathaniel rested easily against her.

"And do you remember how Karen took you to the ocean and you loved the waves. Karen was so special to you...." There was a little gurgle and Nancy looked down at Nathaniel. He was still breathing. "Nathaniel, in just a few minutes you'll leave my arms and go into the arms of Jesus." Nancy kept talking, recounting whatever incident popped into her head.

Dave got up to get another chair for someone and as he returned with it to the room, James was saying. "He's gone. But he passed while you were in the room, before you left. I watched his breathing stop. It was just so peaceful, you didn't know it."

Flowers adorned the rooms of the funeral home where Nancy displayed pictures of her boy on easels and laid out photo albums on tables that celebrated the different chapters of his life. Before the people began to arrive, more and more floral arrangements had to be placed. And then because people knew Nathaniel loved balloons, the funeral home was inundated with helium balloons, hundreds and hundreds of them.

Dave had asked their friends Doug and Vicki to come down from New York to help. Doug did the music for them. Nancy decided to have a scheduled block of time at the visitation where informal sharing could take place. A song was sung. Vicki read from Nathaniel's favorite story, *The Velveteen Rabbit*. The staff from Ridge Crest brought the children with them, all dressed in their finest. Another song was sung followed by more sharing.

The staff from Ridge Crest did a reading, and each paragraph was read by a different staff member. Patty began, "I am the child who cannot talk. You often pity me; I see it in your eyes. You wonder how much I am aware of. I see that as well. I am aware of much... whether you are happy or sad or fearful, patient or impatient, full of love and desire, or if you are just doing your duty by me. I marvel at your frustration, knowing mine to be far greater, for I cannot express myself or my needs as you do...."

Patty sat down, while Trish continued to read, "I do not gift you with clever conversation, cute remarks to be laughed over and repeated. I do not give you answers to your everyday questions, responses over my well being, sharing my needs, or comments about the world about me. I do not give you rewards as defined by the world's standards... great strides in development that you can credit yourself; I do not give you understanding as you know it. You cannot conceive my isolation, so complete it is at times. What I give you is so much more valuable... I give you instead opportunities. Opportunities to discover the depth of your character, not mine; the depth of your love, your commitment, your patience, your abilities; the opportunity to explore your spirit more deeply than you imagined possible. I drive you further than you would ever go on your own, working harder, seeking answers to your many questions with no answers. I am the child who cannot talk."

The poem went on, and new readers got up, repeating the theme. One section began, "I am the child who cannot walk," and told what gifts that child gave. The next paragraph began, "I am the child who is mentally impaired," and explained what this child taught.

The final paragraph began, "I am the disabled child. I am your teacher; if you allow me, I will teach you what is really important in life. I will give you and teach you unconditional love. I gift you with my innocent trust, my dependency upon you. I teach you about how precious this life is and about not taking things for granted. I teach you about forgetting your own needs and desires and dreams. I teach you giving. Most of all I teach you hope and faith." The last reader ended the last sentence of the paragraph: "I am Nathaniel Norris."

Dave's assistant pastor Pete shared his remembrances of Nathaniel. Friends told funny things that happened with Nathaniel. A whole group came up from Dover and shared remembrances. Wayne told about remembering Nathaniel waiting for the school bus. This was all very important to Nancy, because some people in the room hadn't seen Nathaniel in years.

Dale and Marion, who had shared so many experiences with the Norrises at A. I. duPont, came all the way from upstate New York. Nancy knew that it was a sacrifice for Marion to trust her little Marion to others in order for her to come to Nathaniel's funeral, and she loved her for coming.

Jim came from Wisconsin, and Dan from Indiana. Robert came from St. Paul, as did Dave's sister Linda and her family. Dave's brother Bob and his family came from Sioux Falls, South Dakota, and his sister Joanne and her family came from southern Minnesota. It had been less than a year since Dave's sister Pat had died. Her husband Bill was there and would read a Scripture.

Nancy's dad and mom were there as was her brother, David. He would be a pallbearer. Nancy's sister Cathy was working behind the scenes to help organize everything and was a great support at the viewing. While this or that one shared, people could read from the program that told Nathaniel's life story. The last paragraphs read:

> For 13 years Nathaniel loved and was loved. But this week, after 8 weeks of recurrent pneumonia that rarely allowed him out of the Intensive Care Unit at Children's Hospital, the last paragraph in Nathaniel's life story recorded the peaceful breaths of a loving boy cradled in his mother's arms. His dad stroked the brow of his dying son, and as he wrestled with the meaning of his son's life, he recalled the words spoken to a great ballet artist upon the completion of a masterful interpretation. *Why did you dance it in that way?* she was asked.
>
> She only smiled. *If I could tell you, do you suppose I would have danced it?*
>
> The father continued to stroke the boy's hair as his wife

spoke to the child for the last time, tearfully recounting to him his own life story that he had danced before them. *And soon, Nathaniel,* she said softly, *you are going to leave my arms and go into the arms of Jesus.* Several minutes later, so peaceful that it was unnoticed at first, he slipped from his mother's arms and made his way heavenward.

Why did you release your balloon? asked a father to his son, as they walked along at the park. The lad had bought the colorful balloon earlier with his allowance at the cotton candy stand and seemed to treasure it. But now, suddenly, he released it, and it unexpectedly wafted toward the heavens. The boy shrugged his shoulder, searching for a response to his father. *I don't know,* he said. *It just seemed like it wanted to go free.*

Nathaniel's mother left her lifeless son at the hospital and now rode in the passenger side of the car on I-76. *Dave,* she said thoughtfully, *some Scriptures say the dead know nothing, but some people believe they can see us.*

Dave took a breath and began explaining the Ecclesiastes text in terms of the Corinthian text. *He's with the Lord, Nancy. The Scripture is clear. To be absent from the body is to be present with the Lord.* Dave enjoyed the opportunity to talk theology and continued on some technical point, but she was thinking of other things.

She pointed at the clouds. *Look, I bet he went up through that blue patch in the clouds—right there,* she said pointing.

Dave continued, *We'll know each other in heaven, but probably we won't know anything about what is going on here on earth...*

—So he can't see us then? she interrupted. Dave split the difference between his heart and head. *Well there is no Scriptural support...some things the Bible doesn't really spell out....* He continued, but she was absorbed in thought again.

Well, just in case, she said, as she waved a tender good-bye heavenward, looking up at the blue hole in the clouds. A tear rolled down her cheek. *You made it up there before us,*

Nathaniel, but we are going to see you again.

She turned to her husband. *Nathaniel's done suffering now, Dave. I think he just wanted to go home....* She waved again. *I think he just wanted to go home.*

By the graveside, after Bill read a Scripture about the resurrection, people released their balloons. "Fly, Nathaniel, fly!" said Dave spontaneously, not realizing he had said it aloud.

Nancy didn't want to leave the cemetery to go back to the church. She knew that people had brought food to serve and everyone was expecting her there. She realized that those who were gathering up plants and arrangements needed to know what to do with them. And then later that day, she was aware that all of the out-of-town guests would be coming over to the house. She knew that tomorrow she would have to begin to figure out what life looked like without Nathaniel. And yet, she couldn't quite get her feet to leave, to go on to the next thing.

For a moment longer, Nancy just stared at the casket, not wanting them to put it in the ground. But they would have to do it. One of the nurses had cut some of Nathaniel's hair and had given it to Nancy when he died. She was glad she had it. Most of the things that Nathaniel had would be given away, but she wanted to keep a few things. Nancy would keep Nathaniel's cabbage patch doll and some of his special toys. She wanted to keep things that still smelled of Nathaniel, that fresh smell of Nathaniel after a bath—of baby powder on him and fluffy towels and baby shampoo. Yes, she would keep anything that smelled of Nathaniel.

"You doing okay?" said the kind voice of someone next to her. She wasn't sure if this was a hint to move on and greet those in the crowd around her or just something that people said at funerals. It was a good question. And she wasn't sure how to answer it herself. "How was she doing?"

Mostly she was numb. But not so numb as not to feel a pain so deep that it physically hurt. Yet, it was not simply pain. Woven into the fabric of sorrow was something else. She felt it at once. Nathaniel's sweet sounds, words of kindness given and received, tragedies layered on one another, God's comfort and provision, and special friends who offered unconditional love to her and Nathaniel. She felt defeat of course, but one permeated with hope; sorrow certainly, but a sorrow interlaced with joy. "How was she doing?" No single word could capture the feeling; no single emotion could describe it. Then she decided what it was she felt. It was sweet pain.

Chapter 32

"You look a little lost"

After the interment, Nancy sat at a table at church where a meal was being served. Usually, Nancy was aware of the workings of such things, but she wasn't sure who had arranged what. Some servers seemed to have come from her church, and some were from Don's church. People who had left their church for this or that reason now walked in and out of the kitchen. Some people who were there she didn't recognize at all. It didn't matter, really. Nancy was thankful for the act of kindness.

As Dave sat at a table munching on a dessert, he too was amazed by how much was being done by others. He thought of the cost of the funeral. For years, in the back of his mind he had worried about how he would pay for Nathaniel's funeral, and even now he still wasn't sure what the costs were or how it would all get paid. Rhonda was taking care of everything for them.

After the meal, out of town guests came over to Nancy and Dave's house. Additional food and refreshment appeared from parts unknown. Chairs sprouted first out on the deck and then on the front yard. Nancy was happy that her parents had come for the funeral. Even though they were apprehensive about flying, they sat in their living room. Dave randomly thought of the layer of dust on the window sill that no one had time to clean, all the while listening to this or that conversation coming from around the house.

Nancy lined up plants and gave away as many as she could to whomever came over to the house. She gave away a lot of balloons but still had more. All that were left, she put in a bedroom and let

Dave's little nieces and nephews play with them. As conversations took place in the living room, Nancy was heartened by the laugher that came from the other room.

Dave was thankful for all the help that went largely unrecognized. He noticed that Pete, his assistant pastor, had brought all the balloons in his van. Although Pete wasn't present at the house, he and his wife Sheila had been behind the scenes making everything happen. That was normal for them.

Nancy suggested that Dave take the extra balloons to the Children's Hospital, so the next day he drove the van down to the hospital and carried in enough helium balloons to loft a small animal into the sky. He wasn't sure what to do with them and so on impulse headed to the ward where Nathaniel died. A man passed him in the hall, impressed with the display going the other direction. "Wow," he said to Dave. "Whoever those balloons are for must be a very special person."

Dave bit his lip. "Yeah," said Dave, distressed. "Very special."

As the man walked by him tears coursed down Dave's cheeks, and more than anything in the world he just wanted to leave this building. But he forced himself to keep heading to the ward to drop off the balloons in his hand. That much he would do for Nancy... and for Nathaniel.

Not only did people who came to the funeral grieve for Nathaniel, but others grieved as well. Two summers earlier, Nathaniel had gone with his parents to a church camp in Pennsylvania. During the evening service, a little boy named Joshua noticed him. "Mom, what's wrong with that boy? Why doesn't he sing or clap?"

"He would like to," said his mom, "but he can't. Why don't you do it for him?" This was a request that his mother knew had little chance of success. Her four-year-old son was extremely shy and was afraid that people would look at him. Yet, suddenly, he began clapping and singing.

Since that camp, every night at his home in Chambersburg, Pennsylvania, when Josh said his bedtime prayers, along with "bless Mommy, bless Daddy," he added another prayer request, "and Lord, bless Nathaniel Norris."

Joshua was now six, and Nathaniel had passed away. When it was time for his bedtime prayers for that night, his mom and dad decided that they needed to have a talk with their boy. They were just not sure how they were going to do it.

His mother began tentatively, "You know, Josh, Nathaniel has been very sick recently." She was choosing her words carefully. A child's prayers are a special thing, and she wanted her boy to know that God had not failed him despite the fact that Nathaniel had passed away.

"Well, Josh," she continued, "Nathaniel died."

"Finally," said Josh.

"What do you mean, finally?"

Josh responded quickly, "He's healed. Now he can walk and talk."

The day after the funeral everybody had gone home and most of the flurry of activity was over. But for Nancy, life would never be the same. She no longer had to go up to Ridge Crest, run down to the hospital, or even scurry about to help a support group. Because Nathaniel's death was such an abrupt loss, it seemed that the very core of who she was had been somehow whisked away. In the days following the funeral, because everything had changed so radically, she sometimes found it difficult to function.

As Nancy pushed a shopping cart down the aisle at Acme Foods, she was suddenly overwhelmed by the noise of the normal activity around her. People were laughing and asking the butcher to slice up lunch meat while inside she was screaming, "Why does everyone go on like nothing happened. My son died!"

Nancy's next-door neighbor, walked up behind her. Arlene was married to Frank, and they were good neighbors. Frank had retired from the Navy and was home during most days. Sometimes, when Frank was cutting his own grass and could see that the grass was getting a little long on the Norris's lawn, so he just kept going and mowed their lawn as well. Just that week Frank was going to plant a tree in the Norris's yard in honor of Nathaniel. His wife, Arlene, looked into Nancy's shopping cart, which contained only a single item. Nancy was staring blankly at the shelves. "Are you all right?" she asked. "You look a little lost."

Nancy smiled vacantly. "I'm fine. Just fine."

Eastern University had already started for Nancy. She had enrolled sometime back and was now halfway through a master's degree at the school. This semester she had signed up for a research methods class. Within two weeks, she had to pick a topic to research. Nancy now made what seemed to her an obvious choice. She was going to write on a particular kind of grieving: "Mothers now Childless." Her professor, Dr. Chang seemed a little hesitant about such a choice but supported her in this decision. For very personal reasons, Nancy was reticent to share her topic of research with the other students in the class.

Dave had intended to be very consistent in his employment as a security officer. He needed the income and the opportunity for large blocks of study time. However, he also needed to ask a favor from his supervisor. "Craig, can I get two days off at the end of the month?"

"What days?"

"Well, it's a Thursday and Friday. I am flying out to Indiana to teach at a Bible college there."

Craig reminded him that he had a full-time job and had been given his preferred assignment in a building that had very little traffic. Dave thanked him but waited patiently until Craig consented.

Answering a posting in the want ads, Nancy got a job as a substitute teacher at Pathway School, a place that specialized in helping autistic children. The school served children that ranged in age from grade school through high school, so there was plenty of need for substitutes. After all her paperwork was approved, the administrator called Nancy. "There is a good chance we'll call you every week, depending on the need. This week we need you to do a 'one-on-one' with Kevin. He keeps running off."

"Okay," said Nancy, looking forward to the challenge.

Dave was sitting on the couch struggling with his paper on the church father Ignatius. He was working to demonstrate that the hymnic material in his epistle to the church at Rome was representative of a particular genre that preserved an important christological confession. Further, church history had ignored such a confession because the church evolved away from it in its understanding.

He was deep in thought when Nancy walked in and asked, "Hey Dave, have you ever heard of Compassionate Friends?"

"Do you mean like friends who help each other?"

"No, it's an organization of parents who have lost children."

"Oh, that's nice," he said distantly, still engaged in what he was working on.

"Good then," said Nancy. "Get dressed."

"Why?"

"We're going."

"To what?"

"Compassionate Friends. They get together at the Lutheran Church up the hill and the meeting starts in half an hour."

"I have at least twelve hours more of work to do by Monday and...."

"But don't you think we should work through our issues about Nathaniel?"

335

"He just died."

"Eight weeks ago."

Dave smelled danger. There was nothing he could say that would not get him in hot water. He went to the meeting. The men shared in one group and the women shared in another group. It was hard. While there was a kind of release in talking about his son, he wasn't ready to go back.

Nancy found the sharing and support invaluable. She listened. She cried. She shared some more. It was a warm environment. Whereas Dave didn't normally welcome talking about Nathaniel as an ongoing topic of conversation, Nancy received strength from the meeting because she felt understood. As soon as she got home, she circled the bi-monthly meeting on the calendar to make it a permanent part of their lives.

Dave went to Indiana and enjoyed teaching. The school didn't pay very much, especially considering the time it took to grade the papers, but he was glad for the opportunity to stay connected to teaching. He could justify the time grading papers because he could do the work at his security guard desk anyway, so he was sort of "double dipping". Meanwhile he was also finishing up his two papers for Temple.

Nancy hit a brick wall in her research class at Eastern. Several times she sat down at the kitchen table attempting to do work for the class. All the books were in front of her. She had read much but written little.

"How's the paper coming?" Dave asked when he came home. He had left for a meeting several hours before. He walked over to the table where Nancy was working and looked down at her paper. The title sounded good, impressive even: "Mothers Now Childless. Dual Loss of a Child and Parenthood: A Phenomenological Study of Mothers'

Bereavement." It was just that there was so little written on the paper after the title. He decided not to say anything more and walked on by.

"And I disagree," said Dave, countering the critique of the second research paper, one written about the canon of Scripture. He was now presenting his findings to a group of graduate students. "What I am trying to say here is that it wasn't the church in the fourth century that made the writings of Scripture authoritative. Consider the writings of Paul. They were authoritative when he wrote them—they were canon by every meaningful definition of the word."

While Dave cranked ahead in school, he was treading water spiritually. Dave generally would journal in his private time, but his journaling had trickled to a halt. He had no desire to write about Nathaniel, Nancy, or any of the things he had gone through. Further, he was growing very tired of Nancy bringing Nathaniel into as many conversations as possible.

"Do you see the butterfly in the tree that Frank planted in remembrance of Nathaniel?"

"Yeah?"

"Every time I see a butterfly, I think of Nathaniel and how he is changed now. 'Hello Nathaniel.'"

Dave couldn't quite make the connection. He couldn't at all think of Nathaniel by seeing the butterfly. Nancy went to another Compassionate Friends meeting to share the butterfly story. Dave didn't go. It was there that Nancy was comforted by a room full of people who talked, listened, and cried with her. Dave was glad for her.

On Thanksgiving, they drove down to Joe and Rhonda's house in Dover and spent the day with them. Rhonda had sent cards and notes. She was especially sensitive about their loss. Not much needed to be said. Thanksgiving was a time of easy friendship. That weekend Dave put the finishing touches on his papers for his classes at Temple.

"So you've started the research project?" Dr. Heewon Chang asked Nancy.

"Yes," she replied, "but I really need to talk to you about this. I really want to do this, but it's like I have 'brain-freeze.' I know the paper is due next week, but there is no way that I am going to finish it."

Dr. Chang looked at Nancy compassionately. "You've been through a lot," she said. "And this was a big subject to tackle. I will put in for an extension on this. That will give you a little longer to work on it."

And as the ebb and flow of December signaled a break in intensity, for the very first time in a long time, Dave brought a novel to work. It was a work written by Chaim Potok, and it was called *The Gift of Asher Lev.* The book was about a closely-knit Hasidic Jewish community that had emigrated from Eastern Europe to New York City. The Rebbe was the spiritual leader of the community and the individual around whom the community revolved.

The book is told in the first person by a young man named Asher Lev. He had grown up in the community, and his father was a close assistant of the Rebbe. But as an artist, Asher had painted pictures that offended the sensibilities of the community and was ostracized, exiled to France. The book begins with his return to New York City to attend an uncle's funeral.

Dave read the book with fascination. There were struggles with relatives, lawsuits, misunderstandings. On one level, the "gift" of Asher Lev was his creative gift of art, which had resulted in others rejecting him. But as the book progressed, Dave began to realize the author's intention. The book evolves to the point where the Rebbe seems to be asking for Asher to give up his little five-year-old boy to the community so that one day his only son might be the future Rebbe. This would be the "gift" of Asher Lev.

Dave read himself into the pages of the book. The characters from the novel and people from his own life together made appearances on the stage of his mind. The rejection of Asher Lev was the rejection of his father; the character of the Rebbe had on him superimposed both God and his grandfather, and the insistence that Asher give up his son morphed into the loss of Nathaniel. God Himself was brought onto the stage as the One who required that Nathaniel be taken. And perhaps only on that day could Dave begin to grieve his son, for he had thus far been too afraid to deal with his sea of pain. If he took his finger from that dike, all the losses he had sustained might at once wash over him at once, unbidden.

Dave wept. He cried a long time for his losses. He was not altogether ready to deal with all the issues, but there were some important things that he wanted to address with God—for he suddenly blamed God who had allowed all the hurt. "How could you take my son? Is heaven a better place because he is there? Why would it have been such a bad thing if he were still here? I did not give him to You. You took him." And then Dave wept some more.

Nancy did not take a new class at Eastern for the second semester. Rather, she tried to finish the research course she had already begun by completing her project on grieving mothers. Once again she checked out the same books from the library, looked at her stacks of journal articles, shuffled them around the kitchen table and stared at them. And that was all. She continued to go to Compassionate Friends. Dave went another time. While Nancy enjoyed working with the children at Pathway School, she was much less enthusiastic about church work.

On January 27, Dave woke up at 1:30 in the morning. He'd had a dream, one that had was at once vivid and strange. Nathaniel was in the casket and he came back alive. It was a miracle. Dave embraced his son, but as held him, his boy winced with pain. Then it was as if Nathaniel could talk. Dave had never heard him talk. But somehow Nathaniel was able to tell Dave that he wanted to go back to where he was. That it was better there. And Dave said it was okay and that he was glad. And then Dave woke up. He quickly wrote down the dream, deciding that it was from the Lord. And he felt a measure of peace. But it was his dream. It was private. He wouldn't tell Nancy about it. He wouldn't tell anyone at all.

It happened on a Thursday night when Nancy and Dave were driving forty-five minutes away to teach a Bible study. They were working with a family who had not yet become a part of their church but enjoyed the weekly studies. Dave taught the adults. Nancy taught the children. Five minutes from the house, Nancy complained, "Dave, we're wasting our time here," she said.

"What do you mean?" he remarked.

"We've invested a lot of effort in this family, and I'm tired."

"We need to give it some time, Nancy, because…"

"I've given it enough time." That was their last week.

Nancy needed another extension on her paper. Finally, Dave said that Saturdays would be their day for her to finish up. He would sit in the recliner in the living room with his laptop computer. He would wait for her to write things, and then he would type them up on his computer. Line by line, page by page, Nancy eked out the work until it was finally done.

Dave was on the phone. Someone was calling him about something. He put his hand over the mouthpiece and yelled, "Nancy, they want us to have a missionary two weeks from this Sunday night. Does that look good on the calendar for you?" There was such a waving of arms and hand signals from Nancy that Dave told the person he would call them back.

"Isn't that a good Sunday for us?" Dave asked, confused.

"Dave, why do we have to have all these people all the time?"

"Nancy, I cancelled the special speaker a couple weeks ago because it was too much. And this missionary wouldn't be staying at the house."

"But everything involves me and you know it!"

Things were spinning out of control. Of that Dave was sure.

They went to Dr. Canfield who was just about ready to retire. He had helped them before. He had given up his office and was just seeing a few people at his house. He seemed distracted as Nancy and Dave shared their struggles. Without too much listening, he offered a quick solution. Nancy should submit; she had a bad attitude.

Nancy said they were never going back to him.

On the anniversary of Nathaniel's death, the Norrises visited his grave to release balloons. There was a song that Nancy said she really wanted to play. She had been the vice president of a group in the county that planned special events for handicapped children. One event that she so much wanted Nathaniel to participate in was a fashion show. At a previous show, they dressed up the boys in tuxedos, the girls in formal wear, and even the people who pushed the wheelchairs were nicely dressed. They had played the song, popular at the time, "I Believe I Can Fly." But Nathaniel never made it to the fashion show. So, Nancy played the song on a tape recorder, and while balloons floated upward, the lyrics resounded, "I believe I can fly…. I believe I can touch the sky…."

Dave said Nancy should try another counselor and she did. His name was Neil. She wasn't sure what happened. It could be that he had some sort of sleep disorder. She never really knew. But he was so nondirective, that not only did he not have any advice, he would doze off as he tried to write down what she was saying.

Nancy had just a couple more classes to go and she would complete her degree. The pattern was set that on Saturdays Dave sat on the recliner and watched her while she cranked out the work and then typed it up for her. He had now finished his language study and classes. He only had to take his comprehensive exams before he could begin his dissertation.

A few weeks later, Nancy tried another counselor who told her she was mad at God. She didn't go back. Finally, someone at Eastern told her about a lady who was a former pastor's wife, so she went there. Her name was Kathy. After some weeks, Kathy asked if Dave could join Nancy at the sessions. Reluctantly, he agreed.

Chapter 33

"I want my wife back"

"I want my wife back," said Dave. "I want her smiles and laughter again. I need her help at the church. I feel like I am all alone."

The counselor turned to Nancy, who sat next to Dave. "Is that how you see it?"

"I'll tell you one thing," said Nancy passionately. "A person who loses his son shouldn't go on with his life like nothing happened!"

"Now Dave," Kathy began, "Nancy says that when you fly out to Bible school, you're likely as not to just call up and say you're bringing home a bunch of Bible school kids to Philadelphia to do outreach."

"She acts like that's a weekly occurrence. It's not. And it's not as if she has to keep these kids at the house. Other people in the church house them."

"So it doesn't involve Nancy?" said Kathy. Nancy gave Dave a look that said he'd better tell the truth.

"It doesn't now," he replied. "Nancy's withdrawn herself from everything."

Kathy turned to Nancy. "But is that true? You're still teaching at the school for autistic children, aren't you?"

"Yes," said Nancy. "I had started there as a substitute, but now I'm working in a career program. I've been visiting department stores to encourage them to let our kids intern there. That way they can continue to develop the skills we're trying to teach them at school. We're already in two chain stores in the mall, and I do onsite supervision."

"And you enjoy the work?"

"It's challenging. But it's good. I didn't know that I would like these teenagers as much as I do."

"And you're still a group leader at Compassionate Friends?"

"Actually, sometimes I just take a turn helping to facilitate."

"Remind me. That's a support group for parents who have lost a child."

"We do some work with siblings who lose a loved one, but yes, it's mostly for parents."

"And you say that Dave won't go with you?"

"No."

"I've gone."

"Twice!"

"Well, I just don't like spilling my guts to a bunch of men in a circle."

Kathy looked at him. "Dave, do you think this is really healthy? You have to grieve. So, what are you going to do? Are you just going to go faster and faster so you don't crash and burn?"

"No," said Dave. "I grieve. I just do it in my own way. I journal, mostly."

"So you're just dialoging with yourself then? Are you shutting Nancy out from your feelings?"

Dave paused thoughtfully. "I share my feelings with you, don't I, Nancy?"

"Very much so," she said sternly.

Kathy chimed in. "Dave, why are you working so hard anyway? You take on all kinds of extra responsibilities besides doing your doctoral work. Isn't that kind of nutty? I mean, why in the world do you do all these things? I just want to know one thing. Whose approval are you trying to get, anyway? Your father's?"

Dave was about to disagree with Kathy and insist that he had always been this way, but he paused and thought. It was definitely more complicated than that, but he was sure there was a good deal of truth to what she was suggesting. "Well, maybe."

"You're never going to get your father's approval," Kathy declared. "He's dead!" And before Dave could recover, Kathy asked,

"What's this about you not letting Nancy do a seminar at another church?"

"She wants to be gone for weeks!"

"The whole week?"

"No, on Wednesday nights. And that's our educational night. And Nancy's in charge."

"Will they pay her?"

"Yes."

"Do you pay her?"

"No."

"Why not?"

"How can I pay her?" he said in frustration. "I don't have any money to pay her?"

"Then it sounds pretty straightforward to me. You should let her go."

"Kathy, you just don't understand our church culture."

"And what if I did? Who's to say your church culture is the right one?"

Dave paused, exasperated. "Come on. What would I tell the people from the church?"

"That's your problem, not mine. She should go." Dave thought about it for a minute. It was James who had asked for Nancy to come and give the teachers in his church some hands-on help and guidance. James had never done anything to hurt Dave and Nancy. He had only helped. Dave decided that maybe he would let Nancy go, after all. Maybe it would do her some good.

Kathy continued, "So then Nancy, you say you don't like to go to church. There must be something about church you don't like. Do you have a hard time listening to Dave when he speaks?"

"No," she said. "I'd rather listen to him than anyone else."

"Well, what then? Do the people at church speak meanly to you?"

"No. They love me. There was one person who said unkind things, but they're gone now."

"So what is it? Why is it so hard for you to go to church?"

"I can't explain it, really. It just feels like loss… and hurt… and obligation."

"From Dave?"

"Not the loss and hurt... but the obligation part."

"I understand. But there's something more going on here. So are you mad at God?"

"No. I mean, I didn't think I was. I pray and read my Bible. So I don't think so. But maybe I am. I don't know."

"Is it because you no longer have Nathaniel in your arms? Is that it?"

"I don't think so. But I just don't want to go. I don't know what more you want me to say, but that's how it feels."

Kathy then turned to Dave. "So what about you? Are you planning to move to Indiana when you finish your degree?"

"Well, they want me to. Starting last fall, I've been teaching a full-time load there while I am finishing my dissertation. They fly me out and pay me well to teach two full days a week, so I've been able to let my guard job go. The school wants me to come full-time as soon as possible."

"But you don't sound persuaded. You're not convinced that you want to go there?"

"Not entirely, no."

"Well, then what would you do?"

"I'm not sure. There are a couple of possibilities. I'm on a committee that's working to plan a denominational seminary."

"But you sound negative about this. You don't think that the seminary will go?"

"No. It doesn't look like it is going anyplace; I doubt it will."

"Why's that?"

"We have such a love/hate relationship with education in our movement. People think education is pretty dangerous."

"And you don't?"

Dave laughed. "Education can be dangerous. But ignorance can be dangerous, too. I think that way too many people make a false contrast between being spiritual and being educated. They reason, 'You can be one or the other, but you can't be both.'"

"And you don't see it that way."

"Well, I suppose I've met plenty of educated people who are

346

carnal. I don't deny that. But I've also met a lot of ignorant people who are pretty carnal, too. Look, I don't see education as an end in itself. It's just a tool in the toolbox—and it's one we need. But no, I don't think they will ever get this seminary off the ground. I'm not cynical. I'm just no longer as idealistic as I once was."

"What about you?" said Kathy, turning to Nancy. "Talk about your dreams."

"I'll be done with my master's degree in just a few months," replied Nancy.

"Does this conflict with Dave's work?"

"No. He helps me."

"Okay. But then what will you do after you get your degree… what then?"

"I don't know. I guess I'll teach someplace. And I'd like to do some traveling. Yes, I'd really like to do some traveling. In fact, I think I would like to travel around the world."

"Maybe you will," said Kathy, smiling. Then she prompted, "Is that all?"

"Well, someday, maybe, I would like to write Nathaniel's story."

"Give me a break," said Kathy suddenly. "I have asked you for three months in a row to write something about Nathaniel and your loss, and every time you come in here empty-handed. You have yet to write one word."

"I know. I'm sorry."

"But why? Why haven't you written anything?"

"I don't know," said Nancy. "I want to. I can't really explain why I haven't written yet."

"But still, one of your dreams is to write a book about Nathaniel?"

"Sound's crazy, doesn't it?"

"Not at all. Anything's possible."

"But not just any book. I would want it to be real…."

"By that you mean…."

"I wouldn't want to cover up the ugly stuff. It might help people if I were more open to what I felt."

"What do you think about that?" said Kathy, turning to Dave.

"About what?"

"About Nancy writing a book?"

"Great. I'm for it."

"A book about Nathaniel?"

"I would say 'Amen.'"

"But you wouldn't help her write it?"

"You mean... like type it for her?"

"No, like, write it together."

"No."

"But Nancy seems to need your support in this area. You two feed off each other. I'm afraid if you won't help, then...." She paused, looking at Dave.

"Are you kidding? What? No. I said 'No.' It'd be just too painful."

Kathy scribbled something on her notepad and then looked up. "I'm sorry Nancy, but this is probably just one dream you might have to let go."

Nancy received her Masters Degree in Multicultural Education from Eastern University in May 1999, three years after Nathaniel died. Dave finished his Ph.D. in Religion from Temple University in 2000. In 2001 the couple moved to St. Louis where Dave became part of the founding faculty for a seminary started by his denomination. Nancy began teaching at a Bible college located on the same campus.

Nancy and Dave made several failed attempts to write this book. They were only able to make progress on it by going away for a month between semesters. For thirty days, they argued over details, chronology, and who said what to whom. They corrected each other and laughed and cried until they finally completed the first draft. Then after the next semester was over, they carved out a few more weeks in order to rework the whole book. They were greatly aided in this effort by helpful suggestions from friends who assisted them in smoothing out the manuscript.

Nathaniel Abshire Norris was born February 3, 1983. He died September 7, 1996. As this book goes to press, it will be almost thirteen years since he died—as long a time has passed since he died as he actually lived. On the face of it, there is no real justification for a book about Nathaniel, for there was truly nothing remarkable about a little boy who could neither walk nor talk and who had to work so hard at just staying alive. Indeed, if report cards mean anything, then he failed everything. His goals in school were always the same as the year before, and these were goals that he never achieved. He never rolled over, he never bore his own weight, nor did he ever consistently identify sounds or purposefully select the best option when presented with choices. Not a remarkable life at all.

But this would be a very shallow assessment; very shallow indeed. Every life should be celebrated, regardless of failures or successes. Perhaps frailty is not such a bad thing after all; it may very well be that weakness has a whole lot to teach us.

Even a decade after he is gone, it is possible to reflect on Nathaniel's legacy. Like any other boy, he had likes and dislikes, hurts and pleasures. He needed to be included and accepted, and he showed love by gifting others with smiles and hugs and sloppy kisses. In his brokenness he preached two important things: first, celebrate gifts that are so often taken for granted. And even more importantly, if we aren't whole enough to love, then we are not truly whole.

Just as Nancy and Dave were changed by Nathaniel's life, so too, were they changed by his death. After he was gone, they grieved differently, and their individual grief remained a source of on going conflict between them. Indeed, even though they eventually did work hard enough to have a measure of appreciation for what each other was feeling, to this day neither one fully comprehends why the other grieves as they do. On one or two occasions Nancy and Dave have shared their pain with others and called it a marriage seminar. But it was really just weakness made public. And although Nancy lobbies Dave to mention Nathaniel at some point whenever and wherever he speaks, they both carry their hurt privately, hurt that Dave, in particular, does not often care to unwrap.

For the one to whom grief has never been a guest in their home, loss is an incredible mystery; one would think that what Nancy and Dave experienced belongs only to a time now past. One would think that after thirteen years they would get over it—that their grieving would be ended and that their pain would be gone. But one would only think this if one had never lost someone truly special… or if for whatever reason, circumstances prevented that loss from being embraced.

Those of you who are navigating some sort of crises in your life will likely understand that the story of Nathaniel Norris is not merely a chronicle about pain. Rather, it is a narrative of how wonder, delight, and joy may be found in the same house where chaos has chosen to live. In every crisis there is a reason to hope. It is the very nature of neediness to invite compassion and care. In our deepest loneliness, the smallest gift of kindness yields unexpected delight. It is in our darkest places that a small light shines most brightly.

Tragedy also brings with it "God" questions. If God is so loving, then why did He allow bad things to occur? We get angry and then we feel guilty. And sometimes we think that because we have gotten so upset with God that we have already burned our bridges, that we are no longer eligible for divine help. Such thinking may even seem to be confirmed by our experience. God wasn't all that accessible in the time of our greatest need.

But God is not put off by our anger at Him or others, or by our doubt, or even by our habit of unbelief. God is nothing if not constant. However imperfect our faith may be, or however much we fail, God continues with an open invitation. It doesn't require heaps of faith either. Just a small spark. A tiny seed. It's tough to lean into sorrow, to not lose hope. But it is in the small decision to hope, to take baby steps of faith, that we discover incredible joy.

For additional information and pictures of Nathaniel, go to www.nathanielnorris.com.